SPECTACLE AND PUBLIC PERFORMANCE
IN THE LATE MIDDLE AGES AND THE RENAISSANCE

STUDIES IN MEDIEVAL AND REFORMATION TRADITIONS

History, Culture, Religion, Ideas

FOUNDED BY HEIKO A. OBERMAN †

EDITED BY

ANDREW COLIN GOW, Edmonton, Alberta

VOLUME CXIII

ROBERT E. STILLMAN (ED.)

SPECTACLE AND PUBLIC PERFORMANCE IN THE LATE MIDDLE AGES AND THE RENAISSANCE

SPECTACLE AND PUBLIC PERFORMANCE IN THE LATE MIDDLE AGES AND THE RENAISSANCE

EDITED BY

ROBERT E. STILLMAN

BRILL

LEIDEN · BOSTON

2006

Cover illustration: Queen Elizabeth I processing into London the day before her Coronation in 1559. By permission of the College of Arms, MS. M.6., f. 41v.

PR
658
.P25
U55
2004

Library of Congress Cataloging-in-Publication Data

University of Tennessee, Knoxville. Marco Institute for Medieval and Renaissance Studies. Symposium (3rd : 2004)
  Spectacle and public performance in the late Middle Ages and the Renaissance / edited by Robert Stillman.
      p. cm. — (Studies in medieval and Reformation traditions, ISSN 1573-4188 ; v. 113)
  Papers from the 3rd annual symposium of the Marco Institute held in spring, 2004, at the University of Tennessee.
  ISBN 90-04-14928-7 (alk. paper)
  1. English drama—Early modern and Elizabethan, 1500-1600—History and criticism—Congresses. 2. Pageants in literature—Congresses. 3. English drama—17th century—History and criticism—Congresses. 4. Theater—England—History—16th century—Congresses. 5. Theater—England—History—17th century—Congresses. I. Title. II. Series.

  PR658.P25U55 2006
  822'.3093579—dc22

                                                                            2005058258

ISSN 1573-4188
ISBN 90 04 14928 7

To Sam and Alex

"They were train'd together in their childhoods; and there rooted betwixt them then such an affection which cannot choose but branch now."

William Shakespeare, *The Winter's Tale*

CONTENTS

ACKNOWLEDGMENTS

Several people deserve thanks for helping to assemble this volume of essays. First, I am grateful to Mr. Robert Yorke, archivist at the College of Arms in London, for his assistance with securing the right to publish the cover image of Queen Elizabeth I's Coronation procession. I am grateful also for the advice and support of my colleagues at the University of Tennessee Robert Bast and Thomas Heffernan at various stages of this book's composition. My colleague in the English Department Heather Hirschfeld also deserves acknowledgment because of her kind intervention on my behalf in soliciting several excellent contributions that have made the book considerably more substantive than it could have been without her help. Finally, it is my pleasure to thank my friend Anne Lake Prescott of Barnard College for her assistance in identifying Tiffany Alkan's essay, and for what Tiffany describes as her unflagging support, patience and care in reading the essay's several versions.

I would like to acknowledge financial support for the publication of this volume from MARCO, the University of Tennessee's Institute for Medieval and Renaissance Studies, as well as from the University's Exhibit, Performance, and Publications Fund. I need also to acknowledge with thanks the permission granted by Manchester University Press to publish Peter Holland's "Mapping Shakespeare's Britain."

EDITOR'S FOREWORD

As recently as 1972, it was possible for David M. Bergeron to complain that scholars dismiss the spectacles and public entertainments of early modern England as "scarcely worth the trouble of serious study."[1] Three decades later, the case has altered. Contemporary scholars have turned with increasing historical interest and theoretical sophistication to interrogate—and thereby to trouble—critical assumptions about what constitutes fit matter for "serious study," as the vast body of early modern entertainments, civic pageants, festival shows, rituals, masques and plays has been enthusiastically embraced and eagerly anatomized to new critical purposes. Scholarship itself has altered greatly during these decades, and with the steady dislocation of traditional notions about the boundaries that distinguish disciplinary pursuits, especially those boundaries once thought to secure, more or less absolutely, the divide between social and political history, on the one hand, and the literary and performing arts, on the other, attention to the spectacles and public entertainments of early modern England has achieved a fascination, even a sense of urgency that earlier scholarship could hardly have anticipated.

Such fascination grows partly from what Stephen J. Greenblatt defined for the generation that followed as self-fashioning—especially the politically pointed self-fashioning of elites who dramatize in their infinite variety of public displays those imaginary means by which power seeks to contain and control the always unruly body of the state.[2] In the aftermath of the new historicism and the rise of cultural studies, every dramatic performance is an artifact whose making speaks potentially to large concerns about that now familiar triad—gender, race, and class. The new historicism has long ago ceased to be new, but its impact on contemporary critical studies remains arguably strong, even as the need to produce better, more reliable histories

---

[1] *Twentieth-Century Criticism of English Masques, Pageants, and Entertainments: 1558–1642* (San Antonio: Trinity University Press, 1972), Introduction, n.p.

[2] *Renaissance Self-Fashioning: More to Shakespeare* (Chicago: University of Chicago Press, 1980).

has become clear.[3] More recently, the fascination with early modern entertainments derives too from the turn toward religion that distinguishes so much academic work in the period, as scholars are discovering in spectacles and public performances ready vehicles for exploring how religious experience—conceived in the full range of its expressions among the culture's institutions, its codes of behavior, and its structures of belief—is made visible in dramatic displays. Piety is increasingly prominent as a subject of historical interest in relation to political authority, individual agency and subjectivity, and as a dimension of lived experience that merits attention in its own right.[4] Increasingly, too, with the rehabilitation of the aesthetic as a category for scholarly inquiry, such entertainments are proving fertile ground for reopening questions about the nature of authorship, generic distinctions among kinds of dramatic entertainments, and the material conditions—the local contexts and conditions of entertainment practices themselves—that shape specific performances in specific times and places.[5] Contemporary scholars have turned, then, to the study of the spectacles and public performances in late Medieval and Renaissance England for motives nearly as diverse as those bodies of material that they seek by anatomy to understand.

Beyond fascination, the sense of urgency that so often attends these scholarly studies derives arguably from the heterogeneous—even miscegenational—quality of the materials under investigation. By their very nature—whether they emerge as the spectacles crafted by guilds, the cooperatively compiled dramas of professional acting companies, the powerfully encoded products of patronage, or the self-consciously fashioned dramas of the aspiring author, such entertainments are always, as performances that intermingle the visual and the aural, spectacle and music, dance and words, conspicuous illustrations of culture at play in the activities of creating and recreating itself. Conceived by pictorial analogy, such entertainments resemble less

---

[3] See "Introduction: Demanding History" in *A New History of Early English Drama*, ed. John D. Cox and David Scott Kastan (New York: Columbia University Press, 1997), pp. 1–5.

[4] See Debora Kuller Shuger, *Habits of Thought in the English Renaissance: Religion, Politics and the Dominant Culture* (Toronto: University of Toronto Press, 1997; repr. 1990), pp. 1–16.

[5] See, for example, Heather Anne Hirschfeld, *Joint Enterprises: Collaborative Drama and the Institutionalization of the English Renaissance Theater* (Amherst: University of Massachusetts Press, 2004).

Caravaggio's luminously present beings who look ready to step live from the canvas than Giuseppe Archimboldo's factitiously mannered creatures, assembled from the raw materials of nature—vegetables, fish, or stones. Amidst their heterogeneous intermingling of the stuff of culture—song, dance, music, spectacle, and words—we see the "seams" in their making, and experience the promise of discovering (and hence the urgency to discover), as Philip Sidney would write, how and why their makers made them.

It is to that promise of discovery that this volume of essays owes its beginnings. In the spring of 2004, a new institute called MARCO (the Medieval and Renaissance Curriculum and Outreach Program at the University of Tennessee) held its third annual symposium on the topic of "Spectacle and Public Performance in the Middle Ages and the Renaissance." An interdisciplinary collection of major scholars from the United States, Canada, and Great Britain assembled in Knoxville to deliver papers to professors, students, and interested members of the public, and to engage, formally and informally, in discussions both among themselves and with that large and diverse audience. As a creative component of the symposium's activities, two performances were staged by the University of Toronto's *Poculi Ludique Societas*, the Chester *Coming of Antichrist* and George Peele's *The Old Wives Tale*. In turn, the success of those performances helped to swell the size of the audience for the lectures, and to lend to the symposium the feel of a community—not just an academic—event.

Many of the papers in this collection are easily recognized as the products of that particular symposium organized for the needs of that particular audience. With an eye toward making the strange familiar, and with the intention of informing students and the public at large, Richard Emmerson's essay on "Antichrist on Page and Stage in the Later Middle Ages" displays the distinguished scholar working as a distinguished educator, reorganizing large territories of knowledge for fresh explorations in his subject matter. Once again, as the director in charge of staging the Chester *Coming of the Antichrist*, Peter Cockett writes from the vantage of a performance critic, exploring the challenges of balancing a commitment to historical authenticity with the need for dramatic accessibility. In Richard McCoy's essay on "Spectacle and Equivocation in *Macbeth*," the economy of focus throws into sharp relief for its audience of readers—as it did for its original audience of auditors—the significance of a single "secondary" character (Malcolm) for a reassessment of the tragedy's meaning and power as a public performance. In Peter Holland's paper on the mapping of Britain in *King Lear*, early modern cartography supplies a significant storehouse of historical material for illustrating the play's engagement with issues of nationhood, just as it served as a wonderfully lucid device for illuminating the meaning of that engagement for the audience. In turn, Sarah Beckwith's playful and provocative engagement with the language of knowledge, self-knowledge and acknowledgment in *Measure for Measure* recapitulates, as it extends, the clarity of her spoken performance's intellectual engagement with the text. The essays in this collection do not read as the paradigmatically predictable products of the academic conference, and their freedom from that paradigm is arguably a measure of new strength obtained, at least in part, from heightened accessibility. All of the essays printed here have been revised in light of subsequent rethinking on the part of the authors. Once more, several of the essays in the volume were included by invitation, and such essays have given to the collection a greater range than the limited resources of the symposium could afford, and an opportunity to mingle with the views of the internationally established, diverse perspectives from a greater variety of scholars (some younger, some already established themselves) at work in the area.

No volume entitled, *Spectacle and Public Performance in the Late Middle Ages and the Renaissance*, could pretend to treat comprehensively a body of materials so conspicuously vast and heterogeneous. Rather than efforts to survey the territory, the essays published here are to be understood, by contrast, in the best and original sense of the term as "essays," as trials, attempts, experiments to open alternative ways of understanding important aspects of that vast corpus of entertainments, mystery plays, civic pageants, courtly masques and professional dramas that constitute its subject. It is a book that freely crosses traditional period lines, as it includes studies of late Medieval as well as Renaissance entertainments, and a book that seeks to impose no uniform "period" terminology on its authors. When historical boundaries between cultural eras are themselves matters for contemporary critical debate, it makes sense to allow the traditional descriptive terms, "Medieval" and "Renaissance," to coexist as chronological markers (however imprecisely) with that even more difficult-to-define catchall, "early modern."

Once more, the essays in this collection are not organized according to a single critical or historical methodology, even when their subjects are similar in kind. They employ, instead, an eclectic range of interpretive practices, which reflect the variety of interpretive practices now current in the field. For instance, Robert Barrett and I both write about civic entertainments, but to different ends. While my essay seeks to question still-current theoretical accounts of power and agency by examining the staging of debates about words in Elizabeth I's coronation procession, Robert Barrett's careful archival research enacts a historical recovery of the political circumstances that explain the absence of the "Triumphator" in the 1610 *Chester's Triumph in Honor of her Prince*. One paper seeks retrospectively to challenge the ideological determinism of materialist and historicist interpretations of culture, while the other supplements new historical work with additional—and necessary—historical labor. In turn, as illustrious examples of what I have called "the rehabilitation of the aesthetic" in contemporary dramatic criticism, Nora Johnson's theoretically provocative interrogation of the "magic" of authorship in *John a Kent and John a Cumber* finds its complement in Lauren Shohet's rigorous reassessment of genre as a necessary "locale" for reading mid-Caroline masques. Tom Bishop's essay on the aftermaths of English court masques illustrates, in turn, the power of the new materialist criticism both to recover greater knowledge about the staging practices of early modern performances, in the full specificity of their production, and to reflect upon the significance of those practices for understanding the social significance of the genre. And as one more example of the diversity of critical approaches employed in these essays, Tiffany Alkan's paper supplies an intertextual reading of Busirane's mask of Cupid in *The Faerie Queene*, a reading that highlights the indispensability of courtly entertainments for understanding Spenser's literary production, and the dark liminal quality of that production as it is analyzed from anthropological and psycho-sexual perspectives.

All of the essays in this volume have at their center the spectacles and public performances of Medieval and Renaissance England, and that national perspective gives the volume a certain focus. When Peter Holland writes about the mapping of Britain in *Lear* or Richard McCoy about the political dynamics of equivocation in the "Scottish play," a national perspective becomes especially meaningful to the papers' arguments. The volume possesses an important coherence, too, in certain pairings between and among the essays. Most obvious, Richard Emmerson's survey of the Antichrist on page and stage finds a useful partner in Peter Cockett's account of the PLS's (*Poculi Ludique*

Societas's) staging of the Chester *Antichrist*. Three of the volume's essays attend to Shakespeare's public performances—however differently pointed that critical attention proves—and three provide special attention to the Renaissance court masque. Just as interesting, however, and just as significant are those less obvious relationships that bind one essay in the collection to another. Nearly all of these essays supplement their individual readings of individual texts with self-conscious critical reflections about how best to undertake the interpretation of early modern performances, and in the aftermath of those major revisions in hermeneutic theory taking place since the 1980s, such self-consciousness remains one of the distinctive characteristics (and, arguably, one of the strengths) of contemporary critical practice. New critical movements are often productive of new critical pieties—the insistence, for instance, upon reading theater strictly in terms of social or political determinants—and the papers by Johnson and Shohet illustrate pointedly the potential gains of reassessing the new pieties as well as the old.

Other connections bind the essays in the collection. Not surprisingly, religion appears front and center as a prominent issue both for the scholar of Antichrist who illuminates the variety of his late Medieval representations and for the director who ponders how to make the Antichrist's demonic "miracles" meaningful for a contemporary (and mainly) secular audience. Moreover, as an indicator of the turn toward religion in recent criticism, Sarah Beckwith's meditation on *Measure for Measure* performs much of its critical work against the background of early modern inwardness conceived in Christian terms; her argument illuminates what she calls the "peculiarity" of Shakespeare's relation to the Middle Ages, evidenced by his use of theater to combat the skeptical alienation of Renaissance culture and the empty theatricality of mere signs. Partly in response to Beckwith's argument about Shakespeare's use of theater against theatricality, Richard McCoy's essay on *Macbeth* attends to the less radically iconoclastic spokesmen of the Reformed church as a means of contextualizing the value of theatrical signs—the equivocal dissimulations of a Malcolm—to clarify important realities and to reconstitute community. Also, my own effort to interrogate the near-obsessive preoccupation with words in Elizabeth's coronation procession trades centrally on the new prominence of the Word in Protestant England, and the complex epistemological consequences of heightened awareness inside humanist culture about the always conditional relationship between signs and the things they signify.

Other readers of the volume will discover other connections among these essays for themselves. This is not to lay claim to some sort of overarching scheme that unifies its contents. Similar to most collections of its kind, the value of this book depends largely upon the quality of its individual essays, and upon the power of those essays, circulating through scholarly publication, to report, extend, and renew those engaging conversations about the significance of early modern spectacles and public performances, which had their beginnings in MARCO's third annual symposium.

Robert E. Stillman
University of Tennessee, Knoxville

LIST OF CONTRIBUTORS

TIFFANY J. ALKAN is a Ph.D. candidate at Columbia University, where she has been awarded a Whiting Fellowship in support of her dissertation, entitled: *"The Fantastical Dreams of Abbie-Lubbers": Romance and Religion in early modern England.* She has presented her research at several national conferences, including Spenser at Kalamazoo, Sixteenth-Century Studies Conference, GEMCS, and the Shakespeare Association of America Conference.

ROBERT W. BARRETT, JR. is an Assistant Professor of English at the University of Illinois at Urbana-Champaign. He is currently finishing a book on regional writing and identity in Medieval and Renaissance Cheshire and will soon begin work on an edition of the Chester Whitsun plays for the TEAMS Middle English Texts series.

SARAH BECKWITH is Marcello Lotti Professor of English, Theater and Religious Studies at Duke University. She is the author of *Christ's Body* (Routledge, 1993, paperback, 1996), and *Signifying God* (University of Chicago Press, 2001). She is currently writing a book on Shakespeare's romances.

TOM BISHOP is Associate Professor of English at Case Western Reserve University, where his principal teaching is in Shakespeare, Renaissance literature, and post-colonial literature. He holds degrees from Melbourne University and Yale University. His publications include *Shakespeare and the Theatre of Wonder* (Cambridge 1996), *Amores: a verse translation of Ovid* (Carcanet/Routledge, 2003), and essays on Shakespeare, Jonson, Jacobean masques, Elizabethan music, Australian literature, and other subjects. He is coeditor of the *Shakespearean International Yearbook* and is currently working on a book on the poetics of scriptural allusion in Shakespeare.

PETER COCKETT is Assistant Professor in the Department of Theatre and Film at McMaster University. He is also a professional actor and director, working in theatre, film and television in England and Canada. His research is performance-centered and explores the theatre of Medieval and early modern England through theatrical production. He directed the PLS double bill of George Peele's *Old Wives Tale* and the Chester *Play of Antichrist*, which were performed as part of the University of Tennessee's Third Annual MARCO Symposium.

RICHARD K. EMMERSON is Executive Director of the Medieval Academy and Editor of *Speculum*. After taking his Ph.D. at Stanford University, he taught at Walla Walla College, Georgetown University, and Western Washington University, where he chaired its English department. Since coming to the Academy he has taught at Tufts University and Harvard University. He has published five books and numerous articles studying medieval apocalypticism, drama, visionary poetry, and illustrated manuscripts.

PETER HOLLAND is McMeel Family Professor in Shakespeare Studies and Department Chair in the Department of Film, Television and Theatre at the University of Notre Dame. Before moving to Notre Dame in 2002, he was Director of the Shakespeare Institute, Stratford-upon-Avon. He is General Editor of *Shakespeare Survey* and the series 'Redefining British Theatre History' (Palgrave Macmillan) and co-General Editor (with Stanley Wells) of the Oxford Shakespeare Topics series (Oxford University Press).

NORA JOHNSON is Associate Professor of English at Swarthmore College. She is the author of *The Actor as Playwright in Early Modern Drama* (Cambridge, 2003). Her essays and reviews have appeared in *English Literary History, Shakespeare Studies, Theatre Journal*, and *Shakespeare Quarterly*. She is currently at work on a study of Shakespeare and comic performance in nineteenth-century American culture.

RICHARD C. McCoy is Professor of English at Queens College and the Graduate Center, City University of New York. He is the author of several books on Renaissance Literature, including *Alterations of State: Sacred Kingship in the English Reformation* (Columbia 2002), and he is currently working on a study of theatrical faith in Shakespeare.

LAUREN SHOHET, Associate Professor of English at Villanova University, is the author of *Reading Masques: The English Masque and Public Culture in the Seventeenth Century* (Oxford University Press, 2006), and numerous articles on masques, Milton, Shakespeare, and contemporary reimaginings of the Renaissance. She has received fellowships and awards from the National Endowment for the Humanities, the Mellon Foundation, the Folger Shakespeare Library, the Shakespeare Association of America, and the Huntington Library.

ROBERT E. STILLMAN is Professor of English at the University of Tennessee, Knoxville, where he sits on the steering committee for MARCO, an Institute for Medieval and Renaissance Studies. He is the author of several books on Renaissance literature and culture, including *The New Philosophy and Universal Languages in Renaissance England: Bacon, Hobbes, and Wilkins* (Associated University Presses, 1996), and he is now completing a monograph about the piety and politics of Philip Sidney's poetics.

LIST OF ILLUSTRATIONS

Richard K. Emmerson, *Antichrist on Page and Stage in the Later Middle Ages*

Robert E. Stillman, *"Nothing More Nedeful"*

ANTICHRIST ON PAGE AND STAGE IN THE LATER MIDDLE AGES

Richard K. Emmerson

What medieval Christians thought about Antichrist varied greatly depending upon the context in which he was discussed. It mattered significantly whether he appeared in a vernacular poem breathlessly warning of the terrors awaiting the faithful in the Last Days, in a sober Latin theological treatise outlining Christian eschatology, in a heretical sermon condemning ecclesiastical abuses, or in a strident polemical attack on the Jews.[1] While not minimizing the rich variety of popular lore and doctrinal learning surrounding this apocalyptic figure, I wish to trace one particular understanding of Antichrist that had a significant influence on the religious culture of the late Middle Ages. Beginning with patristic commentaries on selected apocalyptic texts and continuing through monastic exegesis of the early Middle Ages to the theological compendia of high medieval scholastics, this understanding became established by the fourteenth century, as is evident in a wide range of sermons, plays, poems, chronicles, and didactic and religious texts as well as many works of art, manuscript illustrations, sculptures, mosaics, and stained glass windows. The Antichrist whom I wish to examine on page and stage was understood not symbolically—as a representative of a religious institution or a particular people or a political force—but as an individual human being, a real person who was expected to appear at a real place in a real time at the end of world history. Most Christians living during the high Middle Ages believed that Antichrist would become Satan's representative in the Last Days, attacking Christianity

---

[1] For these and other understandings of Antichrist, see Horst Dieter Rauh, *Das Bild des Antichrist im Mittelalter: Von Tyconius zum deutschen Symbolismus*, Beiträge zur Geschichte der Philosophie und Theologie des Mittelalters n.F. 9, 2nd ed. (Münster: Aschendorff, 1979); Richard Kenneth Emmerson, *Antichrist in the Middle Ages: A Study of Medieval Apocalypticism, Art, and Literature* (Seattle: University of Washington Press, 1981); Robert E. Lerner, "Antichrists and Antichrist in Joachim of Fiore," *Speculum* 60 (1985): 553–70; Bernard McGinn, *Antichrist: Two Thousand Years of the Human*

and gaining control over the world primarily by four means: by converting Christians through the effective preaching of false doctrine;
by deceiving God's chosen (even the "elect," Matt. 24:24) through
the enactment of "miracles," probably accomplished through demonic
assistance; by bribing officials, both political and ecclesiastic, with
riches and territorial possessions; and by brutally persecuting those
who remained steadfast. He was expected, in other words, to carry
out the last great trial that Christians must endure before the second advent of Christ and the Last Judgment.

My goal in discussing this widely established and popular tradition is to provide a context for understanding the *Coming of Antichrist*,
the penultimate play of the Chester cycle of mystery plays.[2] It was
staged as part of the University of Tennessee MARCO conference,
at which the oral version of this paper was presented. The play's
treatment of the legendary apocalyptic figure will receive attention
throughout this discussion even as analysis focuses on other examples of the popular understanding of Antichrist. As a way of organizing the discussion and surveying the tradition, I will examine a
much longer and not widely known French play, the *Jour du Jugement*.[3]
A full theatrical treatment of the life and career of Antichrist, it is
much more extensively developed than is the Chester pageant, which
as part of a much longer cycle of plays covering salvation history

Fascination with Evil (San Francisco: Harper, 1994); Andrew Colin Gow, *The Red
Jews: Antisemitism in an Apocalyptic Age, 1200–1600* (Leiden: E. J. Brill, 1995); and
Curtis V. Bostick, *The Antichrist and the Lollards: Apocalypticism in Late Medieval and
Reformation England* (Leiden: E. J. Brill, 1998).

[2] *The Chester Mystery Cycle*, ed. R. M. Lumiansky and David Mills, Early English
Text Society, supp. ser. 3 (London: Oxford University Press, 1974); plays from this
cycle will be cited parenthetically by pageant (in Roman numerals) and by lines.
For interpretive studies see Peter W. Travis, *Dramatic Design in the Chester Cycle*
(Chicago: University of Chicago Press, 1982); and David Mills, *Recycling the Cycle:
The City of Chester and its Whitsun Plays* (Toronto: University of Toronto Press, 1998).
For dating and the cycle's sixteenth-century revisions, see Lawrence M. Clopper,
"The History and Development of the Chester Cycle," *Modern Philology* 75 (1978):
219–46; for the reception of its performance in relation to the English Reformation,
see Richard K. Emmerson, "Contextualizing Performance: The Reception of the
Chester 'Antichrist'," *Journal of Medieval and Early Modern Studies* 29 (1999): 89–119.

[3] Edited by Emile Roy, *Jour du Jugement: Mystère français sur le Grand Schisme, Ètudes
sur le théâtre français au xvi*[e] *siècle* (Paris: Emile Bouillon, 1902). Translations are quoted
by line number from Richard K. Emmerson and David Hult, *Antichrist and Judgment
Day: The Middle French Jour du Jugement*, Early European Drama Translation Series
2 (Asheville, N.C.: Pegasus, 1998). The play has recently been re-edited and translated into modern French prose by Jean-Pierre Perrot and Jean-Jacques Nonot, *Le
Jour du Jugement: Mystère du XIV*[e] *siècle* (Chambéry: Éditions Comp'Act, 2000).

from Creation to Doomsday is necessarily much shorter and more
selective in what it stages. The *Jour du Jugement*, composed around
1335,[4] about a century and a half before the Chester play, develops in a highly original, thematically rich, and theatrically spectacular way the medieval Antichrist tradition as well as other popular
expectations regarding the events approaching the end of the world.
It is the only medieval non-cycle play that presents at length two of
the fundamental episodes of Christian eschatology, the appearance
of Antichrist in the Last Days and the Last Judgment.[5] In contrast
to the relatively small cast of seven main and four minor characters
who comprise the Chester Antichrist play, the French play's cast of
ninety-three characters is enormous, including ten devils, ten angels,
and ten kings; the pope, two cardinals, and a bishop; a host of Jews,
soldiers, and other followers of Antichrist; numerous saints of the
New Testament and two Old Testament figures, Enoch and Elijah;
the righteous saved and many more of the evil damned; and Antichrist
and his mother, the "Whore of Babylon," as well as Christ and his
mother, the Virgin Mary. It begins with a sermon that recounts the
Fall of Adam and Eve and other Old and New Testament events
leading to the life of Christ. Although it does not develop the full
biblical tradition at length, as do the several Old and New Testament
plays in the Chester cycle that precede its Antichrist play, the
Preacher's sermon in the *Jour du Jugement* does recall the central
events of salvation history to set its eschatological themes within a
larger biblical context.

More significantly for our introduction to Antichrist on the page
as well as the stage, the unique manuscript of the *Jour du Jugement*
includes numerous beautiful illustrations that may help us visualize
what a late medieval audience might have seen and thought about
Antichrist when viewing the play. After a dramatis personae and
frontispiece depicting the Last Judgment, the mid-fourteenth-century
deluxe manuscript from north-eastern France inscribes the play's

---

[4] For a discussion of its date, provenance, and manuscript see the introduction
to Emmerson and Hult, *Antichrist*, pp. xiii–xvi. Although Roy originally associated
the play with the Great Schism and dated it to 1398, he retracted this view after
Noël Valois, in a review of the edition (*Journal des Savants*, n.s. 1 [1903]: 677–86),
dated the play to ca. 1330 and the manuscript to ca. 1350. Unfortunately, Roy's
erroneous dating is inexplicably repeated in Lynette R. Muir, *The Biblical Drama of
Medieval Europe* (Cambridge: Cambridge University Press, 1995), 150.
[5] For a survey of Antichrist drama see Klaus Aichele, *Das Antichristdrama des
Mittelalters der Reformation und Gegenreformation* (The Hague: Martin Nijhoff, 1974).

dialogue in double columns. Rubrics identify the speakers, and the
dialogue is accompanied by eighty-eight remarkable miniatures placed
one, two, or three to a page.[6] Unfortunately, the play and its manuscript have received little sustained scholarly analysis since it was
first edited in 1902.[7] Furthermore, the images from its manuscript
have never been described at length or analyzed in depth, even
though they constitute the largest and most developed cycle of
Antichrist images in art, in any medium and, as far as I've been
able to determine, from any period.[8] This neglect is in part due to
the unique nature of the manuscript—which is still basically not
known to art historians—and in part to the fact that analyses of
Antichrist in art have tended to emphasize the influence of the many
beautiful illustrated Apocalypses that became very prominent and
important during the high Middle Ages.[9] This scholarly emphasis is
understandable because commentaries on the Apocalypse were crucial

---

[6] For a list of miniatures in relation to the text see Emmerson and Hult, *Antichrist*,
appendix 2, 94–98. Perrot and Nonot reproduce in color twenty-nine miniatures,
and all the miniatures are available in color on Jesse Hurlburt's DScriptorium website project (http://www.byu.edu/~hurlbut/dscriptorium/jugcment/jugement.html).
Roy also lists the miniatures at the conclusion of his edition, 257–59.

[7] In addition to the introductions and commentaries that accompany Roy's edition, Perrot and Nonot's edition and modern French translation, and Emmerson
and Hult's English translation, see Grace Frank, *The Medieval French Drama* (Oxford:
Clarendon, 1954), 131–35, which summarizes the play and corrects Roy; Aichele,
Antichristdrama, 35–39, which outlines the play's scenes; and Emmerson, *Antichrist*,
166–87, which traces the exegetical context of the *Jour du Jugement* and discusses its
relationship to other plays. Muir, *Biblical Drama*, devotes only two sentences to the
play, erroneously describing the Antichrist section as a "preface" to the *Jour du
Jugement* (p. 150). The play is not discussed in Alan Knight, "France," in *The Theatre
of Medieval Europe: New Research in Early Drama*, ed. Eckehard Simon (Cambridge:
Cambridge University Press, 1991), 151–68.

[8] The fullest study of the miniatures, which focuses on their possible relationship
to the play's performance, is Richard K. Emmerson, "Visualizing Performance: The
Miniatures of Besançon MS 579 (*Jour du Jugement*)," *Exemplaria* 11 (1999): 245–72,
from which this present essay occasionally borrows. For Antichrist in medieval art,
see Rosemary Muir Wright, *Art and Antichrist in Medieval Europe* (Manchester: Manchester
University Press, 1995), which does not discuss the *Jour du Jugement* miniatures. See
also Emmerson, *Antichrist*, 108–45; Bernard McGinn, "Portraying Antichrist in the
Middle Ages," in *The Use and Abuse of Eschatology in the Middle Ages*, ed. Werner
Verbeke, et al., Mediaevalia Lovaniensia, series I, studia XV (Leuven: Leuven
University Press, 1988), 1–48; and Richard K. Emmerson, "The Representation of
Antichrist in Hildegard of Bingen's *Scivias*: Image, Word, Commentary, and Visionary
Experience," *Gesta* 41 (2002): 95–110. For continuity of the Antichrist tradition in
Renaissance art, see Jonathan B. Riess, *The Renaissance Antichrist: Luca Signorelli's Orvieto
Frescoes* (Princeton: Princeton University Press, 1995).

[9] One of the most important studies, still valuable, is Jessie Poesch, "Antichrist
Imagery in Anglo-French Apocalypse Manuscripts" (Ph.D. diss., Univ. of Pennsylvania,

in the development of the Antichrist legend.[10] Exegetes identified the various beasts, hellish creatures, and angelic beings from the Book of Revelation as prophetic symbols hinting of the roles that Antichrist and his supernatural supporters and opponents were expected to play in the Last Days. But one result of such emphasis on illustrated Apocalypses is to limit analysis of the rich details of Antichrist's legendary life, which had a wide-ranging iconography extending in interesting ways beyond traditional Apocalypse illustrations, as is particularly evident in the graphic cuts illustrating the German block-book *vitae Antichristi*.[11] Although drawing from many patristic, scholastic, and legendary sources, this popular *vita Antichristi* drew from the *Libellus de Antichristo*, a short compendium of eschatological exegesis, pseudo-prophetic texts, and folklore written around 950 by Abbot Adso for the French Queen, Gerberga.[12] As I have argued elsewhere, the *Libellus*, by ingeniously transforming and inverting the well-established genre of the saints' legend, created in its form and subject matter something like an anti-saint's life.[13] It served as a convenient way to organize what were originally many unrelated events expected in the Last Days, because they could be linked to the life of the leading antagonist of the end-time, Antichrist. Both in Latin and in vernacular versions, the *Libellus* was included in encyclopedic compendia and developed in theological handbooks, influencing many religious,

---

1966); for a survey of manuscripts illustrating the Apocalypse see Richard Kenneth Emmerson and Suzanne Lewis, "Census and Bibliography of Medieval Manuscripts Containing Apocalypse Illustrations, c. 800–1500," *Traditio* 40 (1984): 337–79; 41 (1985): 367–409; and 42 (1986): 443–72. It will be cited as "Census" and manuscript number.

[10] See Emmerson, *Antichrist*, 39–43.

[11] See Karin Boveland, et al., *Der Antichrist und Die Fünfzehn Zeichen vor dem Jüngsten Gericht*, 2 vols. (Hamburg: Friedrich Wittig, 1979). For other non-Apocalypse illustrations, see Richard K. Emmerson, "Beyond the Apocalypse: The Human Antichrist in Late Medieval Illustrated Manuscripts," in *Waiting in Fearful Hope: Approaching the New Millennium*, ed. Christopher Kleinhenz and Fannie LeMoine (Madison: University of Wisconsin Press, 1999), 102–30.

[12] The standard edition is *Adso Dervensis, De ortu et tempore Antichristi*, ed. Daniel Verhelst, Corpus Christianorum Continuatio Mediaevalis 45 (Turnholt: Brepols, 1976). The best translation is by Bernard McGinn, *Apocalyptic Spirituality*, Classics of Western Spirituality (New York: Paulist, 1979), 81–96; John Wright also translates it as an appendix to his *The Play of Antichrist* (Toronto: Pontifical Institute of Mediaeval Studies, 1967), 100–10. On Adso see Robert Konrad, *De ortu et tempore Antichristi: Antichristvorstellung und Geschichtsbild des Abtes Adso von Montier-en-Der*, Münchener historische Studien (Kallmuenz: Lassleben, 1964).

[13] See Richard Kenneth Emmerson, "Antichrist as Anti-Saint: The Significance of Abbot Adso's *Libellus de Antichristo*," *American Benedictine Review* 30 (1979): 175–90.

literary, and visual texts during the high Middle Ages.[14] Expanded
by legendary and folkloristic sources, it provided the basic shape of
the Antichrist tradition, from which various cultural works, such as
the plays we are examining, could draw to develop their own unique
theatrical versions.

For example, the *Jour du Jugement* draws on features of this popular tradition when it treats the origins of Antichrist. After the
Preacher's introductory sermon outlining the major events of salvation history up to the Last Days,[15] the action of the play begins with
a parliament in hell, a rather inauspicious, if spectacular, opening.
Satan, realizing that the end of time is near, rallies his demonic
troops by urging action to produce the greatest weapon they will
marshal against Christianity:

> But before the judgment arrives,
> one of us should become a man
> and go straight to Babylon,
> making sure that, without any delay,
> he manages to bed a woman
> full of every type of disgrace,
> one who has lived all her days
> in a brothel, winter and summer.
> She will be of the lineage of Dan
> and will conceive a son.
> He will call himself Antichrist
> and make the people love him
> through gifts, through fraudulent preaching,
> and through the resuscitation
> of the dead, whom he will bring back to life;
> even the treasures of the world will be,
> in truth, completely at his disposal. (lines 207–23)

The goal is to seduce a Jewish prostitute living in Babylon, the play's
dramatic version of the apocalyptic Whore of Babylon (Rev. 17) and
the way it imaginatively merges two apparently unrelated strands of
exegesis concerning Antichrist's origins—that he will be born of the

---

[14] For the influence of Adso's *Libellus* see Emmerson, *Antichrist*, 74–107. For an
early vernacular version, see Richard K. Emmerson, "From *Epistola* to *Sermo*: The
Old English Version of Adso's *Libellus de Antichristo*," *Journal of English and Germanic
Philology* 82 (1983): 1–10.
[15] For the miniature illustrating the sermon, see Emmerson, "Visualizing Performance,"
267–68 and fig. 10.

Jewish people, specifically from the tribe of Dan; and that he will be born in Babylon.[16]

In the next scene two devils travel to earth, and one, Engignart, discards his hellish costume to take human form. A miniature shows him dressed in the latest style as a modish young man and approaching the prostitute in a garden, recalling the seduction scenes so common in medieval romances.[17] Ranting about her hatred of Christianity, the Babylonian harlot establishes her crucial prophetic pedigree from the tribe of Dan, a lineage clearly in contrast to the house of David that is so fundamental to the genealogy of Jesus (Matt. 1):

> I am a Jew, and I was born
> under the Law that God gave
> to Moses and to the rest of us;
> but I hate the Christians, all of them,
> those people who believe in Jesus Christ,
> for their God is insignificant,
> and I neither esteem him nor fear him in the slightest.
> Let there be no doubt, I am of the lineage of Dan;
> now you, tell me what you are seeking. (lines 293–301)

Engignart, a perfect devil, answers forthrightly, drawing on the language of *fin amours* to explain his "adventure":

> Those are admirable words you have pronounced
> my fair sister; it is from a foreign land
> that I have come here in search of adventure,
> and I also have come to look for a beloved.
> Thus I beg you, with utmost courtesy,
> to agree to be my lady
> and to accept me as your beloved;
> grant that you will take possession of me as you would a lover
> so that with you I may fulfill my pleasure;
> this is what should come from love. (lines 302–11)

The conception of Antichrist follows, which is pictured in a relatively coy miniature showing the devil and Antichrist's mother under bedclothes.[18] The play thus follows the more popular, folkloristic tradition that Antichrist is engendered by a devil, not the orthodox

---

[16] See, for example, Adso's *Libellus de Antichristo*, trans. McGinn, *Apocalyptic Spirituality*, 90–91.

[17] See Emmerson, "Visualizing Performance," fig. 6.

[18] For the conception of Antichrist see Emmerson, "Visualizing Performance," 259–62 and fig. 4.

view that he is fully human but just possessed by a devil.[19] As his prophetic opponent will proclaim in the Chester *Coming of Antichrist*, he may call himself Christ and Messiah, but "Hee ys the devyll" (XXIII: 299)! To my knowledge, the miniature illustrating the *Jour du Jugement* is the first visual depiction of the conception of Antichrist.[20]

The French play's emphasis on the origins of Antichrist is one of the ways in which it differs from the Chester Antichrist play. Since the English play is part of a much longer cycle, it is much shorter and necessarily more selective in staging the tradition. It does not stage Antichrist's conception, birth, or youth, but introduces him at the beginning of his false ministry when he claims to be "Messias, Christ, and most of might" (XXIII:13) and attacks Jesus as a liar who was slain at his command (25–32). He even boasts that he will be loved by all women (40–44), an interesting allusion to Daniel 11:37: "and he shall follow the lust of women. . . ." In contrast to this hurried introduction, the action of the *Jour du Jugement* seems leisurely. For example, it depicts him as a young man being taught by Satan (Fig. 1), who has taken human form. He promises the youth authority over the earth if he consents to a Faustian pact:

> You must renounce God
> and grant everything to me,
> body and soul together. (lines 549–51)

In response, Antichrist takes Satan as his feudal lord: "I hereby become your vassal, in body and in soul" (line 571). This scene is the humanized dramatic equivalent of miniatures depicting Apocalypse 13:2, in which the Dragon, symbolizing Satan, gives authority to the seven-headed beast that rises from the sea, a traditional symbol of Antichrist.[21] In the French play, the passing of authority is dramatized in more personal terms, as the devil teaching his pupil and promising "I shall remain with you never leaving your side" (line

---

[19] On the exegetical discussions, see Emmerson, *Antichrist*, 79–83.

[20] Similar images are included in the fifteenth-century German block-book *vitae Antichristi*; see Boveland, *Der Antichrist*, 2:3, and Emmerson, *Antichrist*, fig. 3. It is also illustrated in a book printed by Wynkyn de Worde, ca. 1525, about the time when the Chester cycle was revised. See Richard K. Emmerson, "Wynkyn de Worde's *Byrthe and Lyfe of Antechryst* and Popular Eschatology on the Eve of the English Reformation," *Mediaevalia* 14 [1991, for 1988]: 281–311, esp. fig. 4.

[21] See, for example, the Cloisters Apocalypse, fol. 22v; facs. ed. in *The Cloisters Apocalypse*, with commentaries by Florens Deuchler, Jeffrey M. Hoffeld, and Helmut Nickel (New York: Metropolitan Museum of Art, 1971).

Fig. 1

579), a way of reminding the audience that notwithstanding his claims to be the Messiah, Antichrist is thoroughly inspired by the devil.[22] The exegetical interpretation and the visual illustration correspond to the dramatic scene, but its effect in the play is to rationalize apocalyptic symbols within a medieval social structure and thus develop a new iconography suitable for the stage.

Another way in which the French play develops popular, if also loathsome, expectations regarding Antichrist's role in the Last Days is in its emphasis upon the Jews as Antichrist's first and most loyal followers. As Adso explains, "all the Jews will flock to him, in the belief that they are receiving God, but rather they will receive the devil."[23] Once Antichrist begins his preaching career, therefore, the Jews are shown as his constant companions. Such is the case throughout the French manuscript's miniatures, even in those illustrating dramatic scenes in which the Jews have no part in the play's action or its dialogue.[24] This anti-Jewish bias informs a unique interpretation of

---

[22] As Adso states, "The devil's power will foster and protect him in his mother's womb and it will always be with him" (McGinn, trans., *Apocalyptic Spirituality*, 90).
[23] Trans. McGinn, *Apocalyptic Spirituality*, 94.
[24] See, for example, Emmerson, "Visualizing Performance," fig. 11.

Der Enndkrift heyffet die juden bezeichen an die ftirn · Vnd uff
die rechten hand/zů einem zeichen das sp an ín glouben·das ftet
geschaben ín Appocalipfi johannis ín Compendio feptmo

Fig. 2

the mark of the beast. Revelation 13 warns that a false prophet beast
"shall make all, both little and great, rich and poor, freemen and
bondmen, to have a character in their right hand, or on their foreheads. And that no man might buy or sell, but he that hath the character, or the name of the beast, or the number of his name" (13:16–17).[25]
The German block-book *vitae Antichristi* repeatedly depict the "mark
of the beast" in the expected way (Fig. 2), showing a seated Antichrist
surrounded by demons and directing his assistants as they mark a convert's forehead. But the *Jour du Jugement* spins this text by staging a
scene in which Antichrist has coins minted with his image embossed,
as pictured in another miniature illustrating its manuscript.[26] It first
shows the leader of the Jews, Annes, urging Antichrist to

> Have coins minted
> upon which your image is engraved,
> and as soon as they are made
> have it announced that everyone should take one
> as a sign that they are under your banner. (lines 640–44)

---

[25] All biblical citations are to the Douay-Rheims translation of the Vulgate, *The
Holy Bible* (rpt. Rockford, Ill.: Tan Books, 1989).
[26] For this miniature, see Emmerson, "Visualizing Performance," fig. 3.

A workman standing to the right hammers the image onto coins, while the devil Pluto stands behind him. In the next miniature Pluto reads a proclamation given to him by Annes. It orders the entire world to use the coins and display them as a sign of loyalty to Antichrist, threatening that "whomever is found or taken into custody/ without the ensign will be accused/ of disloyalty and put to death" (lines 687–89). Clearly the mark of the beast plays a central role in the play, but it is here imprinted on coins rather than on the foreheads or hands of Antichrist's followers, a dramatically effective way of handling the enigmatic apocalyptic text and making it believable for a contemporary audience.

All are also warned that anyone who raises the price of these coins artificially will be imprisoned (lines 658–61), probably alluding to economic events in mid-fourteenth-century France. This focus on economic issues seems connected to the play's fixation on the eschatological role of the Jews. It is no coincidence that the *Jour du Jugement* strongly condemns usury, probably another reference to contemporary economic issues and yet another way in which it can attack the Jews.[27] This condemnation is evident in a particularly harsh scene in which Christ in judgment fiercely condemns to hell a usurer and his entire family and household, who are shown rising from the dead (Fig. 3).

> You neglected my command
> and lived by usury,
> all four of you, this you all know well.
> Body and soul together, each as a complete individual,
> I hereby give the four of you to the Devil. (lines 2070–74)

Interestingly, the Usurer is also the last human to speak in the play; at the very conclusion of the Last Judgment he mourns:

> Alas! What sorrow! Alas! Alas!
> I have been dispatched to the eternal presence
> Of the king of every iniquity
> And shall be toasted on every side. (lines 2408–11)

---

[27] For a similar linking in the visual arts, see Sara Lipton, *Images of Intolerance: The Representation of Jews and Judaism in the Bible moralisée* (Berkeley: University of California Press, 1999). Lipton notes that in these deluxe illustrated Bibles "a series of similar metaphoric condensations (of greed and idolatry, of avarice and the Antichrist) represents the nexus of Judaism, usury, and avarice not simply as non-Christian but as actively and willfully anti-Christian" (40).

Fig. 3

Ending with the Usurer's punishment links the play's economic and anti-Jewish elements. This unrelenting anti-Semitism is one of the most troubling ways in which the *Jour du Jugement* differs in tone from the *Coming of Antichrist*. Although the Chester play depicts Antichrist as Jewish—he refers to "my people of Jewes," XXIII (33 and 229)—it does not stage Jewish caricatures who are unrelentingly evil, conspire against Christians, or motivate the vicious action of the play.

The *Jour du Jugement* manuscript also includes several miniatures that accentuate Antichrist's tremendous deceit and that warn that he will successfully convert the entire world. Antichrist's growing hegemony is staged through his preaching of false doctrine shortly after he is instructed by Satan, the first of the four ways in which the apocalyptic deceiver is expected to sway the unwary.[28] But Antichrist's most effective stage tricks are his apparent miracles, such as the restoration of sight to a blind man (lines 606–29, Fig. 4) and curing a leper (lines 696–743), which he accomplishes with theatrical flair. One of the questions regarding Antichrist debated by medieval theologians was the source and extent of his miraculous power. Was

---

[28] For an illustration of his preaching, see Emmerson, "Visualizing Performance," fig. 11.

Fig. 4

he able to accomplish numerous supernatural marvels through the power of the devil working in him? Or were they all fake, simply illusions, in the case of this play, sheer stage magic? Of particular concern was Antichrist's amazing power to raise the dead, the ultimate miracle. Some theologians argued that Antichrist really would be able to raise the dead, whereas others said it would be accomplished through magic or demonic possession.[29] This miracle is made a central scene in both the *Jour du Jugement* and the *Coming of Antichrist*. In the French play, Antichrist, following the suggestion of an evil bishop (lines 756–67), proceeds to a graveyard, where he apparently resurrects a dead man, calling out: "Body, pick yourself up instantly!" (line 786). A miniature depicts him as he rises from a tomb, hands clasped in worship of Antichrist.[30] The Chester *Coming of Antichrist* similarly makes the resurrection of two men the primary sign of Antichrist's divinity:

> Whether I in my godhead bee
> by verey signe you shall see.

---

[29] On this debate see Emmerson, *Antichrist*, 92–94.
[30] See facsimile 2 in Emmerson and Hult, *Antichrist and Judgment Day*, xxxvi.

> Ryse up, dead men, and honour me
> and knowe me for your lord. (XXIII, 101–104)

But it is important that this so-called miracle not be left unchal-
lenged by the action of either play. Chester reveals the falsity of the
fake resurrections when Elijah, challenging their genuineness, offers
the two resurrected men bread consecrated in the name of the Trinity,
and they must turn away in fear:

> Alas, put that bread out of my sight!
> To looke on hit I am not light.
> That print that ys upon hit pight,
> hit puttes me to great feere. (XXIII, 577–80)

This unmasking is particularly appropriate in the dramatic context
of the Chester play, since it is part of what was originally a Corpus
Christi cycle, drama associated with the celebration of the Eucharist.
Given the theatrical effectiveness of the false miracle, those apparently
raised from the dead must, in some way, be unmasked, because the
miracle of resurrection is finally just too powerful for Antichrist's
appropriation, whether on page or stage. The French play also ultimately assures its audience that this apparent miracle is, in fact, a
fake, that indeed the dead body has not been resurrected but has
been possessed by a devil. Thus, a later scene near the end of the
play, after the death of Antichrist, depicts Beelzebub leaving the body
of the dead man.[31] The rubric notes that the devil "speaks in the
Resurrected Body," admitting:

> I have brought this body to its feet
> And yet it is lacking the breath of life:
> Whatever words he has spoken
> are my doing, for thus I have guided him. (lines 1600–1603)

The miniature shows a grisly demon leaving the body while a crowd,
modeling the audience's reaction, stares in amazement.

But before this miracle is proven false, Antichrist is able to convert the entire world. The *Jour du Jugement* symbolically depicts his
secular hegemony by staging the conversion of a group of ten kings
who are shown pledging allegiance to Antichrist (Fig. 5). These characters are the play's representation of the ten horns of the beast of

---

[31] Emmerson, "Visualizing Performance," fig. 9.

Fig. 5

Revelation 13, which exegetes identified as the major kingdoms expected to rule the world in the time of Antichrist. The Chester *Antichrist*, with its much smaller cast, stages only four kings, perhaps symbolizing the four corners of the world rather than the ten horns of the beast but also those, like the Jews, who believe "that Christ ys not common yet" (XXIII, 62). But no matter the number of kings, the symbolic import is the same, to represent the totality of Antichrist's power. In both plays Antichrist gains political and secular support by means of his false teaching and miraculous powers and in Chester he distributes territories to the four kings:

> To thee I give Lombardee;
> and to thee Denmarke and Hungarye;
> and take thou Pathmos and Italie;
> and Roome yt shalbe thine. (XXIII, 241–44)

In the *Jour du Jugement*, he is also able to gain religious support, converting important ecclesiastics such as an unscrupulous bishop, who is amazed by Antichrist's supernatural powers, and coercing two cowardly cardinals with threats (Fig. 6): "I will have you drawn by horses/if you do not convert to me" (lines 1376–77). After the first

Fig. 6

cardinal agrees to follow Antichrist, the deceiver calls on yet another way in which he consolidates his power, by tendering bribes:

> Dear gentle friend, I in turn give to you
> more land and riches
> than you could ever have possessed.
> All that I have will be yours. (lines 1394–97)

Antichrist thus establishes his authority within the Church hierarchy quite effectively. Only the pope, who is dispatched to prison, remains steadfast.

Although not as detailed as the numerous miniatures accompanying the *Jour du Jugement*, illustrated Apocalypses do reveal how medieval artists imagined some central features of the Antichrist tradition. Exemplifying such manuscripts are the Anglo-French Apocalypses, a visual tradition of the mid-thirteenth century and after whose early cycles of images predate the French play by about a century.[32] Their relationship to the biblical text typifies the complex ways in which the Antichrist tradition seeks both to represent the literal details of

---

[32] For these manuscripts see Suzanne Lewis, *Reading Images: Narrative Discourse and Reception in the Thirteenth-Century Illuminated Apocalypse* (Cambridge: Cambridge University Press, 1995); "Census," nos. 38–117; and Wright, *Art and Antichrist*, 115–43.

apocalyptic narrative and to decipher its often fantastic imagery, for these Apocalypses combine a relatively close illustration of the biblical text with interpretations based on earlier Apocalypse commentaries, both Latin and French. The most common biblical source for the development of Antichrist iconography is Revelation 11. Scripture describes how Two Witnesses will come to preach in the Last Days (11:3) and will be killed by a beast that arises from the abyss (11:7). Early commentators identified the Two Witnesses as the Old Testament patriarch Enoch and the prophet Elijah, righteous men taken to heaven without suffering death. According to this tradition, they wait in the Earthly Paradise until the Last Days, when they will return to earth to preach against Antichrist, who is symbolized by the beast arising from the abyss.[33] Thus the Chester cycle introduces them near the conclusion of its *Harrowing of Hell* pageant, where Adam, newly released by Christ from hell, sees the witnesses in the Earthly Paradise. As Elijah explains:

> Yea, bodily death, leeve thou mee,
> yett never suffred wee,
> but here ordaynt we are to bee
> tyll Antechriste come with hise.
> To fight against us shall hee
> and slea us in this holye cittye;
> but sekerly, within dayes three
> and a halfe, we shall ryse. (XVII, 245–52)

This brief scene, immediately preceding the cycle's *Resurrection* play, anticipates their appearance later in the cycle when they return to earth shortly before the General Resurrection.

The *Jour du Jugement* also identifies the Two Witnesses as Enoch and Elijah and associates them with the Earthly Paradise. In its first miniature after the staging of the birth of Antichrist, the manuscript depicts Enoch and Elijah standing within a walled garden—probably an allusion to the Earthly Paradise—while an angel calls them in a song to come forth.[34] They then begin preaching in opposition to Antichrist. These scenes are introduced relatively early in the play and serve the dramatic purpose of allowing time to pass between the birth of Antichrist and the beginning of his adult career. Otherwise,

---

[33] On the exegesis see Emmerson, *Antichrist*, 95–101.
[34] See Emmerson, "Visualizing Performance," fig. 7. For the manuscript's music see the analysis by Keith Glaeske in Emmerson and Hult, *Antichrist*, appendix 3, 99–101.

their preaching, although important to the play's plot, is relatively
brief. In contrast, the preaching of Enoch and Elijah and their dis-
pute with Antichrist constitute the longest and most important section of the Chester *Coming of Antichrist*.[35] Although modern audiences
may wonder why their vigorous theological debate is so lengthy and
perhaps even question its effectiveness in performance, it is crucial
to the play's representation of this most theatrical of deceivers. One
of the biggest challenges in any staging of the figure of Antichrist is
to characterize him both as Christ-like and as demonically inspired.
It must convince the audience that Antichrist, when he claims "Ego
sum Christus" (I am Christ, Matt. 24:5), will indeed fool even the
elect, while also assuring the audience that, no matter how many
on stage are fooled, Antichrist really is not the Messiah. Chester
accomplishes this simultaneous characterization by having Antichrist
open the play speaking in Latin, allowing him to appropriate the
authority of the ecclesiastical language to make outrageous claims of
being divine.[36] At the same time, a ridiculously confusing doctrine
is attributed to him as he debates the Two Witnesses. His convoluted
theology, which must have seemed absurd to medieval Christians—
for example, at one point he asks, "What ys the Trinitye for to
saye?" (XXIII, 491)—cues the audience to recognize his deceit, even
as the characters in the play are fooled. The debate ultimately turns
into a shouting match before the Doctor advises Antichrist to kill
the Two Witnesses, a reminder that, notwithstanding his pretentions
to imitate the life of Christ, he is a vicious persecutor, as he is often
portrayed in medieval art.[37]

---

[35] On the significance of the Two Witnesses to the play and its relation to the
cycle as a whole, see Richard K. Emmerson, "'Nowe Ys Common This Daye':
Enoch and Elias, Antichrist, and the Structure of the Chester Cycle," in *"Homo,
Memento Finis": The Iconography of Just Judgment in Medieval Art and Drama*, ed. David
Bevington, Early Drama, Art and Music, Monograph Series 5 (Kalamazoo: Medieval
Institute Publications, 1985), 89–120.

[36] On the use of Latin in other medieval plays depicting evil characters, see
Richard K. Emmerson, "'Englysch Laten' and 'Franch': Demonic Language in
Medieval Drama," in *The Devil, Heresy, and Witchcraft in the Middle Ages: Essays in
Honor of Jeffrey B. Russell*, ed. Alberto Ferreiro (Leiden: E. J. Brill, 1998), 305–26.

[37] See, for example, the full-folio miniature illustrating the *Livre de la Vigne Nostre
Seigneur* (Oxford, Bodleian Library, Douce 134, fol. 30r), a French manuscript from
the 1460s that depicts, in stark detail, a series of tortures, mutilations, and excruciating
deaths overseen by Antichrist. For a reproduction, see Emmerson, *Antichrist*, fig. 6;
for this manuscript, see Frances Carey, ed., *The Apocalypse and the Shape of Things to
Come* (London: British Museum Press, 1999), 93–94, cat. no. 22; and Wright, *Art
and Antichrist*, 170–71 and illus. 47, 48.

The *Jour du Jugement* separates the original preaching of Enoch and Elijah from the representation of their death, treating their sermon as an introductory warning before staging Antichrist's own preaching, miracles, and persecutions. Much later in the play, after Antichrist has converted the ten kings, the action returns to Enoch and Elijah. The Jews betray them, labeling them "false preachers," "feigned hermits," "traitors," "hypocrites," "fraudulent betrayers," "sons of bitches," "sinful dogs," "filthy traitors and renegades, disloyal, vile, abject, and foul" (lines 1046–48, 1061, 1070–72). Two knights are summoned to arrest the prophets and take them to face Antichrist, who after listening to them states:

> Deceitful hypocrites, putrid churls,
> you are telling lies. I am the son
> of God, who can do anything; and I made
> all things along with Him. (lines 1122–25)

After a relatively short debate, Antichrist loses his patience and orders their execution.[38] The play then again moves away from the prophets to depict Antichrist's confrontation with the cardinals and pope, another theatrically effective way of representing the passage of time prophesied by the biblical account: "And after three days and a half, the spirit of life from God entered into them. And they stood upon their feet, and great fear fell upon them that saw them. And they heard a great voice from heaven, saying to them: Come up hither. And they went up to heaven in a cloud: and their enemies saw them" (Rev. 11:11–12). The miniature representing their resurrection by an angel, however, shows them not rising up into heaven but moving toward heaven's gate on the left.[39] The artist of the *Jour du Jugement* manuscript departs from traditional iconography perhaps to represent a scene as acted out on stage, where the two prophets move stage left towards a Gothic structure representing heaven.

In both plays the deaths of Enoch and Elijah culminate Antichrist's deceit and cruelty and serve as turning points in the action. The crucial significance of the Two Witnesses in the dramatic tradition is not unusual, for their death at the hands of Antichrist or his minions is central to apocalyptic iconography. In fact, in one strand of Anglo-French Apocalypses it served as the context for the development of

---

[38] See Emmerson, "Visualizing Performance," fig. 2.
[39] See Emmerson, "Visualizing Performance," fig. 8.

mini-picture cycles portraying the deceits and persecutions of Antichrist. One of the most interesting of these is found in the Wellcome Apocalypse, a German manuscript dated about 1420 that interleaves within its sequence of biblical illustrations several scenes warning of Antichrist's future evil.[40] Its account begins by picturing the traditional understanding of Apocalypse 11, showing the Two Witnesses, identified specifically as Enoch and Elijah, as they come forward to challenge the deceiver. In the next miniature (Fig. 7), a crowned Antichrist, enthroned and holding a sword, orders them killed by his henchmen, one of whom stabs a decapitated witness while the other swings his sword toward the head of the second prophet, who kneels in prayer. The lower register of the miniature then depicts their resurrection and assumption into heaven, following the apocalyptic text quite closely by depicting Enoch and Elijah in the upper left rising in a cloud, while a great earthquake destroys one tenth of the city, as prophesied (Rev. 11:13).

The following miniatures, however, are not based on the biblical account. Instead, the next five pages of this illustrated Apocalypse insert a legendary visual life of Antichrist between the biblical account of chapters 11 and 12, a series of images based, ultimately, on Adso's *Libellus de Antichristo* and later more extensive versions of the Antichrist legend rather than on scripture. A series of three scenes per folio detail the deeds of Antichrist as they were popularly imagined during the high Middle Ages. One folio, for instance, shows Antichrist in its top register burning books, to destroy the doctrine of true Christianity, and rebuilding the temple in Jerusalem, which he then appropriates, a symbolic representation of the "abomination of desolation" (Matt. 24:15).[41] The next two registers of the miniature depict various supernatural, sometimes absurd, marvels that Antichrist performs to fool his followers. Among these, the middle register shows a tree growing upside-down, with its roots in the air, a symbol of the upside-down unnatural world of the Last Days that Antichrist

---

[40] On the Wellcome Apocalypse, see Emmerson, *Antichrist*, 126–44 passim and illus. 11; "Census," no. 128; and Carey, ed., *Apocalypse*, 90–91, cat. no. 20.

[41] For a reproduction of this folio, see Wright, *Art and Antichrist*, illus. 49. As Wright notes (174), the main source of the inscriptions accompanying the Antichrist images is Hugh of Strasbourg's *Compendium Theologicae Veritatis*. Similar scenes are also included in de Worde's *Byrthe and Lyfe of Antechryst*; see Emmerson, "Wynkyn de Worde's *Byrthe and Lyfe of Antechryst*," fig. 8.

Fig. 7

performs in the Chester Antichrist play. There his stunt is part of
his campaign to convert the four kings, as he boasts, from heresy:

> Nowe wyl I turne, all through my might,
> trees downe, the rootes upright—
> that ys marveyle to your sight—
> and fruyt groinge upon.
> So shall they growe and multiplye
> through my might and my maisterye.
> I put you owt of heresye
> to leeve me upon. (XXIII, 81–88)[42]

The lower register of this folio depicts yet more unnatural marvels,
such as Antichrist's extracting a knight from an egg. More seriously,
it also illustrates a troubling supernatural sign, his bringing fire down
from heaven, a power attributed to the false prophet beast in
Apocalypse 13:13: "And he did great signs, so that he made also
fire to come down from heaven unto the earth in the sight of men."
This event was traditionally interpreted as another of his many ways
in which the pseudo-Christ deceitfully patterned his life on key events
in the life of Christ, in this case performing a pseudo-Pentecost.[43]
Such parodies of biblical events are particularly effective in the *Coming
of Antichrist*, since they recall earlier cycle plays the audience would
have just seen that staged genuine events from Christ's life, from his
Crucifixion (XVI) and *Resurrection* (XVIII) to *Pentecost* (XXI). Thus
Antichrist now pretends to die, ludicrously crying "I dye, I dye! Nowe
am I dead!" (XXIII, 133), and the four kings bury him and await
his resurrection in three days, as promised. He then rises, receives
the adoration of the kings, goes to the temple to be worshipped, further blasphemes, and then performs the pseudo-Pentecost:

> I will nowe send my holye ghooste.
> You kinges, also to you I tell
> to knowe me lord of mightes moste
> of heaven, yearth, and hell. (XXIII, 193–96)

Antichrist's faked resurrection and his pseudo-Pentecost—both pictured
(Fig. 8) in a German block-book *vita Antichristi* that emphasizes their

---

[42] This event is depicted in other Apocalypses that insert a brief *vita Antichristi*
after chapter 11. For example, see Pierpont Morgan Library, M.524, fol. 7r
(Emmerson, *Antichrist*, fig. 4); and London, British Library Add. MS 19896, fol. 8v
(Carey, ed., *Apocalypse*, 125, no. 1; "Census," no. 127).

[43] This scene is also illustrated in the German block-book *vitae Antichristi*; see
Emmerson, *Antichrist*, fig. 9.

Der Entkrist erstet au dem dritten tag. Vnd spricht zů den fürsten vnd herren vnd zů allem anderm volck. Secht das ich wor er got vnd mensch byn. Vnd alsdann so knuwen sy für in nider vnd betten in an

Der Entkrist macht durch die krafft des tüfels vnd durch zouberig das feür von hymel vellet vff syn junger. des vberhebē sy sich denn vnd sprechen sy syn besser dann die junger vnsers herren cristi ihesu die den heiligen geist empfiengen.

Fig. 8

demonic origins—are stunning examples of his success in mimicking
Christ and deceiving Jews and Christians alike.

The visual life of Antichrist inserted within the Wellcome Apocalypse
depicts several other deeds of Antichrist on two facing folios, each
illustrating a series of events in three registers.[44] The first folio in its
top register details a series of gruesome tortures against those who
remain faithful to the true Christ. A man is skinned alive, another
has a metal rod drilled into his skull, and others are fed to wild ani-
mals. In the middle register Antichrist's followers celebrate as Enoch
and Elijah are decapitated, and in the lower register Antichrist pretends to die and be resurrected. In the top register of the facing
folio, Antichrist attempts his last impudent parody of events from
the life of Christ, a pseudo-Ascension, but his blasphemy here finally
ends. After attempting to rise to heaven from the Mount of Olives,
Antichrist falls headlong from the arms of demons after being struck
down by an angel.[45] In the middle register, Enoch and Elijah reap-
pear after Antichrist's death to preach to those who are feasting as
in the days of Noah, warning them to prepare for the return of
Christ. Finally, the folio's lower register depicts the signs of Doomsday,
certain evidence that the end is imminent. Medieval eschatology
included the popular belief that judgment day would be preceded
by numerous cataclysmic signs that would provide warnings of the
end, and there developed a tradition, attributed to St. Jerome, that
cosmic and supernatural signs would warn the world of the return
of Christ on each of the fifteen days before Doomsday.[46] The German
block-book *vitae Antichristi*, for example, illustrate all fifteen signs at
the conclusion of their Antichrist sequence (Fig. 9) and before depicting the Last Judgment, and the Fifteen Signs of Doomsday also
appear in *The Prophets of Antichrist*, the pageant preceding the Antichrist

---

[44] The manuscript opening is illustrated in Carey, ed., *Apocalypse*, 91, no. 20.

[45] For this scene, see also Emmerson, *Antichrist*, fig. 11; and Wright, *Art and Antichrist*, illus. 50. Similar depictions of Antichrist's fall are included in the German block-book *vitae Antichristi* (see Boveland, ed., *Der Antichrist*, 2:24), the *Nuremberg Chronicle* printed by Anton Koberger in 1493 (see Carey, ed., *Apocalypse*, 110, fig. 6), Signorelli's *Antichrist* fresco at Orvieto (see Reiss, *Renaissance Antichrist*, fig. 4), and the early six-teenth-century *Byrthe and Lyfe of Antechryst* (see Emmerson, "Wynkyn de Worde's *Byrthe and Lyfe of Antechryst*," fig. 12).

[46] See William Heist, *The Fifteen Signs before Doomsday* (East Lansing: Michigan State College Press, 1952). The signs are fully illustrated in the Oxford *Vigne* manu-script and in the famous *Pricke of Conscience* windows of All Saints, North Street, York.

Fig. 9

play in the Chester cycle. It introduces the dramatic depiction of the false Christ of the last days just as the Old Testament prophets are often staged to introduce the plays depicting the nativity of the true Christ. These signs are enumerated by the play's Expositor, who describes each sign and then addresses the audience, urging them to remain faithful and concluding with a warning:

> Nowe have I tould you, in good faye,
> the tokens to come before doomesdaye.
> God give you grace to do so aye
> that you them worthye bee
> to come to the blysse that lasteth aye.
> As mych as here wee and our playe,
> of Antechristes signes you shall assaye.
> Hee comes! Soone you shall see! (XXII, 333–40)

The signs of doomsday in the Chester cycle introduce the *Coming of Antichrist* rather than conclude it because the *Prophets of Antichrist* initiates the cycle's shift from early Christian to eschatological events, preparing the audience for both Antichrist and Doomsday.

The *Coming of Antichrist* concludes quickly after Antichrist orders the death of Enoch and Elijah. According to the play's Latin rubric, Michael, holding a sword in his right hand, approaches immediately after the death of the two prophets and addresses Antichrist, sending him to the devil:

> Antechriste, nowe ys common this daye.
> Reigne no lenger nowe thou maye.
> Hee that hath led thee alwaye,
> nowe him thou must goe to. (XXIII, 625–28)

With the conclusion of his speech, Michael kills Antichrist. A mid-fifteenth-century Carthusian miscellany roughly contemporary with the early development of the Chester cycle represents the sequencing of events staged by the *Coming of Antichrist*.[47] In images based on the Middle English version of the Pseudo-Methodius *Revelations*, the Yorkshire manuscript depicts a tyrannical Antichrist seated on a throne and ordering the death of Enoch and Elijah. Juxtaposed immediately to the right of this scene is the death of the pseudo-Christ, a visual reminder of the way in which the Chester cycle links the execution of the Two Witnesses with Antichrist's death. The miniature depicts Michael standing behind the throne of Antichrist and poking him with a long spear as he falls forward into hell. Christ watches from above, the "breath of his mouth" (2 Thess. 2:8) falling down like hail onto the doomed deceiver. The conclusion of Chester similarly shows the triumph of good over evil. After Michael wields his sword, Antichrist ludicrously cries for help from "Sathanas and Lucyfere!/Belzebub, bould batchellere!" (XXIII, 645–46), whereupon two demons emerge from hell to haul him away. This is where the Chester play briefly explains Antichrist's parentage and devilish power, features of the tradition that receive much greater attention in the *Jour du Jugement*. As in the cycle of images portraying the life of Antichrist in the Wellcome Apocalypse, Enoch and Elijah then return from the dead. They praise God, an effective dramatic contrast to Antichrist's pathetic rants as he is hauled to hell. Michael then

---

[47] See James Hogg, *An Illustrated Yorkshire Carthusian Religious Miscellany, British Library London Additional MS. 37049*, Analecta Cartusiana 95 (Salzburg: Institut für Anglistik und Amerikanistik, 1981). For the depiction of Antichrist's death, see Emmerson, "Beyond the Apocalypse," fig. 5.8.

addresses the two prophets. Noting that after their long wait in the Earthly Paradise and their combat against Antichrist they have earned "heaven-blysse" (XXIII, 717), he takes them to heaven. Their ascension ends the play, which is followed by the cycle's final play, the *Last Judgment*.

Although much more leisurely, the *Jour du Jugement* similarly links the death of Enoch and Elijah to the conclusion of Antichrist's power. After the prophets are taken to heaven, the Jew Malaquim reports to Antichrist:

> I bring you dreadful news.
> I am being eaten up with great pain and fury,
> because those men you had killed the other day
> have come back from the dead.
> This is an event that you cannot keep
> from being known throughout the city.
> I can assure you that there are now a good two thousand
> who know about it, and who, having rejected
> your law, believe in Jesus Christ.
> This is turning into a great disaster for you. (lines 1446–55)

Antichrist boastfully brushes off this concern, claiming that their resurrection is a gimmick he has devised to root out any remaining Christians. Nevertheless, his control of the play's action has now been terminated. St. John comes on stage to distribute vials of wrath to angels, whom God commands to "Go and spread my wrath over the earth" (line 1505; cf. Rev. 16:1). The fourth angel, holding his vial, then states:

> As for me, I will pour out mine
> over Antichrist, who proclaimed himself
> to be the Son of God, and who thus ridiculed
> the true God of all creation. His fate will indeed be horrible,
> and issue from the sun itself, which will
> become so blazing that he will be snuffed out
> by the uncontrollable heat. (lines 1556–63)

The angel alludes to the plague that results from the pouring out of the fourth vial of wrath, when power is given to the sun to scorch all mankind (Rev. 16:8–9). But the accompanying miniature (Fig. 10) focuses specifically on Antichrist, showing a vial being poured onto his head as he falls over backward to his death. The sun blazes

Fig. 10

above, while Annes, Antichrist's first Jewish supporter, watches. He finally recognizes the false Messiah's deceit:

> I can see that we have been betrayed.
> I don't even have the time to repent,
> for that God who tells no lies
> has already sentenced us. (lines 1570–73)

But it is too late. The play leaves the Jews hopeless even before facing their judgment.

After Antichrist's other followers mourn their perverseness and some, such as the blind man and leper, even beg forgiveness, the action shifts to heaven. Several saints and Mary now act as intercessors with Christ before the General Resurrection and judgment are staged. The movement to Doomsday thus takes place seamlessly in the *Jour du Jugement* as its eschatological narrative continues without break, a miniature establishing the authority of the true Christ, who reveals his wounds while angels hold the signs of the cross. Like the Chester play, in other words, the *Jour du Jugement* is traditional in understanding Antichrist as an eschatological figure who will appear just before the conclusion of human history, not as a generalized symbol of evil, an institution, or a despised people. Both plays thus follow a rich medieval tradition discovered in the Bible by means of vigorous exegesis, developed through numerous apocryphal and legendary accounts, depicted in rich Apocalypse manuscripts, and effectively represented in the late Middle Ages on both page and stage as vivid warnings of the trials awaiting the faithful in the Last Days.

STAGING *ANTICHRIST* AND THE PERFORMANCE OF MIRACLES

Peter Cockett

As part of the MARCO symposium on "Spectacle and Public Performance" at the University of Tennessee, Knoxville in April of 2004, the PLS (the University of Toronto's Medieval and Renaissance Players) performed the Chester *Coming of Antichrist* and George Peele's *The Old Wives Tale*. I was the director of both productions that were chosen, with the theme of the conference in mind, for their spectacular content. This paper is an examination of a process: the decision-making that informed our production of *Antichrist* as it pertains specifically to the production and performance of miracles in medieval theatre. It will examine the significance and consequences of production choices made and those considered and rejected. On the one hand, my analysis will be specific to the play and explore the manner in which the theatrical producer of *Antichrist* can and should manipulate responses to the play's miracles. This aspect of the paper addresses recent critical discussion of the play's attitude to and treatment of theatrical signs. On the other hand, a secondary intent of this paper is to give critical perspective on the process of performance-centered research itself, offering insight into the PLS's methodology, and the direction of our future labors. Of necessity the paper at times will take the form of a personal account of the directorial process.

The PLS has been a driving force in the research of medieval and Renaissance drama through performance for over three decades.[1] The company's production of the *Castle of Perseverance* and their two productions of the York Cycle stand as landmark achievements in the field. The company was originally formed by participants in a

---

[1] In this account of the company's development I rely on David Klausner's paper presented at the MARCO symposium, "Performing the Middle Ages: What Do We Think We Are Doing?," and on conversations with the company chair, Alexandra F. Johnston.

graduate seminar on medieval performance taught by Professor John Lyerle at the University of Toronto in 1964. The initials of the PLS derived from Professor Lyerle's Seminar but the group also styled itself a Latin name the *Poculi Ludique Societas* that can be roughly translated as "the drinking and playing society." The name gives an accurate impression of the spirit in which the company was formed. Initial work was characterized by wide-eyed enthusiasm as the company staged plays without concern for, or indeed awareness of, the difference between contemporary performance practice and the original performance conditions. While the performativity of the supposedly primitive medieval play texts was a revelation at the time, it quickly became apparent that research into the original performance conditions was urgently required. This led to the foundation of the REED project under the direction of Alexandra F. Johnston, an active member of PLS and now the company chair. The increasing knowledge of the historical theatrical context led to a more cautious and conservative production philosophy as the company aimed for complete authenticity to the original performance conditions. It soon became apparent, however, that knowledge of theatrical history can never be exhaustive and this realization, coupled with the influence of poststructural theory, led to the abandonment of authenticity as a goal in favor of what we now refer to as historically-informed performance. The PLS is presently in the process of clarifying its research criteria and production practices in this latest stage of its development.

Since one cannot hope to recreate authentically a moment of theatrical history, how is the work of the company different from the work of other theatrical producers of early drama, like the Stratford Shakespeare Festival, or the RSC? Our work is distinguished from these companies by its academic context and its concern for the relationship between the play texts and their original production environment. But what implications do these differences in context and concern have for the production process? What relationship should there be between the texts of the plays, contextual research material, and the creative choices made in production? And what authority can our productions have in the scholarly community? What role, that is, can they play in developing scholarly understanding of early theatre?

In the context of the ongoing company debate, MARCO's invitation to perform Chester's *Coming of Antichrist* was fortuitous and fortunate. Although we had produced the play relatively recently, it was still high on the company's "wish list" due to the controversial nature of the PLS's most recent production. Scott Moore's production in 2001 was a radical reinterpretation of the play in which Antichrist was played as a television evangelist and the dead were dressed as comical Egyptian mummies, one of which lost a detachable arm in an extended dance sequence. The company response to this production was divided. Scott's intention was to put the Christian beliefs behind the original under critical light, and many felt that his eclectic and postmodern approach to the play was invigorating and enlightening, arguing that it made history "perform" for a modern audience. The more conservative members of the company felt that this approach was out of keeping with the tenets of the PLS because the production departed too far from the historical context of the original. Scott's production has since become a lightning rod of debate in the company and a regular reference point in our continuing efforts to define ourselves as a theater company and research institution.

I personally favor the more conservative approach to our work. My interest in the PLS is primarily academic, and while my experience in the professional theater is essential to my process, my approach to PLS productions is distinct from my work with other companies, and the difference is one of intent. My work for PLS is primarily motivated by a desire to understand the significance of the plays in their original context. The two approaches, of course, are not exclusive. As medieval playwrights were well aware, performance of historical material is a dynamic means to bring the past into contact with the present. They approached the task with as much gusto and creativity as Scott did in his reworking of the *Antichrist*. My approach is more restrictive as the creative process is undertaken with constant deference to the historical context of the original. While I aim to engage the audience with the play, it is the relationship between the created live performance and my knowledge of the original performance context that particularly fascinates me and drives my work on PLS productions. MARCO's request for a production that respected the conditions of the original performance thus matched well with my own inclinations.

That the production would form part of a conference on theatrical spectacle made the project all the more attractive. I had just finished directing the Digby *Mary Magdalene* for the company's Saints'

Play Festival and had been inspired by Theresa Coletti's keynote paper at the festival that explored the play's engagement with the contemporary theological controversy surrounding theatrical images through a comparison with the Chester *Coming of Antichrist*.[2] Coletti argues that both plays encode "issues that were central to practices of representing the sacred in the religious theater of late medieval England."[3] In the Digby *Mary Magdalene* the pagan rituals in the temple of Marseilles are burlesque inversions of Christian practice that imply a relationship between sacred images and idolatry. This implicit challenge to the spiritual efficacy of the dramatic image is juxtaposed with the numerous miracles stage-managed by Jesus in the play and most importantly with the sacrament of the Eucharist performed for Mary by the priest directly before her death.[4]

In *Antichrist*, the power of the sacrament is also juxtaposed with dramatic spectacle. Antichrist uses a series of miracles to convince the four kings that he is Christ: he raises men from the dead, he dies and resurrects himself, and he sends *"forth his Spirit"* (sd. 196) to the four kings once they have accepted his divinity. All this staged spectacle amounts to, in Peter W. Travis' words, "a burlesque of the cycle itself—which has just completed its own sped-up version of Christ's life, employing the 'magic' and 'fraud' of theatrical deception."[5] Within the play itself Antichrist's theatrical trickery is juxtaposed with a performance of the sacrament of the Eucharist. Enoch and Elijah expose the fraudulent miracles by offering a Eucharistic host to the men raised from the dead by Antichrist. The dead men cannot bear to look at the host, Antichrist's true nature is revealed, and the four kings convert to Christianity. The Chester dramatist has therefore set the Antichrist's deceptive theatrical images against the Eucharistic host as sign of spiritual truth. In doing so, Travis argues that the Chester dramatist "conceded everything to the

---

[2] "Theology, Theatricality, and the Digby *Saint Mary Magdalene*," a paper presented at the PLS Saint's Play Festival, sponsored by the Councillor Jackman Program for the Arts, Victoria College, University of Toronto, May 2003. This paper has since been published in altered form as a chapter of her latest book, *Mary Magdalene and the Drama of Saints* (Philadelphia: University of Pennsylvania Press, 2004), pp. 190–217. I would like to thank Theresa for allowing me access to her paper prior to publication.

[3] Coletti, p. 191.

[4] Coletti, pp. 199–202.

[5] *Dramatic Design in the Chester Cycle* (Chicago: University of Chicago Press, 1982), p. 236.

iconoclasts"[6] and suggests that the *Coming of Antichrist* works to purify the dramatic image in preparation for the cycle's final play of the *Last Judgment*. Antichrist is both master manipulator of the dramatic image and a dramatic image himself, and in performing his defeat "the play manages . . . to 'do down' its own adversary."[7]

> What survives after this comic purgation is the dramatic world intact, purified by its self-profanation, its identity and value as a 'sign' now to be judged in context with that other surviving and more sacred sign, the sacrament of the eucharistic Host.[8]

This is a persuasive argument that articulates a significant function for the play in the cycle as a whole, but the distinction between signs is not as clear-cut as he implies since the "sacred sign" of the host is also contained within the theatrical representation. Presuming it was not an actual consecrated host, then it is only the representation of such a host and thus a carnal sign of a carnal sign of a spiritual truth. The cleansing process therefore is not complete, nor could it be.

Coletti addresses the semiological issue by embracing Sarah Beckwith's analysis of the York Cycle in the context of late medieval sacramentality.[9] Beckwith argues that contradictory responses to images and signs are "intrinsic to symbolic formation as such, and a component part of the sacramental culture enacted in these plays."[10] Sacramentality is a particular way of understanding the signifying process, in which "it is the change in the person, not the ritual object, that is the significant and transformative moment."[11] At Mass, therefore, the Eucharistic host attains its spiritual efficacy through the response of the congregation. The fact that the "ritual object" of the host in *Coming of Antichrist* is a representation of the Eucharist is less problematic in the context of a sacramental culture that embraces the difference between sign and signified. However, since the spiritual efficacy of the ritual object is dependent on its reception, how did the production generate the appropriate response in

---

[6] Ibid., p. 240.
[7] Ibid.
[8] Ibid.
[9] "Sacrum Signum: Sacramentality and Dissent in the York's Theatre of Corpus Christi," *Criticism and Dissent in the Middle Ages* (Cambridge: Cambridge University Press, 1996).
[10] Ibid., p. 265.
[11] Ibid., p. 266.

its audience? And how did it ensure the audience's response to the Antichrist's miracles was distinct from its response to the prophets' presentation of the Eucharist?

Directing *The Coming of Antichrist* offered me the chance to explore these questions in practice and from the point of view of the theatrical producer. Richard K Emmerson's essay, "Contextualizing Performance: The Reception of the Chester *Antichrist*," explores possible changes in the reception of the play over the course of its history. Drawing on reception theory, Emmerson argues that, as the cultural valency of Antichrist shifted, the consequent change in the community of readers that made up the audience would have led to divergent readings of the play in performance. My work, in contrast, focuses on the initial "readers" of the text—those responsible for the theatrical production,[12] and how their choices might influence the secondary readers in the audience. My production process was thus informed by a specific question: is it possible to distinguish between miracles on the stage intended to represent spiritual truth and the deceptive versions of those miracles presented by Antichrist? My primary goal in the production was to maintain an awareness of the diabolical intent behind the Antichrist's rhetoric and his performance of miracles, and this called for production choices that removed ambivalence from the signifying process. Given complete artistic freedom, this would have been relatively easy to achieve. As the example of Scott Moore's previous production revealed, it is possible to change radically the intended meaning of a play through manipulation of the production process. This is one of the joys and attractions of classical theatre, but in my production I was intent on exploring the role theatrical production can play in influencing the interpretation of its signs while respecting the text of the play, contextual information on contemporary representation of Antichrist, and what we can deduce and presume about the didactic intentions of the playwright. This attitude to the text and historical context limited the freedom of my creative response to the play, but, I hope,

[12] See Marvin Carlson, "Audience and the Reading of Performance," *Interpreting the Theatrical Past: Essays in the Historiography of Performance*, ed. Thomas Postlewait and Bruce A. McGonachie (Iowa City: University of Iowa Press, 1989), pp. 82–98. Carlson refers to the "two readings" of the play involved in theatrical communication, both of which constitute what Tony Bennett refers to as "productive activations" of meaning (p. 86). See also Tony Bennett, "Text, Readers, Reading Formations," *Literature and History* 16, no. 1 (1983): 3–17.

increased the value of the production as scholarly investigation. The following analysis describes my production process and the principles that informed my decision-making. It examines the choices to be made in any theatrical representation of the Antichrist, and considers the effect of those choices on the reception of his miracles and the distinction between sacred and false signs.

Scott's choice to have Antichrist played as a television evangelist was a good one in that it served his purpose and responded to cues in the text. Antichrist is his own evangelist. The play opens with a sermon advocating his power and righteousness with specific, if misguided, reference to scriptural authority. The connotations of tele-evangelism, at least for an audience of liberal Torontonians, created a critical relationship between the figure of Antichrist and contemporary Christianity that belittled both. This served Scott's didactic goals, but it clearly works against the intent of the original performance. But how exactly would Antichrist have been represented in late medieval Chester? And might there have been a similar ironic relationship between the representation of Antichrist and his words and actions on the stage? Richard K. Emmerson's extensive work on the figure of Antichrist in medieval art and literature has illuminated the multivalency and the semantic temporality of the Antichrist as cultural sign.[13] With a risk of oversimplification, interpretations of the Antichrist can be reduced to three basic options: the Antichrist is either a devil, a man, or a metaphor for a social institution such as the Catholic Church, as he became to Protestants during the Reformation. Emmerson argues that later performances of the Chester play would have identified Antichrist with the Catholic church,[14] but for our production we adopted David Mills's edition of the play, which is based on the early Peniarth manuscript and imagined a

---

[13] Richard Kenneth Emmerson, *Antichrist in the Middle Ages: A Study of Medieval Apocalypticism, Art, and Literature* (Seattle: University of Washington Press, 1981). Emmerson has also explored the manner in which the Chester *Coming of Antichrist* participates in contemporary interpretations of Antichrist: "'Nowe ys common this daye': Enoch and Elias, Antichrist, and the Structure of the Chester Cycle," in *The Chester Mystery Cycle: A Casebook*, ed. Kevin J. Harty (New York: Garland Publishing, 1993), pp. 171–198. Pages cited refer to this edition. The essay was originally printed in *Homo, Memento Finis: The Iconography of Just Judgment in Medieval Art and Drama*, ed. David Bevington (Kalamazoo: Medieval Institute, Western Michigan University, 1985), pp. 89–120.

[14] "Contextualizing Performance: The Reception of the Chester *Antichrist*," *Journal of Medieval and Early Modern Studies* 29.1 (1999): 106–111.

pre-Reformation production, thus excluding the connection between
Antichrist and Catholicism. In this early version of the text Emmerson
asserts with considerable authority that Antichrist is represented as
a man.[15] Although this is the interpretive option that we finally settled upon as the basis of our production, the alternative possibilities
warrant further consideration.

The representation of Antichrist as a devil carries least textual and
contextual authority. The prophets Enoch and Elijah use multiple
epithets in reference to the Antichrist, many of which identify him
directly or closely with the devil, and yet they do not give us a clear
idea of his appearance. At line 299 Elijah informs the kings that he
is "the Devil," and Enoch refers to him as "a fiend, comen to annoy"
(477) and "false fiend" at line 336. Later they refer to him less
directly as the "verray Devil's limb" (341), and "the Devil's own
nurry" (354). The prophets' references connect the Chester Antichrist
with the popular interpretation of Antichrist's heritage as the son of
the devil and the Whore of Babylon.[16] In fact, the first Devil explicitly takes credit for parenting Antichrist "in clean whoredom" (674).
In illustrations of this story, however, although the devil features
prominently, often hovering above or behind Antichrist, Antichrist
usually appears as a man.[17] Emmerson argues that even those manuscripts that "envision him as a normal man, emphasize his very
close relationship with the devil," alerting the reader to his "double
nature."[18] For example, the Bodleian Douce 134 depicts Antichrist
with the "the face of a young man," but above his head "sits a grin-
ning red-faced, two horned devil's head."[19]

The close visual association of Antichrist and devil was appealing
to me as it would serve the objective of my production. To represent Antichrist as a devil one would give the actor a devilish mask,
of which there are many in the PLS storerooms, and the mask would
clearly indicate Antichrist's diabolical nature even as he attempted
to persuade the kings that he was the true Christ. This interpretation would complement the strategy of the playwright in establishing the significance of the Antichrist for the audience before the play

[15] Ibid., 98. All references to the play are from David Mills, *The Chester Mystery
Cycle* (East Lansing: Colleagues Press, 1992).
[16] Emmerson, *Antichrist in the Middle Ages*, pp. 79–83.
[17] Ibid., pp. 126–7.
[18] Ibid., p. 127.
[19] Ibid.

begins: the play was preceded by *The Prophets of Antichrist* that tells us clearly who he is and what he is going to do. In principle, there should be no doubt in the audience's mind that his words are lies and his miracles illusions. The use of an actor in devil-mask would maintain focus on the Antichrist as devil regardless of his rhetorical efforts to persuade us to the contrary. As a counter product of this choice, the kings would seem more credulous and potentially ludicrous generating a laughter that could serve the didactic intent by ridiculing the follies of gullible sinners.

The text does not offer indisputable evidence on the nature of Antichrist's costume, and as we know that Christ was sometimes performed with a face masked or painted gold, it remains a possibility that Antichrist may have been masked in some way.[20] Enoch tells us that Antichrist "sits so grizzly and so grim" (342), a description that would be supported by an actor wearing a "grizzly" devilish mask. We considered creating a double mask with a golden front that could be removed to reveal the devil "within." If the golden front only partly covered the devil's mask, leaving his horns for example uncovered, the audience would be constantly aware of the Antichrist's "double nature." This remains to me an intriguing possibility that would have produced an informative reception dynamic for the Antichrist and his miracles. Ultimately, however, there was not enough textual or contextual support for such an interpretation. The prophets connect Antichrist with the devil, but they also delineate an alternative relationship between Antichrist as man, and the devil as his master and the source of his power. Elijah, for example, says he works "through the Fiend's craft." Elijah's reference to "this man" cited above is also strong evidence for this interpretation, as are his following lines: "Thou callest thee 'King' and 'Lord of all'?/A fiend is thee within!" (466–7). Elijah's distinction between the claims Antichrist has made and the truth "within" asserts a difference between the human appearance of Antichrist and his devilish identity lurking beneath. On this evidence, we decided to represent Antichrist as a man.

Having decided that Antichrist was to appear as a man, however, we were faced with a further decision: what kind of a man? Again, the source material offers more than one option for his depiction.

---

[20] The post-Reformation Banns in Mills's *Chester Mystery Cycle* refer to the "face-gilt" (201) used by the actors playing the "Godhead" (199).

Antichrist is pictured as a royal tyrant and as a pseudo-Christ, and the Chester text implies that he is both.[21] Following his opening Latin stanza, Antichrist introduces himself as follows:

> All ledes in land now be light
> that will be ruled throughout the right.
> Your saviour now in your sight
> here you may safely see.
> Messias, Christ, and most of might,
> that in the Law was you behight,
> all Mankind to joy to dight
> is comen, for I am he. (9–16)

This is apparently the pseudo-Christ, a bringer of "joy" not violence, but in the fourth stanza he complains about the impostor "Jesu" (26), who was "slain through virtue of [his] sond" (31). He is therefore a "'Messias'" that brings joy and violence. His tyrannical nature becomes increasingly apparent as the play proceeds, but what impression should we give of him when he first enters the stage? What should he wear? Again, the text gives us no clear indicators on this issue. Even in the reference to the Antichrist sitting "so grizzly and so grim," it is unclear whether Enoch is describing his fierce appearance or his attitude. Since contemporary art depicts Antichrist both as pseudo-Christ and royal tyrant, and given the absence of local art depicting these scenes, the matter remains open to speculation.[22]

The evidence in support of Antichrist as tyrannical king is perhaps the strongest. Antichrist's repeated reference to his "might" and his "posty" are signs of his pride and power, but that power is often quite explicitly spiritual rather than material power. He threatens the prophets with physical violence, promising to bring them "sorrow and care" (364), saying they will "hastily hong" (373) and that he will "make" them "lout full low" (391). However, this tyrannical attitude is matched, if not exceeded, by the prophets own threats of violence. Enoch, for example, says: "I would thy body were from thy head/twenty mile from it laid,/till I it brought again!" (368–370). If prophets can speak in this way, then so could a pseudo-Christ. Antichrist's final violence ultimately reveals him as the tyrant: the stage direction tells us that he kills the kings and the prophets with "*the sword*" (sd. 626),

---

[21] For description of the variety of representations of Antichrist, see Emmerson, *Antichrist in the Middle Ages*, pp. 124–145.

[22] Emmerson, "Nowe is common this daye," p. 173.

but this is the first mention of a sword in the text. Has Antichrist carried the sword from the beginning of the play? Does he pick it up at this moment as he finally reveals his true nature? Again, although the evidence implies that Antichrist appears as a royal tyrant, it is not conclusive. Taking his cue from the pre-Reformation Banns which describe the Dyer's guild's pageant wagon as a "wurthy cariage/that is A thing of grett costage,"[23] David Mills imagines the play would have been "costumed with some splendour."[24] This interpretation of the evidence implies an Antichrist dressed in some material grandeur, a royal tyrant rather than a pseudo-Christ. This is the choice that we made, but the evidence is still not decisive.

It would be possible, for example, to dress Antichrist in humble attire and set him upon a regally appointed carriage. This alternative is also a compelling one that deserves further consideration. Travis and Emmerson have shown how the play invites comparison between Antichrist and the Christ that appeared in the previous pageants of the cycle.[25] Antichrist performs an *imitatio christi* and his life follows exegetical tradition by imitating the saint's vita. At the same time, the dramatist clearly establishes the biblical and diabolical provenance of the Antichrist in the previous play *The Prophets of the Antichrist*. This pageant finishes with the line: "he comes, soon you shall see!"[26] and dressing Antichrist in identical fashion to Christ would have created a compelling moment for the audience that had witnessed the preceding pageants, creating a double vision, challenging them to distinguish the true Christ from the impostor, and leading them to question the veracity of the theatrical image in just the manner that Travis suggests.[27] The extent of this effect in performance is yet to be tested and in my mind warrants a further production. My own production choice was informed by my desire to work against potential ambivalence in the representation of the play's signs and thus we dressed the Antichrist as a royal tyrant. This choice, therefore, while it was influenced by the evidence in the text, and by the contextual evidence of the pre-Reformation Banns, was

---

[23] In *Chester*, ed. Lawrence M. Clopper, Records of Early English Drama (Toronto: University of Toronto Press, 1979), p. 38.
[24] *The Chester Mystery Cycle*, p. 388.
[25] Travis, pp. 238–41. Emmerson, "Nowe ys common."
[26] *The Prophets of the Antichrist*, in David Mills, line 340.
[27] See Travis's discussion of this moment and its significance, *Dramatic Design*, pp. 230–1.

ultimately motivated by the criteria for the production. The choice
served to maintain a distinction between the false miracles of Antichrist
and the true miracle of the Eucharist.

I cast Kyle Macdonald as Antichrist, an actor with a powerful
physical presence and commanding voice. Our costume designer and
Artistic Director, Linda Phillips, dressed him in a richly embroidered
red tunic and draped him in a black velvet cloak, creating an image
of opulence and material power. He also prominently carried a sword
and when he first referred to himself as "*Christus, vester salvator*" (8)
he raised the sword in the air. The stage image thus undermined
his rhetorical claim. When Antichrist claimed to be Christ, the bringer
of joy, Antichrist's appearance and domineering presence on the
stage created an ironic relationship between word and image. And
when he articulated his material power the theatrical image supported his words, confirming the didactic truth of his identity and
his intentions. The costume decisions identified Antichrist as a mortal and material king using arts of deception to persuade the kings
and the audience that he is Christ. The costume worked therefore
in the same way as his name works in the text, or as the title does,
creating an interpretive frame that continuously refers the audience
to his diabolical intentions. This is especially significant when it is
noted that the first character to name him Antichrist in the play is
St Michael right at the end. In performance, the audiences are less
aware of play titles and unaware of speech headings and Antichrist's
royal costume served as a constant reminder of the diabolical identity of this man who claimed to be Christ.

My work with Kyle on the development of his character followed
a similar direction but took an unexpected turn. To serve my objective, I wanted to make the Antichrist appear suspect at all times and
I therefore encouraged Kyle to give his evangelism the quality of a
cheesy magician or a second-hand car salesman. Kyle resisted this
direction, feeling that it undermined his character, removing the serious intent behind Antichrist's words. My concept had much in common with Leslie Howard Martin's interpretation of the play as an
antic interlude in which Antichrist plays the ridiculous "noisy tyrant"
in the mold of Herod.[28] Kyle's interpretation of the role has more

---

[28] "Comic Eschatology in the Chester *Coming of Antichrist*," *Comparative Drama* 5,
no. 3 (1971): 169.

STAGING ANTICHRIST AND THE PERFORMANCE OF MIRACLES

in common with Travis, who questions how ridiculous Herod would have been in performance and argues for a more serious and disturbing Antichrist. The play's text supports both interpretations and over the rehearsal process we gradually worked our way towards a creative compromise that responded to the text while maintaining my production objective as far as possible.

The playwright's comic intent is indicated most tellingly by the presence of a "gag" that still occurs in comic routines today. Confronted by the belligerent prophets, Antichrist asks his Counsellor for help. The Counsellor, a little confused by his master's sudden uncertainty, simply suggests that Antichrist should use his power to curse them because "those whom thou cursest, they are but dead" (439). Antichrist responds:

> The same I purposed, lieve thou me.
> All things I know through my posty.
> But yet thy wit I thought to see,
> what was thine intent. (442–5)

Which is as much to say: "That's what I was planning to do, I know everything of course, and I was just checking to see if *you* were smart enough to think of it!" The presence of one of the oldest jokes in the book is an indicator of a degree of comic intent in the writing of the play. However, the text is not exactly full of such gags. Much of the play is taken up with theological argument and in our attempts to maintain my comic interpretation of the role we had to work hard to discover opportunities for humor in the text. For example, we created comic business around the Antichrist's citation of scripture. Each time he quoted from the Bible we had his Counsellor check the reference in a Bible he was carrying. Finding the citation was correct, he gave an approving nod to Antichrist who smiled in self-satisfaction. When Antichrist miscites his reference to Daniel at line 56, the Counsellor started to correct him only to be silenced by a withering gaze from his master. Although this constitutes a creative addition to the text, I believe it was in keeping with the spirit of the original. When played as part of the entire cycle, Antichrist's references to scripture would have reminded the audience of the preceding pageant *The Prophets of Antichrist* in which the biblical prophets are brought to life on the stage and foretell the arrival of Antichrist on earth and in the succeeding pageant. There is an ironic relationship between the Antichrist's use of the Bible and the Chester playwright's, since Antichrist is using scripture to prove his godhead, while the playwright used it to establish the exegetical evidence for Antichrist's diabolical provenance. Our creative business with the Counsellor recreated this irony for a modern audience that had not witnessed *The Prophets of Antichrist*. Antichrist was attempting to use the Bible to establish his identity as Christ, but we made it clear that this was showmanship rather than exegesis. Antichrist quoted scripture with the smug satisfaction of an egotistical scholar, and expected applause and approval in response. The comic irony again undermined Antichrist's rhetorical efforts and sustained the audience's awareness of him as Antichrist rather than Christ.

We took a similar approach to the performance of Antichrist's miracles. The parameters of our production limited our ability to recreate the special effects likely used in the original. Medieval theater practitioners could call on elaborate pyrotechnics to represent the scenes of the Pentecost and Antichrist's imitation of the same. We had used modern pyrotechnics for the miracles in *Mary Magdalene* but felt that it would be unadvisable to bring explosive devices into the US at the present time. Instead, Antichrist's imitation of the Pentecost was achieved using red spotlights. Antichrist summoned his power using a mock incantation and then pointed to four lights in quick succession which illuminated the awaiting kings. Antichrist's pointing brought the audience's attention to the stage mechanics behind the miracle and Antichrist was thus represented as a showman and deliberate manipulator of theatrical signs.[29]

The simple and self-conscious use of lighting served our goals but by medieval standards it was relatively unspectacular and we wanted to have at least one miracle depend on an elaborate stage effect. To this purpose we created an extra miracle that is implied by Antichrist's words, but not indicated in stage directions. Antichrist says:

> Now will I turn, all through my might,
> trees down, the roots upright—
> that is marvel to my sight—
> and fruit growing upon. (81–4)

This marvel is depicted in many contemporary illustrations but the lack of stage direction leaves it unclear whether it was part of the

---

[29] In retrospect, a similar effect could have been achieved without resorting to modern stage lighting by creating a clumsy imitation of the Pentecost by using pieces of red tissue on the end of stiff wires, for example.

Chester pageant. We had already decided that the cross needed for the *Old Wives Tale* to establish a location for Erestus would be on stage for Antichrist to reduce the amount of stage management needed between the shows.[30] This gave us an opportunity we could not resist.[31] We rigged the cross so that on Antichrist's command, and with a tug of a rope from backstage, it could invert. We attached a small leafy tree to its back, which helped establish the country setting in *Old Wives Tale*, but could also represent the inverted tree of Antichrist's marvel. The effect was surprising and spectacular and was always met with a round of applause. Kyle encouraged this response by approaching the audience with arms outstretched and a large smile, inviting their approval. The fact that it was a cross as well as a tree that was inverted made the anti-Christian nature of the miracle apparent, and Antichrist's delight in his own showmanship exposed the miracle as a piece of theatrical trickery.

The remaining miracles were relatively easy to execute. The raising of the dead only calls for two actors to appear out of a grave or tomb. However, the style in which this action is performed can create radically different effects. Our dead were so decrepit that they could barely walk and spoke in creaky "horror movie" voices; only the gullible kings would be fooled by such a miracle. The effect of Antichrist's death is also dependent on his performance style. Kyle performed his death as high melodrama mixed with a heavy dose of slapstick. Antichrist's lines support such an approach: "I die, I die, now I am dead," and we added lighting and sound effects to exaggerate the effect. Before dying, Antichrist looked up at the lighting box as he performed his mock incantation. Each "I die" was then timed with thunder and lightening. After the second "I die," Antichrist fell to the ground as if dead, at which point the mischievous stage manager, otherwise known as God, released a further bolt of lightning which jolted Antichrist up from the ground to shout his final "now I am dead" with his fist raised in the air. One final bolt of lightning then struck him back to the ground. Our Antichrist was not even in control of his own miracles and was thus

---

[30] A stage direction in *The Old Wives Tale* indicates the presence of a cross. It reads: "*Enter the OLD MAN at the cross.*" George Peele, *The Old Wife's Tale*, ed. Charles Whitworth (London: A&C Black, 1996), sd. after 133.

[31] This idea arose in rehearsals and was first suggested by Kyle Macdonald. I would like to take this opportunity to credit his creativity and dedication in bringing Antichrist to life on the stage.

further exposed as a fraud. For his resurrection Antichrist emerged out of the tomb wrapped in a shroud with arms outstretched in imitation of a comic book mummy and making noises to match. He approached the kings, suddenly regained his vigour, threw off the shroud and cried a joyous: "I rise!" The effect of the miracles was comic and while they fooled the gullible kings the audience could see through the deceptive tactics used by Antichrist. Our production choices therefore ensured that the miracles remained only comically grotesque versions of Christ's miracles not to be mistaken for the real thing or even confused with theatrical representations of the real thing. Clearly no claim for authenticity can be made for the production choices described above, but it is evident that within the parameters of medieval theater, the theatrical producer could have created similar comic business to maintain a distinction between the kinds of theatrical signs that he was producing.

In contrast to the comic grotesquery of Antichrist's miracles, the prophets' Eucharistic miracle was performed with simplicity and sincerity. Enoch carefully produced a host from within a pouch and held it gently before his fellow prophet. Elijah then blessed it reverently, and consecrated it with the words:

> 'In nomine patris' that all hath wrought
> 'Et Filii Virginus' that dear us bought
> 'Et Spiritus Sancti' is all my thought,
> 'One God and Persons three.' (573–6)

There is no indication in the text at this point for stage action. The first Dead simply responds in horror: "Alas! Put that bread out of my sight!" (579). The second Dead tells us that the "bread to [him] is so bright" (584), but there is no stage direction indicating a theatrical special effect to support his perception. We considered creating a Eucharist that could be lit from within but chose to take the lack of stage direction as an indication that no special effect would have been used. Although this decision was made out of respect for the text, in retrospect it limited the effectiveness of the experiment. The theatrical trickery of the Antichrist was now juxtaposed with a straightforward performance of the sacrament of the Eucharist and not with the theatrical representation of a visible miracle, as would have been seen elsewhere in the cycle in the original production. Our choice helped maintain a distinction between true sign and false but the true sign was not spectacular. The issue of how the original production might have distinguished, say, Christ's Pentecost from Antichrist's, remains unresolved. Might it have been possible to create a truly stunning effect for the Eucharist that filled the audience with wonder and a sense of mystery? How would this have redefined the nature of theatrical signs in the cycle? These questions and possibilities establish the need for further performance-centered research and I will return to them at the end of this paper.

In our production, the comic interpretation of Antichrist's ministry did serve therefore to expose Antichrist's spectacular signs as fraudulent, but a comic interpretation of Antichrist is not sustainable throughout. Kyle's reluctance to play Antichrist solely as a cheesy magician or secondhand car salesman was a sensitive response to the text and served as an important check on my research agenda. Performance is a powerful interpretive tool and can be used to make a text more or less say whatever we want it to say. Anthony Gash is alert to the interpretive power of performance in his assessment of the subversive possibilities of *Mankind*.[32] This potential, however, can easily undermine the value of performance-centered historical research. Experimentation and imagination are key to our undertaking but unless they are exercised conservatively, with respect for the structure of the text as a whole and for the contextual data available on its original production, the value of the productions as research is substantially diminished. The production choices outlined above were made to test a theory about the producers' ability to affect the reception of theatrical signs. They were made in the spirit of experimentation, but they were also made cautiously and we remained open to the pressures of the text. As we rehearsed, it became clear that there was simply not enough comic material in the text itself to maintain interest through the entire play. Furthermore, the slaughter of the kings and the prophets at the end, although it could be funny, clearly should not be. Kyle's real concern was that the intention behind Antichrist's rhetoric and spectacle should not be trivialized. A cheesy magician wants to entertain his audience, a secondhand car salesman wants to sell cars, but Antichrist wants to bring mankind to damnation. The stakes are a little higher. The rhetorical battle with the prophets is by far the most difficult part

---

[32] "Carnival Against Lent: The Ambivalence of Medieval Drama," in *Medieval Literature: Criticism, Ideology, and History*, ed. David Aers (Brighton: Harvester, 1986), pp. 74–98.

of the play to bring off in performance, since (aside from an attempted joke about the Trinity) the dialogue is a heated but rather repetitive theological debate. Attempts to inject humor into this section failed to maintain interest, a sure sign that we were working against the intentions of the text. This section became more engaging, however, when all parties engaged with the consequences of their debate and thereby turned the theological discourse into a dramatic struggle for power.[33]

Allowing Kyle to develop the serious intent behind the Antichrist's performance changed the dynamics of the comedy. He no longer appeared quite as ridiculous since his antics had a serious purpose. Kyle demanded that his character be taken seriously and this demand was extended to the audience as Kyle directed his powers of persuasion towards them from the outset of the play. Martin argues that Antichrist does not address the audience directly until after the prophets arrive,[34] but the opening line of the play is inclusive: "All ledes in lond now be light." "All ledes" is an oddly generic term to use if his words are directed only to the four kings.[35] The lack of specificity implies Antichrist is addressing the audience and this interpretation had significant consequences for the production. Martin believes that there would have been an ironic distance between audience and Antichrist, and that he would have been the object of their mocking laughter.[36] In our production, Antichrist attempted to charm the audience, to seduce them to his side, at the same time that he seduced the kings. Our production choices aimed to encourage the audience to separate themselves from the gullible kings on the stage, but allowing Antichrist access to the audience disrupted this effect. Antichrist was charming, and while often ridiculous, his miracles were fun. The series of comic theatrical spectacles staged to convince the kings of his power, also entertained the audience, and while

---

[33] This really only worked in our performance in Tennessee when I finally released the prophets from the pressure to maintain a degree of Christ-like passivity and allowed them to be as threatening and aggressive as Antichrist.

[34] "Comic Eschatology," 172–3.

[35] In fact, the opening four stanzas reveal a spatial and temporal flexibility. His lines appear to be addressed to the Christian audience of Chester and the four kings who are imagined as existing some time in the apocalyptic future. For example, when he refers to Jesus as "one who ligged him here," where is "here"? Are we to imagine he is speaking in Jerusalem, or is he referring to the performance of Jesus's crucifixion recently witnessed in the streets of Chester? The answer, most likely, is both.

[36] "Comic Eschatology," 173–4.

they may see through his illusions, his charisma and entertainment value encouraged them to embrace him.

I am relying here on conversations with audience members and especially on class discussion with my undergraduate students.[37] On the whole, the distinction between the vacuity of the Antichrist's miracles and the substance of the Eucharistic miracle was clear to the audience and I had thus achieved my intended effect. However, most audience members surveyed admitted that they were drawn to Antichrist all the same. To a certain extent this can be attributed to the inclinations of a contemporary and largely non-Christian audience, but further discussion revealed that it was also due to the charismatic power of the actor playing the role. I had students report that they found Antichrist so charismatic that they were entirely disinterested in the "drier" prophets and wanted Antichrist to beat St. Michael at the end. However, the most interesting response came from a practicing Christian who felt that Antichrist was directly challenging his faith, and while he was aware of Antichrist's charismatic appeal, he felt that it was his duty to resist him. This student's experience is comparable to that imagined by Travis where the audience is called on to exercise "all the powers of human discrimination."[38] However, since the deception of Antichrist's miracles was apparent and the audience was repeatedly reminded of Antichrist's true identity and the actual motivation behind his words, the audience was not really called upon to discriminate true sign from false: our production choices had done much of that work already. And yet, the spectators were subject to the persuasive charisma of Antichrist's physical presence. For my Christian student, the truth was readily apparent, but he still had to resist the charismatic appeal of the liar on stage. The play, therefore, did not call upon his powers of discrimination, but it did call on the strength of his faith.

Because of limited historical evidence, no single production, and indeed, no single argument about a production, can ever be definitive. Performance choices of necessity will remain partly speculative, but the performance-centred research of the PLS can still play a crucial role in the effort to recover the theatrical past. Our production, I believe, revealed that while one cannot remove the ambiguity from

---

[37] I would like to thank students of ENG332Y: English Drama to 1642, class of 2004, for their insightful responses to the production.
[38] Travis, p. 235.

the representation of miracles in this play, particular choices can be used to encourage a high degree of distinction between false miracles and true. That said, this would have been far more difficult to maintain if we had chosen to use a special effect to represent the Eucharist. Since the cycle as a whole contains many such divinely inspired miracles, it remains to be discovered how elaborate spectacle used to represent true miracles might be distinguished from Antichrist's. Furthermore, my experience with elaborate stage effects in *Mary Magdalene* tells me that audiences are far more likely to applaud the ingenuity of the effect than appreciate its spiritual significance. The challenge presented by Sarah Beckwith's understanding of the sacramentality of theater is to create theatrical miracles that encourage a spiritual transformation in the beholder. I am left with a desire to produce the play again and find a model of performance that allows me to experiment with the effect of different production choices in front of an audience. The PLS has now instituted a yearly workshop to facilitate such experimentation. The play could be performed on alternate nights with Antichrist in a mask, dressed as Christ, and as a tyrant. We might feature a special effect for the Eucharist one night and use our simpler version on another. This experimental approach could be coupled with a more structured assessment of audience response. Ideally, of course, the production should be seen as part of a performance of the entire cycle.[39] The discoveries of my production of *Antichrist* are therefore, clearly provisional. However, I believe they indicate that neither Martin's comic interpretation of the play, nor Travis's interpretation of the play as a deliberate challenge to the signifying process of religious theater itself, are fully satisfactory. Antichrist is comic at times, but an entirely comic interpretation is not supportable; and while the play does provide much meat for iconoclastic arguments, the producer of the play need not, as Travis implies, concede "everything to the iconoclasts."

---

[39] The Chester Cycle is on the company's "wish list" of major productions, although as yet there are no concrete plans. Please visit our website for news on upcoming productions and conferences at http://www.chass.utoronto.ca/~plspls.

"NOTHING MORE NEDEFUL": POLITICS AND THE RHETORIC OF ACCOMMODATION IN QUEEN ELIZABETH I's CORONATION PROCESSION

Robert E. Stillman

> You know Nahum Tate wrote *King Lear* in 1681 and his improvements took the form (besides a happy ending) of reducing the occurrences of the word 'if' from 247 to 33.
> —Anne Carson, *Beauty of the Husband*
>
> Your if is the only peacemaker; much virtue in if.
> —William Shakespeare, *As You Like It*

On 14 January 1559, the day before her coronation, Elizabeth Tudor made a royal passage through the streets of London. The pageants organized for the occasion pay spectacular tribute to the authority of the new monarch whose political credentials they everywhere enthusiastically but anxiously advertise. The enthusiasm for the new Protestant Queen was tempered by anxiety about the precariousness of her position. A young female sovereign opposed by powerful Catholic adversaries at home and abroad, challenged by a patronizing nobility, in charge of a state forever on the razor's edge of bankruptcy and civil war, with no standing army and no organized police force, had great need of political reinforcement. To secure that reinforcement, Elizabeth turned early and late in her reign to the rhetorical talents of her humanistically trained advisors, courtiers, and poets.[1] History demanded it.

Elizabeth's coronation passage is a model of humanist rhetorical display. Its pageants are splendidly persuasive vehicles for enlisting the support of the citizenry for the crown; they are celebrations of the Queen and her sovereignty; and they represent a sustained effort on the part of its organizers to give salutary advice to the new monarch. Its principal rhetorical motives are those of persuading,

---

[1] For Elizabeth's political vulnerability at the outset of her reign, see Stephen Alford, *The Early Elizabethan Polity: William Cecil and the British Succession Crisis, 1558–1569* (Cambridge: Cambridge Univ. Press, 1998), and Stephen Greenblatt, "Invisible Bullets: Renaissance Authority and Its Subversion," *Glyph* 8 (1981), 40–61.

celebrating, and advising, and these diverse motives combine to present the appearance of a unified rhetorical display. "Blessing tonges"
speak for "true hertes" in a single act of homage to Elizabeth. At
the foundation of that act of homage is the promise that Elizabeth,
as Truth the daughter of Time and bearer of the Word, will make
salvation from the chaos of recent English history available to all.[2]

The rhetoric that informs *The Quenes Majesties Passage* represents
the ideology of the Elizabethan state at the moment of its inception
and derives its authority direct from the *verbum dei*. As such, it constitutes an essential component of what Jacques Lacan and his most
influential political student, Louis Althusser, might call the symbolic
order of Elizabethan England, the language of power that (in Lacanian
terms) subjects and determines the desires of individual citizens in
accordance to its demands. From this vantage, Elizabeth's coronation procession emerges as a ritualized portrayal of the imaginary
relations between the monarch and her subjects that present themselves
as if they depict the deeper, invisible realities of social existence.[3]

However, if the *Passage* provides thereby what can be conceived
in theoretical terms as a map of the culture's political unconscious,
it is a map whose topography is shaped by the historically specific
linguistic assumptions of the English humanists. Awareness about

---

[2] *The Quenes Maiesties Passage through the Citie of London to Westminster the Day before
her Coronacion*, ed. James M. Osborn (New Haven: Yale Univ. Press, 1960), p. 29.
For a modern spelling, full critical edition of the *Passage*, complete with a comprehensive scholarly introduction, see Germaine Warkentin's *The Queen's Majesty's Passage
& Related Documents*, assisted by John Carmi Parsons (Toronto: Centre for Reformation
and Renaissance Studies, 2004). For a recent study contrasting Mulcaster's version
of the Queen's passage with the rival accounts of the Mantuan ambassador and a
Roman Catholic Merchant Taylor, see Sandra Logan, "Making History: The
Rhetorical and Historical Occasion of Elizabeth Tudor's Coronation Entry," *Journal
of Medieval and Early Modern Studies*, 31 no. 2 (2001), 251–82. For studies of the
Passage in relation to previous coronation displays, see especially: Sydney Anglo,
Spectacle, Pageantry, and Early Tudor Policy (Oxford: Clarendon Press, 1969); David M.
Bergeron, *English Civic Pageantry, 1558–1642* (London: Edward Arnold, 1971); Jean
Wilson, *Entertainments for Elizabeth I* (Totowa, NJ: Rowman and Littlefield, 1980),
and Dale Hoak, "The Coronations of Edward VI, Mary I, and Elizabeth I, and
the Transformation of the Tudor Monarchy," in *Westminster Abbey Reformed 1540–1640*,
ed. C. S. Knighton and Richard Mortimer (Aldershot: Ashgate, 2003), 114–51. See
too Richard L. DeMolen, "Richard Mulcaster and Elizabethan Pageantry," *SEL*
14, no. 2 (Spring 1974), 209–22 and David M. Bergeron, "Elizabeth's Coronation
Entry (1559): New Manuscript Evidence," *ELR* 8, no. 1 (Winter 1978), 3–8.
[3] See Louis Althusser, "Ideology and Ideological State Apparatuses" in *Lenin and
Philosophy and Other Essays*, trans. Ben Brewster (New York and London: Monthly
Review Press, 1971), pp. 127–86.

those assumptions gives both better historical substance to abstract Lacanian discourse about the symbolic order (providing a specific cultural context for understanding how such an order functions) and an historical corrective to theoretically inflexible claims about the determining power of ideologies.[4] As Elizabeth assumes a plurality of roles within the *Passage*'s script, as subject of its celebratory rhetoric, object of its rhetorical persuasions, and spectacularly independent reader of its advisory content, she at once illuminates the growing political importance of humanist hermeneutics and the real complexity of an early modern culture that resists the simplifications sometimes imposed upon it by postmodern theory. The rhetorical work of celebrating, persuading and advising proceeds so urgently in *The Quenes Majesties Passage* not as a confident icon of the state's power to *determine* subjection to its authority, or (to use sixteenth-century parlance) as an image of the power of words to constrain things. By contrast, such rhetoric achieves meaning and urgency precisely because of those shadows of uncertainty that darken the labors of its humanist makers—precisely because of those makers' consciousness about their own lack of determinative power to constrain by words the realm of things, either London's civic world and its citizens or still more vitally that Queen who would not be subjected.[5] Celebration, persuasion, and advice are necessary precisely because words have no determinative power. In that conditional, uncertain

---

[4] For a critique of Althusser, at once sympathetic to his concept of ideology and critical of its untestable denial of all agency to individuals, see Michel Pecheux, *Language, Semantics, and Ideology*, trans. Harbans Nagpal (London: Macmillan, 1982), pp. 133–70. For an extension of Althusserian theory to cultural and literary analysis, see Frederic Jameson, *The Political Unconscious: Narrative as a Socially Symbolic Act* (Ithaca, NY: Cornell Univ. Press, 1981).

[5] See Mark Breitenberg's influential critique of the *Passage*'s sustained preoccupation with words and things, "'. . . the hole matter opened': Iconic Representation and Interpretation in 'The Quenes Majesties Passage'," *Criticism* 28, no. 1 (1986): 1–25. Drawing upon Foucault's now familiar account of "the Renaissance *episteme*," Breitenberg characterizes the *Passage* as an example of "iconic representation," in which a "natural" language of similitude and correspondence reflects and thereby sustains similitude and correspondence in the hierarchy of the state. In iconic representation, "language *resembles* rather than *signifies*" and it does so transparently, copiously, and unproblematically. Breitenberg's emphasis on the iconic character of the *Passage* complements Clifford Geertz's attention to its charismatic quality as the foundation of the cult of the imperial virgin, *Local Knowledge: Further Essays in Interpretive Anthropology* (New York: Basic Books, 1983), pp. 121–46.

For a variety of more recent critics, the *Passage* has been interpreted less as an example of iconic representation than as an instance of pragmatic political rhetoric. Richard C. McCoy calls attention to Elizabeth's characteristically Tudor "ceremonial

space between words and things, like that space between the Word and the Queen, there was both fear and freedom: the fear of anarchy (a chaos at once rhetorical and political) and the freedom to read and to act otherwise.

1. *Eloquence and the Rhetoric of Accommodation*

Elizabeth entrusted the organization of her passage to men of substance and standing: to Richard Hilles, M. P., a Merchant Taylor and a newly returned Marian exile; to Lionell Ducket, a Mercer and afterward Lord Mayor; to Francis Robinson, a Grocer; and to Richard Grafton, a chronicler and guildsman who enjoyed royal favor under Henry VIII and Edward VI. Only nine days after the event, an extended account of the Queen Majesty's passage was rushed into print by Richard Mulcaster, first headmaster of the Merchant Taylors' School and later an M. P. (Then as now, speedy propaganda was successful propaganda.) That individuals in such positions of authority should own and be eager to display humanist credentials, was a commonplace of Elizabethan culture. George Pettie marked one familiar route to advancement when he wrote: "Alas you wyll be but ungentle Gentlemen, yf you be no Schollers: you wyll doo your

pragmatism" in subordinating the potentially Catholic-seeming ritual of the coronation to the previous day's civic progress (250), "'Thou Idol Ceremony': Elizabeth I, *The Henriad*, and the Rites of the English Monarchy," *Urban Life in the Renaissance*, eds. Susan Zimmerman and Ronald F. E. Weissman (Newark, NJ: Univ. of Delaware Press, 1989), 240–66. In turn, Steven Mullaney highlights the *Passage* as an instance of theatrical and political "negotiation" between Elizabeth and the city for power (p. 24), *The Place of the Stage* (Chicago, IL: Univ. of Chicago Press, 1988). Mary Hill Cole reads the *Passage* rhetorically as well, commenting on the organizers' efforts to offer the Queen "instruction in how to rule," *The Portable Queen: Elizabeth I and the Politics of Ceremony* (Amherst, MA: Univ. of Massachusetts Press, 1999), p. 18. In turn, Susan Frye has focused critical attention on the "gendered exchanges that produced the text and that an uncritical reading imposes on its audience," *Elizabeth I: The Competition for Representation* (New York: Oxford Univ. Press, 1993), p. 25.
    Especially interesting for my argument (by contrast to Breitenberg) is Frye's attention to what she calls the *Passage*'s "unstable media of description and allegorical device" (p. 33). Far from creating an untroubled iconic surface, the *Passage*'s allegorical language by "splitting traditional signifiers and their signifieds reminded people that such connections are in fact arbitrary," thereby giving rise to a text in which "the instability of language . . . perpetually undermines its authoritative use" (35). I hasten to agree with Frye about the *Passage*'s "unstable media," but I locate an explanation for that instability elsewhere: not in inherent qualities of allegorical symbols, but rather in the historically specific assumptions of contemporary English humanists about the conditional relationship between *res et verba*.

Prince but simple service, you wyll stande your Countrey but in slender steade, you wyll bryng your selves but to small preferment, yf you be no Schollers."[6] Humanist learning and state service made a ready partnership.

By the time that Henry Peacham described "eloquent orators" as "props . . . to uphold a State, and the only keys to bring in tune a discordant commonwealth" (1622), he was giving voice to a long-standing cultural concern of humanist thought about the persuasive power of the word.[7] Persuasion made for politically powerful language since the rhetorician was conventionally endowed with the power to move people's minds and to influence moral choices, but he had another kind of power as well, less frequently noted, and arguably even more fundamental to the civilizing operation of society—the ability to promote the willing accommodation of citizens to their social callings, to playing their parts in the civic drama. For Cicero, accommodation was at once a rhetorical virtue—the orator's skill in

---

Some better approach to those linguistic issues posed so centrally by the *Passage* is required, one that takes into account both its moments of startling iconic significance (as Breitenberg and Geertz have emphasized) and its strongly pragmatic, rhetorical character as the construction of learned humanist discourse (as McCoy, Mullaney, and Frye have argued). Foucault's analysis of what Breitenberg calls the Renaissance episteme has long since lost its currency among historians of language, who argue for a less totalizing, more diverse, more intense competition among contrasting ideas about language and knowledge in the early modern period, a period in which words are variously conceived in iconic terms (as signatures that picture "naturally" the essence of things) and in conventionally rhetorical terms (as signs whose meanings are fixed by human agreement). (See, for instance, Margreta De Grazia's "The Secularization of Language in the Seventeenth Century," *Journal of the History of Ideas* 41, no. 2 (1980), 319–30 and Robert E. Stillman, *The New Philosophy and Universal Languages in Seventeenth-Century England* [Lewisburg, PA: Bucknell Univ. Press, 1995], pp. 278–80). Such diversity of historical attitude towards language figures importantly as a context for appreciating the complicated intermingling of the piously iconic and the politically pragmatic in Elizabeth's *Passage*. There is a *meaningful* difference between celebrating the Queen as the fulfillment of a saving narrative scripted iconically in the true text of history by God, and in presenting Elizabeth with a vision of that narrative as a piece of pragmatic political persuasion. An adequate account of the *Passage* needs to make sense of that difference and the conjunction between the iconic and the rhetorical so crucial to its production.

[6] *The Civile Conversation of M. Steeven Guazzo*, tr. George Pettie (London: Richard Watkins, 1581), p. 1v. For an exemplary instance of the political importance of scholarship in the Elizabethan state, see Paul E. J. Hammer, "The Earl of Essex, Fulke Greville, and the Employment of Scholars," *Studies in Philology* 91 (Spring 1994), 167–80.

[7] *The Complete Gentleman* in *The Complete Gentleman, The Truth or Our Time, and The Art of Living in London*, ed. Virgil B. Heltzel (Ithaca, NY: Cornell Univ. Press, 1962), p. 18.

adjusting his rhetoric to the particular circumstances of his topic—
and a political necessity, the individual's willingness to adjust behavior to an appropriate role in society. Accommodation persuades,
rather than compels. After all, it is the distinguishing characteristic
of a civilized (as opposed to a brutish) existence. When Cicero spec-
ulates upon the origins of civilized life in *De oratore*, he asks, while
reflecting about rhetoric: "what other power could have been strong
enough either to gather scattered humanity into one place, or to
lead it out of its brutish existence in the wilderness up to our present condition of civilization as men and as citizens?"[8] Implied in
Cicero's question is a certain awareness that civilization requires
unpleasant renunciations, but the celebration of the individual as citizen leaves such implications deeply submerged in the text. Cicero's
celebration of rhetoric is conditioned instead by his experience of
civil war, those "*graves communium temporum*" (disastrous times of public
peril), which frame his defense of the orator's civilizing skills against
a background of primitive anarchy both as distant memory and alternative future (1.1.2).

The civilizing virtues of such rhetorical acts of accommodation
are explicitly foregrounded by Thomas Wilson, the politically savvy
author of one of Elizabethan England's most interesting studies in
sociolinguistics, *The Arte of Rhetorique*. As if recalling Cicero's words,
Wilson engages in some telling amplifications of his own as he celebrates the rhetorical arts at the outset of his treatise:[9]

> Neither can I see that menne could have bene broughte by anye other
> meanes to lyve together in felowshyppe of life, to mayntayne Cities,
> to deale trulye, and willyngelye to obeye one another, if menne at the
> firste hadde not by Art and eloquence, persuaded that, which they ful
> oft found out by reason. . . . Who would digge and delve from morne
> till evening? Whom woulde travaile and toyle with the sweate of his
> browes? Yea, who woulde for his kynges pleasure adventure and hasarde
> his life, if witte hadde not so wonne men, that they thought nothing
> more nedefull in this world, nor anye thing whereunto they were more

---

[8] *De oratore*, trans. H. Rackham, 2 vols. (Cambridge, MA: Harvard Univ. Press;
London: William Heinemann, 1952). 1. 8. 33: "quae vis alia potuit aut dispersos
homines unum in locum congregare, aut a fera agrestique vita ad hunc humanum
cultum civilemque deducere. . . ."

[9] *The Arte of Rhetorique*, ed. Thomas J. Derrick (New York and London: Garland,
1982), pp. 19–20. Just as emphatically for Wilson as for Cicero, rhetoric's power
derives not from compulsion or subjection; instead, rhetoric calls, wins, trains, and
(at its most forceful!) binds, persons who might (brutish alternative this!) be otherwise enticed or compelled.

bounden: then here to live in their duty, and to traine their whole lyfe accordynge to their callynge. Therfore where as menne are in manye thynges weake by Nature and subjecte to much infirmitye: I thinke in this one pointe they passe all other Creatures livynge, that they have the gift of speache and reason.

Wilson champions civilization as eagerly as Cicero. Every sentence of his paragraph is shadowed by a similar horror of the brutish. Like Cicero, Wilson admires society's fellowship and appreciates its arts. Yet as he marvels at the complex organization of civilized life, he records in explicit detail and with the greatest amazement those repeated acts of accommodation that make a hierarchically organized society possible—the strenuous labors of farmers, the perilous hazards of soldiers. What Wilson calls attention to by such means is the indispensable role that rhetoric plays within a complex social order in making such acts of accommodation appear both necessary and desirable: "they thought nothing more nedefull in this world, nor anye thyng whereunto they were more bounden." Wilson's reflections about the persuasive power of rhetoric originate, like Cicero's, in his commitment to the practical necessity of the social order, a commitment reinforced by the piously Protestant overtones of his conclusion with its emphasis on attending to one's "calling." Like Cicero's, too, such meditations are best comprehended in light of that dark vision of brutish existence, the anarchy of the uncivilized, which both shadows and conditions them. Speech and reason are great prizes ("I thinke," says Wilson) because Nature subjects humankind "to much miserie." For Wilson as for Cicero—both political exiles, both survivors of failed regimes, both educated pragmatists who celebrate the rhetorical arts as vehicles for the reconstitution of political order—rhetoric achieves its urgency precisely because of the uncertainty of things and the uncertainty of words (barely acknowledged by the barely hesitant "I thinke") always to exert their power over things. The need for accommodation is conditioned by the lived experience of uncertainty.[10]

---

[10] Kathy Eden, Peter Mack and Kees Meerhoff have drawn attention to a remarkable series of transformations in reading practices over the course of the sixteenth century in which Melanchthon's rhetorical and dialectical theory played a major role—and it is from Melanchthon principally that Wilson's art derives. Eden's *Hermeneutics and the Rhetorical Tradition* argues concisely and cogently for a humanist rehabilitation during the sixteenth century of the classical tradition of *interpretatio scripti*—what she calls "a loosely organized set of rules for interpreting the written materials pertinent to legal cases, such as laws, wills, and contracts" (New Haven,

2. *"Nedeful"* Accommodations and Rhetorical Conditions

Elizabeth's passage through the city of London is staged as high royal drama, "wherein was shewed," as Mulcaster writes, "the wonderfull spectacle, of a noble hearted princesse toward her most loving people . . ." (28). The mutual regard of sovereign and subjects, as an exemplary instance of a decorous politics, is repeatedly reinforced in Mulcaster's account by his emphasis on the ideal decorum maintained within the pageants' rhetorical artistry. As "blessing tonges" speak for "true hertes," godly words derive from pious intentions as one instance of the *Passage's* preoccupation with the appropriate matching of words and things.[11] In turn, Mulcaster's emphasis on decorum is just one element in a self-conscious strategy on the part of the organizers generally to celebrate their own rhetorical skills as they celebrate, persuade, and advise the Queen and her citizens. Always, for example, a premium is placed upon the rhetorical virtue of *claritas*, as in pageant after pageant, refined Latin verses are translated into plain English words; individual details of dress and spectacle explicitly interpreted; and potentially shadowy allegorical displays transposed into transparent exemplary shows. Transparency is at once, like decorum, a rhetorical and political ideal, especially for Elizabeth herself, who struggles in pageant after pageant to listen

---

CN and London: Yale Univ. Press, 1997), p. 7. Formulated by Cicero and Quintillian, those rules included: attention to historical and textual context; analysis of complete works with an eye to the "economy" or the persuasive arrangement of the work's parts; and concern for authorial intention and decorum as touchstones of analysis. Eden especially highlights the importance of "accommodation" to this tradition: the emphasis of the church fathers and their influential Reformed student, Melanchthon, on interpretation as an activity that makes readers at home in the text, encouraging them toward spiritual journeys of their own. See too Mack, "Rudolf Agricola's Reading of Literature," *JWCI* 48 (1985), 23–41; Mack, *Renaissance Argument: Valla and Agricola in the Traditions of Rhetoric and Dialectic* (Leiden and New York: E. J. Brill, 1993); and Meerhof's "Logic and Eloquence: A Ramusian Revolution?," *Argumentation* 5 (1991), 357–74; "Melanchthon lecteur d'Agricola: rhetorique et analyse textuelle," in *Reforme-Humanisme-Renaissance*, 16, no. 30 (1990), 5–22; and "The Significance of Melanchthon's Rhetoric" in *Renaissance Rhetoric*, ed. Peter Mack (New York: St. Martin's Press, 1994), pp. 46–62.

[11] When Mulcaster describes the assembled cast of virtues and vices who parade before Elizabeth in the second pageant, he takes special note of their dress, commenting that: "Eche of these personages according to their proper names and properties, had not onelie their names in plaine and perfit writing set upon their breastes easelie to be read of all, but also every one of them was aptelie and properlie apparelled, so that his apparell and name did agree to expresse the same person, that in title he represented" (33). The proper matching of words and things is an effort to guarantee the pageant's artistry and truth, its rhetorical rightness.

attentively and to respond clearly. Even more obvious for a contemporary audience would have been the organizers' pride in the coherence of the pageants' rhetorical organization. As Sydney Anglo noted some years past, these coronation proceedings differ most conspicuously from those of the early Tudor monarchs by virtue of the extraordinary care taken with their organization.[12] Not surprisingly, again, their strategic unity of design is explicitly associated with the vision of a unified Elizabethan polity, the rebirth of the *respublica bene instituta*—that "flourishing commonweale" hailed in the climactic fourth pageant (47). Amidst all this evidence of self-conscious rhetorical display, this celebration of decorum, *claritas*, and coherence, what does surprise is the repeated deferral of that vision of the unified polity into an indeterminate and uncertain future, the repeated insistence that all the best blessings desired by the best hearts (for sovereign and citizen alike) are conditional. Shadows of uncertainty continually cloud the pageants.

The first of the *Passage*'s five pageants glorifies the Queen's royal lineage. Elizabeth's entourage pauses in front of a platform on which are represented the founders of the Tudor line, Henry VII and his Queen, Elizabeth of York; above them are placed images of Henry VIII and Queen Anne, Elizabeth's parents; and at the summit of the platform, as if ascending from the glories beneath, appears an image of Elizabeth herself. Excluded from this carefully conceived spectacle are any troubling memories of the tragically short reign of Edward VI or the bloody martyrdoms of Mary Tudor's rule. The exclusion is calculated, since—to borrow Mulcaster's words—"unitie was the ende wherat the whole devise shotte" (33). Elizabeth is celebrated not simply as a Tudor, but also as a Tudor in the great line of monarchs who bring concord to history. As "the onelye heire of Henrie the eight," Elizabeth descends from both the houses of York and Lancaster, whose disputes had fueled the Wars of the Roses, and since she is herself a product of the "knitting up of concorde" ending those wars, it is hoped that she "might maintaine the same among her subjectes" (33). In the elusive language of pageantry, Elizabeth is at once celebrated as the bestower of concord and pointedly advised, in an idealized dramatization of the virtue, to realize that concord in present English history. "So now that jarre shall

---

[12] Anglo, p. 353: "structurally, this entry was superior to anything seen in London since 1501."

stint, and quietnes encrease, We trust, O noble Queene, thou *wilt* be cause alone" (emphasis mine, 35). As the rhetoric makes clear, concord is a future event, an event very much conditional in kind.

A sovereign's right to rule depends traditionally on her possession of the appropriate royal virtues, and the next pageants appear specifically designed to endow Elizabeth with those virtues. The Queen is witness to a spectacle in which "a childe representing her maiesties person, placed in a seate of governement, [is] supported by certaine vertues, which suppressed other vices under their seate...." (37). Pure Religion, Love of Subjects, Wisdom, and Justice truimph over such conventional evils as Rebellion, Insolence, Folly, and Vainglory. Once again, Elizabeth is celebrated as the possessor of royal virtues that legitimize her power, only to be strongly advised, in the conditional language of accommodation, to maintain her power by exercising those virtues, lest.... The consequences are too obvious to mention. "Like as by vertues (which doe aboundantly appere in her grace) the Queenes maiestie was established in the seate of governement: so she should syt fast in the same *so long as* she embraced vertue and helde vice under foote" (emphasis mine, 40). The need to celebrate is tempered by the need to advise; the desire to persuade the citizenry of the sovereign's worthiness is balanced by the urge to persuade the sovereign to maintain that worthiness in her person. There is real tension among these diverse rhetorical motives, and that tension manifests itself again in the third pageant. On this occasion, eight children representing the eight beatitudes address the Queen directly and, as Mulcaster writes, "put her grace in mind, that as her good doinges before had geven just occasion, why that these blessinges might fall upon her, that so if her grace did contrive in her goodness as she had entred, she shoulde hope for the fruit of these promises due unto them..." (42). Celebration, admonition, and persuasion are mingled in a complex moment whose force and urgency depend on the conditional quality of the rhetoric.

The climax of Elizabeth's passage through the city of London is achieved in the fourth and crucial pageant designed to celebrate Elizabeth's coronation. At the "litle conduit in cheape," the Queen sees "two hylles or mountaynes of convenient heyghte" (44, 46). One of these "was made cragged, barreyn, and stonye, in the whiche was erected one tree, artificiallye made, all withered and deadde, with braunches accordinglye" (46). The mountain is an image of "*Ruinosa Respublica*, A decayed common weale" (46–47). The other mountain "was made fayre, freshe, grene, and beawtifull, the grounde thereof full of flowres and beawtie, and on the same was erected also one tree very freshe and fayre" (47). The second is an image of "*Respublica bene instituta.* A flourishing commonweale" (47). Between these two mountains, there is "one hollowe place or cave, with doore and locke enclosed" (47). Out of this cave, immediately before the Queen's arrival, comes old man Time leading his daughter, Truth. Truth holds "a booke in her hande upon the which was written, *Verbum veritatis,* the woorde of trueth" (48). As Elizabeth approaches, the child hands her a copy of what Mulcaster informs us is "the Byble in Englishe" (44).

The fourth pageant bristles with allusions to recent Tudor history. In a bold act of rhetorical recovery, the organizers of the passage borrow the motto that had served as the primary vehicle of state propaganda under the Catholic Mary Tudor, "*veritas filia temporis,*" and apply it in an emblematic display to their new Protestant sovereign, Elizabeth.[13] This is recovery, rather than theft, since the motto had originally surfaced in sixteenth-century cultural politics as part of the Reformation's assault upon that bride of Satan, the Catholic Church. Its first apppearance in England, as Fritz Saxl points out, on the verso of the title page of William Marshall's *Goodly Prymer in Englyshe* (1535), occurs contemporaneously with Henry VIII's divorce of the English Church from Rome (Saxl, 203). The broader historical purpose of this recovery is clear. After its unjust imprisonment in the dark cave of Catholic error, Protestant truth has at last appeared with Elizabeth's coronation to transform a ruined republic into a flourishing commonwealth.

The pageant redresses with its allusive spectacle a second injustice, more minor in kind, but equally significant, because of the evidence it supplies about the enormous political consequence generated in this humanist cultural context by arguments about words. In 1554,

---

[13] Fritz Saxl, "*Veritas Filia Temporis*" in *Philosophy and History: Essays Presented to Ernst Cassirer,* ed. Raymond Klibansky and H. J. Paton (New York, Evanston, and London: Harper and Row, 1963), p. 207. See too Donald Gordon, "'*Veritas Filia Temporis*': Hadrianus Junius and Geoffrey Whitney," *JWCI* 3 (1939–40), 228–40. For the continuing importance of the topic for Elizabeth, see Patricia Howard, "Time in the Entertainments for Queen Elizabeth I: 1590–1602," *University of Toronto Quarterly* 65 (1996), 467–81. On the complicated political relationship between Elizabeth and her religious councillors, see Margaret Christian, "Elizabeth's Preachers and the Government of Women: Refining and Correcting a Queen," *Sixteenth-Century Journal* 24, no. 3 (1993), 561–76.

some of the same individuals who organized Elizabeth's passage had
been employed to devise pageants in celebration of the marriage of
Philip and Mary. At one point in their transit through London, Philip
and Mary were greeted by celebratory images of Henry VIII and
Edward VI. In his depiction of Henry, an unfortunate painter had
made the mistake of placing a copy of the *verbum dei* in the sovereign's hands, only to find himself severely reprimanded by the Bishop
of Winchester for practicing "agaynst the quenes catholike pro-
ceedinges."[14] Forced to undo his semiological *faux pas*, the painter
substituted a glove for the book. By placing the Bible in Henry's
hands rather than the Queen's, the painter had removed the main
source of religious and political authority from the sovereign to her
father, and more important, from the Catholic tradition to the
Protestant. In Henry's hands, the Bible is automatically a Reformation
document and an English text. When five years later the organizers
of the coronation pageants redressed this injustice to the painter and
to Protestantism, they made clear that the *verbum veritatis* that passed
into Elizabeth's hands was the "Byble in Englishe." As the language
of the humanist tradition, Latin was revered as an instrument for
placing the English in touch with the world of the classic, the genuine, the culturally valued, but as the language of Catholicism, it
was also marked as the tongue of the beast. English is the right
medium for Protestantism. This double attitude among the Protestant
humanists is reflected in the presence of Latin and English versions
of all of the passage's poems and emblematic names. The tie to the
classical past is acknowledged, as the bonds with Rome are broken.
It is well to remember that one of Elizabeth's first proclamations as
Queen, revoking Mary's ban against the vernacular Bible, was to
order that "the English letanie [be] read accordinglie as was used
in hir graces chappell in churches through the citie of London. And
likewise the epistle and gospell of the daie began to be read in the
same churches at masse time in the English toong. . . ."[15] The dethrone-
ment of Latin as the language of spiritual truth was but one element in the broader program of selective iconoclasm that marked
the early months of Elizabeth's reign. In January of 1559, the Spanish

---

[14] See Anglo, p. 329. He is quoting from the so-called *Chronicle of Queen Jane and Queen Mary*.

[15] Raphael Holinshed, *Holinshed's Chronicles of England, Scotland, and Ireland*, ed. H. Ellis (London: J. Johnson, et al., 1807–08), vol. 4, 158.

ambassador's distaste for the institution of English Litanies was compounded by his disgust at the defacement of "the statue of St. Thomas stoned and beheaded," and by his horror at court mummeries portraying "crows in the habits of Cardinals, . . . asses habited as Bishops, and . . . wolves representing Abbots."[16] The Reformation inspired a revolution not just theological, but also semiological.

The extraordinary political consequence of words is apparent in the political disputes that they occasion, and even more directly in the humanists' efforts to reinforce their representational power. Everywhere the pageantry of Elizabeth's passage reflects the diligent labors of humanist rhetoric—bolstered by a Protestant faith in the Word—to match properly and persuasively *res et verba*. The genealogical pageant with which Elizabeth's passage begins illustrates the point well. As Mulcaster indicates, the pageant is nothing more than an extended and spectacular pun "grounded upon the Queenes majesties name" (33). As he explains: "For like as the long warre betwene the two houses of Yorke and Lancastre then ended, when Elizabeth doughter to Edwarde the fourthe matched in mariage with Henry the seventhe heyre to the house of Launcaster: so synce that the Queenes maiesties name was Elizabeth . . . it was devised that like as Elizabeth was the first occasion of concorde, so she another Elizabeth might maintaine the same among her subjectes . . ." (33). One Elizabeth brought peace, why not another? Mulcaster's characterization of the pageant's rhetoric is fascinating and important. He at once hints at and resists an iconic interpretation of Elizabeth's name, which in this ritual context might readily be made to carry strong magical associations. Considered iconically, the name "Elizabeth" is no mere neutral sign, but a historically loaded signature whose saving significance and power can be evoked as if they might magically influence the present—as if, providentially scripted in her name as a second Elizabeth, was the salvation history that she now enacts. Considered rhetorically, by contrast, Elizabeth's name is simply and conventionally a sign, the basis or groundplot of a fictional invention; the pageant is "grounded," Mulcaster writes, upon her name, reminding us in his very vocabulary, once again, of the artfulness of the pageant's rhetorical construction, its status as something invented or made up. Mulcaster's characterization of this act of naming is so

[16] *Calendar of State Papers and Manuscripts (Venice), 1558–1580*, ed. Rawdon Brown and G. Cavendish Bentinck (London: Eyre and Spottiswood, 1890), 7. 11.

telling because—minor moment as it might first appear—it affords
evidence of the humanist's own self-consciousness about a gap yawn-
ing between the realm of signatures and signs, icons and images, the
ideal narrative of salvation history and the ordinary, always uncertain realm of human history. The hope is that "quietnes encrease,"
but that hope is conditioned by events in an indeterminate future:
"We trust, O noble Queene, thou *wilt* be cause alone" (emphasis
mine, 35). The urgency of humanist rhetoric derives from the necessity of filling that gap, of making causeways over an abyss separating the signature from the sign, icon and image, divine history and
human history—an abyss always visible in humanist projects to restore
to harmony the divided realms of words and things.

3. *Words and Things/The Word and the Queen*

Language is made up of two principal parts, as any Elizabethan who
read his Cicero would have known: "matter and words, and the
words cannot fall into place if you remove the matter, nor can the
matter have clarity if you withdraw the words."[17] What is basically
a grammatical distinction in this passage from Cicero, a means of
analyzing speech in terms of *res et verba*, came to be applied as a
frequently used standard in a variety of other disciplinary domains.
It is a stylistic slogan, a means for advising the writer, as Quintilian
does, to be "careful in his choice of words" and to be "even more
concerned about his subject matter."[18] Good writing is a matter of
matching the right words to the right things. Matching words and
things also has important moral implications, especially for the

---

[17] Cicero, III. v. 19–20: "Nam cum omnis ex re atque verbis constet oratio,
neque verba sedem habere possunt si rem subtraxeris neque res lumen si verba
semoveris," p. 16. For a still useful background study of the topic, see A. C. Howell,
"*Res et Verba*: Words and Things," *ELH* 13, n. 2 (March 1946), 131–42. For a
review of Italian Renaissance criticism on the subject, see Bernard Weinberg, *A
History of Literary Criticism in the Italian Renaissance*, 2 vols. (Chicago, IL: Chicago Univ.
Press; Toronto: Univ. of Toronto Press, 1961). "*Res et verba*" cannot always be accurately translated by the phrase "words and things." For *res* refers not merely to
physical objects or events, but to the matter that the individual wishes to express.
As a result *res et verba* is often better translated as "words and matter," or even
"words and reasons."
[18] *Institutio oratoria*, trans. H. E. Butler, 4 vols. (London: William Heinemann; New
York: G. P. Putnam, 1921), VIII, Pr. 20–21: "Curam ergo verborum, rerum volo
esse sollicitudinem."

sixteenth-century Horatian writers who adopted the phrase *res et verba* as their battle cry. The decorum of good speech is reflected in decorously good behavior, especially if the individual is instructed by poetry that combines the *utile et dulce* in the *res et verba*: "For every poem . . . consists of words and things. The things are those same moral precepts, and the words [the delightfull elements] are the diction itself."[19] Once more, by the Renaissance, the distinction between words and things had been elevated to a standard of epistemological evaluation. As Scaliger writes in an important and influential discussion of language in his *Poetice*: "Truth, in turn, is agreement between that which is said about a thing and the thing itself."[20] Matching words and things is an act of judgment. As a group, the humanists make few large claims for the kind of logically absolute correspondence between the structure of language and the structure of the world that so preoccupied the scholastic philosophers; as rhetoricians concerned with the practical consequences of knowledge, probable correspondences sufficed. Nonetheless, the comprehensiveness of the humanist formula of decorum is striking: achieving the right balance between *res et verba* is an essential standard of stylistic excellence, moral worth, and good judgment. Its achievement is the mark of eloquence; the good writer, the good person, and the good thinker will labor for it.[21]

When Mulcaster dwells upon the dress of the pageant's performers, the names assigned to them, or the actions they perform, therefore, he does more than praise the artistry of the events. By highlighting the effort to achieve a decorous harmony between words and things,

---

[19] Giovanni Britannico Da Brescia, *Poemata* (Milan, 1518 edn.), p. cxxxvi: "omne enim poema rebus et verbis constat: res enim sunt praecepta: verba vero ipsa oratorio." Quoted by Weinberg, 1: 93.

[20] *Select Translations from Scaliger's Poetics*, trans. Frederick Morgan Padelford (New York: H. Holt, 1905), Bk. 1, ch. 1, p. 3. Julius Caesar Scaliger, *Poetices Libri Septem* (Lyon, 1561; Frederich Fromman Verlag: Stuttgart-Bad Cannstatt, 1964, facsim. edn.), p. 2: "Veritatis aut, orationis aequatio cum re."

[21] I hasten to note my agreement with Arthur F. Kinney that "the dangers of a permanent and exclusive faith in eloquence had been the birthright of humanism alongside the glorious possibilities of rhetoric," *Humanist Poetics* (Amherst, MA: Univ. of Massachusetts Press, 1986), pp. 17–18. See also Richard Waswo's argument that implied in the philosophy of Lorenzo Valla, the exegetical commentaries of Luther, and the plays of Shakespeare is an anticipation of "one of the major revolutions of twentieth-century thought: the shift from referential to relational semantics, from regarding the meaning of language as a given object of reference to regarding it as a dynamic function of use." He argues that this shift is "a definitive feature of the Renaissance," *Language and Meaning in the Renaissance* (Princeton, NJ: Princeton Univ. Press, 1987), p. 13.

he marks the coronation pageants in their entirety as a product of humanist eloquence, complete with fit style, sound morals, and good judgment. The rhetoric of Elizabeth's pageants gains authority by virtue of its eloquence, even as this eloquent harmony of words and things aspires to locate its reflection and justification in God's Word. Roger Ascham strikes a familiar note from the English humanist tradition when he writes: "I never knew yet scholer, that gave himself to . . . folowe chieflie those three Authors [Plato, Aristotle, and Cicero] but he proved, both learned, wise, and also an honest man, if he joyned with all the trewe doctrine of Gods holie Bible, without the which, the other three, be but the fine edge tooles in a fole or mad mans hand."[22] It would have pleased Ascham to find the chief homage accorded to words in these coronation events paid to the *verbum veritatis*, a complex symbol whose significance merits careful attention.

The *verbum veritatis* that passes into Elizabeth's hands at the climax of these pageants is a copy of the scriptures, an English Bible whose muscular Protestantism supplies powerful support to the native church, just as it provides, conventionally, a set of standards for the moral, spiritual, and political government of the state. Within the specific context of the fourth pageant's emblematic narrative, the presence of this literal embodiment of the *verbum veritatis* forms part of what Mulcaster might call the apt and proper apparel of Truth, as a decorous representation of Truth's authority and of the authority of the Queen who receives the book from her.

Signs repeatedly point upwards in this pageant. As the scriptural manifestation of God's Word, the *verbum veritatis* is itself a representation of another representation in a specular hierarchy whose summit is God the Father. In the wider context of Renaissance Protestant thought, as Philippe de Mornay makes clear in a text later translated into Elizabethan English, *The Trewenesse of the Christian Religion*, Christ is "the Sonne, the Word, or the Speech; namely, the lively and perfect image and wisedome of the Father."[23] The Bible, then, as one perfect image of God's Word, relates, most importantly, the story of that other perfect image, Christ, and the descent of the healing Word into human history. By associating Elizabeth with the

---

[22] *The Scholemaster* (1570), ed. Edward Arber. English Reprints (London: Constable, 1927), pp. 118–19.
[23] *A Woorke Concerning the Trewenesse of the Christian Religion*, trans. Sir Philip Sidney (?) and Arthur Golding (Delmar, NY: Scholars' Facsimiles & Reprints, 1976), p. 57.

verbum veritatis and the saving fiction by which Christianity offers relief from the sin and death of history, the coronation ritual of the fourth pageant seemingly endows her with divine authority as a sovereign power who brings concord to the troubled state.

It is important to pursue the logic by which such associations become possible within Protestant humanist thought. Christ is a god of many names. As Mornay writes, "Also we call him Logos, which some translate *Word* or *Speech*, and othersome Reason" (59). The doctrine of the *logos*, as articulated in John's gospel, is an effort to personalize in God the pure form and pure intellect of Greek philosophy, but it left Christian commentators like Mornay with the need to puzzle over the distinction between the Logos as Speech and the Logos as Reason. In order to reconcile any possible discrepancy between the two, Mornay explains that: "When we call him [Christ] Speech or Word, it is according to the doctrine of the Philosophers, who have marked that there is in man a dubble Speech; the one in the mynd, which thy call the inward Speech, which wee conceyve afore we utter it; and the other the sounding image thereof, which is uttered by our mouth and is termed the Speech of the Voyce" (59). In Mornay's terms, reason is not something different from speech, but a particular form of it, as "the speech of the mynd" (59). Christ can be called "Speech or Word" because he "is the perfect image of [God's] understanding, and God's understanding is God himself." He can be called "Reason, because Reason is as ye would say the Daughter, Speech or worde of the understanding; and we say that by the same Speech or word, God made al things" (60). What is so interesting and important about Mornay's argument is that Christ achieves his divine status as the Logos because God operates according to sound principles of humanist rhetoric: the word and the thing are one. As God's Word, Christ embodies God's power. Mornay makes the analogy between divine wisdom and human practice explicit: "For Wisedome (even in man) is nothing els but a haviour proceeding of diverse Concepts or inward speeches, whereby our mynde is perfected in the knowledge of high things" (60). The analogy between divine speech and human speech seeks to dispel for the Protestant humanist some of those insecurities potentially inherent within an epistemology guaranteeing the merely probable correspondence of words and things. Wisdom is a matter of matching the right *verbum* to the right *res*, for God and man. In the course of elevating a humanist rhetorical principle to the status of a theological

principle, Mornay illustrates how divine authority is supplied to contemporary humanist discourse.

A pious linguistics serves political ends. This is a truth that Richard
Grafton—one of the pageants' humanist makers—knew well. When
in 1539 he published the first edition of The Great Bible, he commissioned a woodcut for the title page, commonly assumed to be by
Hans Holbein.[24] Holbein's woodcut is a monument to the power of
the *verbum dei* to enlist the accommodation of citizens to the state,
and as such it represents an early version of the spectacular employment of the *verbum veritatis* in Elizabeth's passage. (See Figure 1.) At
the top of the woodcut sits Henry VIII, by far the largest figure in
the picture. Enthroned in imperial splendor, Henry holds two copies
of the *verbum dei*. The classical emblems of monarchical power, the
book and the sword, are replaced by the new emblem of sovereign
authority, God's Word. To either side of the King stand Cranmer
(left) and Cromwell (right) who receive copies of the *verbum dei* from
Henry and, as chief authorities in the English Church, distribute
them appropriately to the citizens below. The organization of the
woodcut is plainly hierarchical, as is its political lesson. Above Henry's
head, and gazing down upon the King with obvious approval, appears
Christ in the clouds. As Henry displays his obedience to the Word,
so he teaches his citizens obedience to himself.

Holbein's woodcut affords an excellent example of the function
that Michel Foucault identifies as essential to the operation of authority
in the state, the effacement of "the domination intrinsic to power."[25]
Power is always more potent when it appears to belong to someone
else, in this instance, to Christ rather than to Henry, though there
can be no mistaking whose authority this woodcut ultimately supports. When the assembled crowd shouts approval from below, their
mouths are filled not with hosannas to heaven, but instead with "*Vivat
Rex*" and "God save the Kynge." No wonder. They are simply (if

---

[24] See Roy C. Strong, *Holbein and Henry VIII* (London: Routledge & Kegan Paul
for the Paul Mellon Foundation for British Art, 1967) and David Piper, "Hans
Holbein the Younger in England," *Journal of the Royal Society of Arts* 111 (1963),
736–55.

[25] *Power/Knowledge: Selected Interviews and Other Writings, 1972–1977*, ed. Colin Gordon
and trans. Colin Gordon, Leo Marshall, et al. (New York: Pantheon Books, 1972).
He writes: "the essential function of the discourse and techniques of right has been
to efface the domination intrinsic to power in order to present the latter at the
level of appearance under two different aspects: on the one hand, as the legitimate
rights of sovereignty, and on the other, as the legal obligation to obey it," p. 95.

Figure 1. Title page of The Great Bible (1541 edition). In disgrace, Cromwell has lost his insignia.

enthusiastically) repeating the lessons that have been handed down
from on high. From the mouths of Cromwell, Cranmer, and More
(bottom left), and even from the lips of Christ, biblical quotations
issue in support of the monarchy. More's citation is typical: "I exhort
therefore, that, first of all, supplicating prayers, intercessions, and
giving of thanks, be made for all men; For kings, and *for* all that
are in authority" (I Tim. 2:1–2). It is telling, therefore, about the
self-effacing function of power in its denial of the domination intrinsic to it, that the biblical quotation given to Henry comes from the
humbled King Darius after Daniel's release from the lions' den.
Humbled into acknowledging the power of the one supreme God,
Darius proclaims: "I make a decree. That in every dominion of my
kingdom men tremble and fear before the God of Daniel: for he is
the living God, and stedfast for ever, and his kingdom *that* which
shall not be destroyed, and his dominion *shall be even* unto the end"
(Daniel 6:26). Darius's obedience to God is the biblical type of
Henry's, and only because this obedience has been offered, the iconol-
ogy suggests, does Henry acquire the power to reign in his state. A
pious linguistics supplies the logic of the idealized and imaginary
relations among savior, sovereign, and subject at the foundation of
Henry's "dominion . . . *even* unto the end."

   The effacement of the domination intrinsic to power plays an
important, but different role in Elizabeth's passage. The emblematic
display of the fourth pageant is unrelentingly romantic. Truth, a
helpless young girl imprisoned in a deep, dark cave emerges at just
the right time to deliver a copy of the *verbum veritatis* into the hands
of a young virgin Queen, who, though oppressed by enemies at
home and abroad, pledges herself—with God's help—to restore
England to a flourishing commonwealth. Such is the stuff of romance
narrative, even melodrama. The impression of the Queen's vulnerability is matched only by her piety as she graciously accepts the
Bible from the hands of Truth, then enthusiastically clasps that Bible
to her breast. Henry holds the Word like a sword, brandishing his
Bible as if it were an instrument of battle. Elizabeth embraces the
Word as a lost daughter might embrace her parent, as a source of
nurture and support. In the process, once again, a humble accommodation of the sovereign to God empowers by the effacement of
power. Mulcaster makes the logic of this presentation clear when he
writes: "But because princes be set in their seate by gods appoint-
ing . . . they must first and chieflie tender the glory of him, from

whom their glorie issueth" (63). As he proceeds to argue, Elizabeth deserves special praise in this regard since "God will undoubtedly preserve so worthy a prince, which at hys honor so reverently taketh her beginning. For this saying is true, and written in the boke of Truth. He that first seketh the kingdome of God, shall have all other thinges cast unto him . . ." (64). All other things, indeed.

At the moment of its genesis, Elizabethan culture displays its social structure and sovereign, and pronounces them good. The narrative of the fourth pageant creates in its celebration of the Word an idealized relationship among savior, sovereign, and citizen. The nature of that relationship, like the Protestant theology upon which it is founded, is hierarchical and speculary. Just as God's Word finds its perfect image in Christ and the Bible, so the bearer of God's Word, Truth, selects seemingly the perfect image of herself as the historical bearer of that Word, Elizabeth. As the ritual action strongly suggests, the Queen *is* the Truth that restores the flourishing commonwealth. The word and the thing are one. (So, too, the Word and the Queen.) In this way, the rhetorical assumptions of the humanist tradition, with its energetic pursuit of the right *verbum* for the right *res*, become essential both to the conceptualization of the divine order and to the representation of political relations in the state.

Only in light of this apparent identification of Elizabeth as the Truth does the other speculary function of the fourth pageant reveal its full significance. As Elizabeth piously embraces the Word of God, she supplies a mirror image for the necessary and desirable embrace by the citizens of herself, as the bearer of the Word. Truth's daughter becomes England's champion, triumphing beyond all expectation, as a dramatic realization of the imaginary social identities provided to Elizabeth, that magically empowered child of Truth, and her grateful citizens. As Louis Althusser writes in his adaptation of Lacanian theory to the study of social practices, an ideologically motivated ritual brings with it "the absolute guarantee that everything really is so, and that on condition that subjects recognize what they are and behave accordingly, everything will be all right: Amen— 'So be it'" (180–81). The success of prayer, as Althusser acknowledges, is conditional. Thomas Wilson would have written more simply and more concretely, with a sharp eye for the tortured labor of farmers and the perilous hazards of soldiers, that it is by such rhetorical means that individuals are persuaded that there is nothing more "nedeful" in this world. Wilson would have noted, too, with a sharp eye for the "infirmitye" of the human condition, that whatever the persuasiveness of those rhetorical means, however binding the words, the circumstances of an uncertain and indeterminate world could always effect a different conclusion.

4. Concluding Differently: Eloquent Magic/Eloquent Rhetoric

As Victoria Kahn has effectively argued, the rhetorical ideals of Renaissance humanism disclose a problem inherent in the humanist program itself: inside the humanist celebration of decorum, the right matching of *res et verba*, are potentially problematic epistemological implications. "The ideal practice of the orator," Kahn writes, is inseparable from "the faculty of prudence."[26] Both the orator and the pragmatic statesman share as their primary concern "the domain of probability" (35). The humanist's preoccupation with decorum, with the matching of words and things, is not intended to secure "exact correspondence to some fixed theoretical truth or ethics," but instead to establish "a practical truth" that promotes "the maintenance of a social and political community" (43). The problem inherent in this understanding of decorum and the probable truths it supplies, according to Kahn, is that "The legitimacy of the prudential judgement's claim to be something more than mere subjective preference . . . is ultimately an article of faith that by definition cannot justify itself before the court of skepticism" (46). Her point is right on target: the last refuge of a probabilistic epistemology is often an "article of faith." While Kahn is clearly correct to identify as one major consequence of this problem the emergence in the late Renaissance of a strong skeptical tradition that spawned "an eventual questioning of [the humanists'] own practical criterion of truth," there was a second, distinct consequence of the humanists' commitment to a probabilistic epistemology, especially within fictions inspired by humanist principles: the busy transformation of those articles of faith into iconic representations of Truth.[27]

---

[26] *Rhetoric, Prudence, and Skepticism in the Renaissance* (Ithaca, NY and London: Cornell Univ. Press, 1985), p. 35.

[27] Kahn, p. 48. For a useful discussion about how seriously we should take representations of monarchs as sacred, see Helen Hackett, "Dreams or Designs, Cults or Constructions? The Study of the Images of Monarchs," *The Historical Journal* 44, no. 3 (2001), 811–23. Because of the merely probabilistic claims of humanist

Within Elizabeth's Passage that potential problematic manifests itself clearly in the division between alternative ways of understanding its climactic fourth pageant. Consider again the significance of Truth's presentation of the *verbum veritatis* to Elizabeth, and note the discrepant awareness—the multiplication of perspectives—created by the emblematic events. In the masque-like merger of the historical world with the fictional realm at the moment that the Elizabeth receives the Bible from the hands of Truth, the pageant assumes a near-magical appearance, as if the Word and the Queen have then and there restored England to a flourishing commonwealth. The Queen adopts the character of Truth in a moment of second incarnation—a sign of the vehemence of the cultural desire at work here to insure, absolutely and unequivocally, the ontological reality of an Elizabethan "*Respublica bene instituta.*" From this perspective, the pageant achieves an iconic status, as if the ritual representation of events were a transparent depiction of the shaping hand of God at work. But this is only one perspective from which to interpret the unfolding show, and an inevitably partial one at that. From the vantage of the historically specific circumstances of the pageant's performance, the Bible's placement in the hands of Elizabeth appears less iconic than pragmatic, less like a magical event, and more like the anxious admonition of humanist advisors about that new, imperiled, all-too-vulnerable Queen's need to champion the Protestant cause. The show manifests itself as politics *tout court*, a pointed piece of advice from worried advisors, who dress Elizabeth in the apparel of truth because historical conditions require it.

Situated then on that ambiguous borderline between the iconic and the historical, between magic and metaphor, the pageant possesses an irreducible doubleness that defines its complex rhetorical character. As pragmatically motivated praise and persuasion, the *Passage*'s events appear to function prudentially (in Kahn's terms) to promote "the maintenance of a social and political community." As piously inspired iconic celebrations, the pageants appear to function magically in order to mark-in-the-making the birth of a new cultural

epistemology, the realization of an Elizabethan "*Respublica bene instituta*," however vehemently desired as an ontological reality, can be represented only as an act of faith, the oneness of the Word and the Queen. Persuasive advice is at best salutary to its achievement. The always limiting circumstances of historical life demand accommodation—accommodations on the part of sovereign and citizen that these humanist makers urgently persuade, but cannot compel.

order. The *Passage*'s rhetoric is by turns pragmatic and iconic, moving between contrasting poles of expressive potential, in complex moments of praise, persuasion, and advice. The promise of unity between "blessing tongues" and "true hearts" in an idealized *Respublica bene instituta* is conditioned by the urgently experienced need to create a causeway across the abyss, to bridge the gap between metaphor and magic, the historical and the iconic. Discrepant awareness leads to a renewed sense of the necessity of rhetoric in a ritual progress that continually foregrounds, in its double vision, the gap between the Word as Icon and the word as human speech and reason.

Roy Strong has argued in his study of the cult of Elizabeth that a primary characteristic of her ritual images "lay in [their] capacity to be read and re-read many ways and never to present a single outright statement which left no room for manoeuvre."[28] If Strong is right to assert that the multivalent significance of the ritual image often comprises part of its strength, as a convenient tool for dramatizing multiple meanings, such multivalence bears importantly on how best to understand the ideological character of Elizabeth's *Passage*. The coronation rituals arguably both afford and invite a multiplicity of responses by fostering what I have called discrepant awareness, and such multiple meanings seem inimical to ideological readings of a deterministic kind. Claims to the deterministic power of ideologies are always theoretically suspect since they are by definition unprovable.[29] But such claims seem especially incautious when applied to a text like this one for two important reasons: they mistake the origin and character of the *Passage*'s rhetorical power, which derive so substantially from foregrounding the gap between iconic representations of the Word and human words, from the self-conscious reminders of the *Passage*'s humanist makers about the merely conditional force of their speeches and reasons. (Determinism does poorly in the space of the conditional). Second, while Althusser is useful for clarifying

---

[28] Roy Strong, *The Cult of Elizabeth: Elizabethan Portraiture and Pageantry* (Wallop, Hampshire: Thames and Hudson, 1977), p. 112. From a different perspective, Louis A. Montrose attributes such multiplicity of meaning to the state's "limited" and "uncertain" power "to control the signifying process," "Idols of the Queen: Policy, Gender, and the Picturing of Queen Elizabeth I," *Representations* 68 (1999), 108–61.

[29] By definition, such claims are unprovable because there can never be any place *beyond* or *outside* the determining boundaries of ideology from which to speak or to write, unless (as a contemporary act of faith, Althusser-style), one ascribes to dialectical materialism as an authentically scientific, objective discourse. See Pecheux, pp. 133–70.

the power of accommodation as a rhetorical and political goal in these coronation rituals, such deterministic claims would inevitably misrepresent the *Passage*'s most important spectator and star, the Queen herself. For Elizabeth possesses an irreducible doubleness parallel in kind to the rhetorical strategies of these humanist makers, a doubleness illuminated by the roles she plays throughout the coronation proceedings.

The Queen is both spectator and star, audience and actor, both a reader of signatures and a master/mistress of signs—contrasting roles that point, once again, to real complexity in these ritual events. As audience, Elizabeth is led, sometimes passively it seems, from display to emblematic display and instructed by ritual images about how to read her own royal virtues, secular and religious. Such ritual images are presented sometimes as commonplaces of textbook moral advice, virtues that she is advised and persuaded to assume. At other moments, those images assume the likeness of signatures— seeming symbols of a historical identity, already divinely ordained, to which she is asked to accommodate herself. Elizabeth not only reads signatures about herself, but also is clearly advised to see herself as a signature, as a Queen whose historical role has been written in God's book: as the steadfast Deborah, for instance, she is a woman providentially scripted to guide the children of the new (Protestant!) Israel. These are additional reminders about the potential power of accommodation to control and constrain both the citizens and the sovereign, the young virgin Queen Elizabeth.

At the same time, and true to character, Elizabeth knows well how to parlay roles from audience to actor, spectator to star. Mulcaster's account of the coronation pageants emphasizes repeatedly Elizabeth's delight in histrionic display. As a child addresses a poem to her, she adopts a "marvelous change in looke" and a "rejoysing visage" (30). When Truth hands her the Bible, Elizabeth "received the booke, kyssed it, and with both her handes held up the same, and so laid it upon her brest, with great thankes to the citie" (48). She even makes some unscheduled departures from the script, staging miniature dramas of her own. When the fourth pageant is interrupted by the arrival of a gift of 1000 gold marks from the city aldermen, Elizabeth seizes the opportunity to announce: "I wil be as good unto you, as ever quene was to her people. No wille in me can lacke, neither doe I trust shall ther lacke any power" (46). Quickly taking advantage of the situation, she parlays the city's gift of gold

into a promise of royal munificence and a reminder of royal sovereignty: the receipt of the gift is made conditional on the acknowledgment of her power. Her assumption of agency, beyond the limits
of those humanist makers' script, is striking and dramatic. Elizabeth
is more than a reader of signatures. She is also a politically adept
master/mistress of signs.[30]

Consider at our own historical juncture Elizabeth in the *Quenes
Majesties Passage* as she is led station by station to heed the lessons
of concord or to learn the political blessings of beatitudes, and it
requires no great leap of imagination to recall the icon-like face of
that newly crowned Queen haunting the screen of Shekhar Kapur's
1998 film, *Elizabeth I*. Kate Blanchett's Elizabeth is a butterfly frozen
by a circus calliope, a woman paralyzed by the patriarchal ideology
of an oppressive culture who finds herself consigned to a lifeless
future. Blanchett is the very definition of the sovereign subjected to
Althusserian interpellation: a puppet who learns too well from her
masters to pull strings for herself. For audiences of a different generation, Blanchett's Elizabeth comes as something of a shock, accustomed as they are to images of Glenda Jackson, playing an Elizabeth
who is the very image of the enlightenment's liberal subject—tem-
peramental but charming, wise and witty, always a powerful independent agent who by ruling herself learns to rule others. At those
moments of the *Passage* where the Queen lingers, with politically calculated effect, to dramatize her enthusiasm at the displays' unfolding, or especially at those times where she departs meaningfully from
the script—pausing, for instance, among the aldermen to trade symbolic capital for capital both material and political in kind—Glenda
Jackson's Elizabeth seems still a skillful embodiment of such agency.[31]

My purpose in juxtaposing these two cinematic images of Elizabeth,
each of which accords with a certain aspect of the Queen's representation in Mulcaster's *Passage*, is to highlight the complexity of her
historical image as it unfolds in the coronation pageants and the

---

[30] For a recent article highlighting Elizabeth's success in negotiating humanist
practices of counsel to assume a powerful "array of active roles . . . within the political system," see Mary Thomas Crane, "'*Video et Taceo*': Elizabeth I and the Rhetoric
of Counsel," *Studies in English Literature* 28, no. 1 (1988), 1–15.
[31] For a helpful review of contemporary cinematic Elizabeths, see Renee Pigeon's
"'No Man's Elizabeth': The Virgin Queen in Recent Films" in *Retrovisions: Reinventing
the Past in Film and Fiction* (London: Pluto, 2001), pp. 8–24.

indispensability of a rhetorical analysis for rendering that representation intelligible. The doubleness of Elizabeth's roles as audience
and actor, spectator and star, parallels the rhetorical doubleness
organizing the *Passage* at large. The Queen is comprehensible as neither the fully determined subject of Althusserian theory nor as the
independent agent of liberal critique, no more than the *Passage*'s
rhetoric is intelligible as either iconic or pragmatic. Instead, what is
crucial to comprehending the *Passage*'s rhetorical organization is
arguably crucial to understanding the issues of subjectivity and power
posed therein—an appreciation of irreducible doubleness, which analysis proceeds to eliminate only at the cost of its own intelligibility.
The ideologically charged power of ritual images and the limited
persuasiveness of ordinary words, the conditioning agency of accommodation and the always conditional freedom of individuals to act
otherwise—the history is complicated by seemingly irreconcilable
extremes that elude our capacity, here and now, to name or to define
adequately. At the edge of understanding, poised at the brink of our
own abyss of historical comprehension, we fall back upon consider-
ations about words (so much like the humanist makers!) because it
is there, we remain persuaded, that the complexities of things are
discovered and conditioned.

BRITOMART'S BACKWARD GLANCE IN SPENSER'S *FAERIE QUEENE*: LIMINAL TRIUMPHS/DARK EROTICS IN BUSIRANE'S MASK OF CUPID

Tiffany J. Alkan

In the climax of Edmund Spenser's third book of *The Faerie Queene*, Britomart—the heroine and knight of chastity—battles Busirane, a wicked enchanter whom she must vanquish. Her mission to rescue the lovely (but unheroic) Amoret depends on her ability to withstand the terrifying and perverse mask of Cupid, a triumphal pageant and wedding mask executed by Busirane's sorcery. Britomart succeeds and leaves the house of Busirane, leading the enchanter himself captive, bound by his own great chain. Amoret follows and as they return through the great halls, the "goodly roomes" and glory of Busirane's hall decay (III.xii.42).[1] Then, at the apex of the chaste heroine's triumph, something strange happens. The vanishing of the "so rich and royally arayd" evil palace "that fraud did frame" provokes not victorious elation, but instead Britomart's consternation (III.xii.42, 43). Her reaction, "That sight of such a chaunge her much dismayd," seems a paradoxical moment (III.xii.42).[2] Why should she lament the erasure of a hall, no matter how "rich and royally arayd," wherein she had grappled with and defeated the "vile villany" of Busirane's mask (III.xii.42/35)?

Britomart's keen dismay parallels many readers' nervousness when the final rushing stanzas of Book III unravel the previous two cantos' elaborately textured verbal tapestries. Her behavior in Book III's final canto perplexes critics, who seek to situate the mask of Cupid in Amoret's fearful fantasies of love.[3] Although long a critical locus

---

[1] *Spenser: The Faerie Queene*, ed. A. C. Hamilton (New York: Longman, 1977). Citations are to book, canto, and stanza and are hereafter included in text.

[2] Spenser uses "dismayd" frequently as a participle adjective with a range of meanings. Its meaning here seems closest to the OED definition of "overwhelmed by fear; appalled" as when Britomart first sees the fire burning before Busirane's castle in III.xi.22, "Greatly thereat was Britomart dismayd." It suggests a loss of courage and the feeling of being undone and paralyzed by fear. The pun in "dismayd" takes on a darker meaning at the end of Canto xii.

[3] Triumphs, pageants, "disguising," mummery, and masks are spectacles that modern historians typically distinguish. To the Elizabethans, however, the terms were

in Spenser scholarship, Busirane's halls and mask bear more explanation, explanation that attention to the realm of Renaissance performance arts can best supply. Amoret plays a focal role as the
rescued virgin, but we must also remember that Busirane's enchantments are quite as much about Britomart.[4] Once more, Britomart's
is a liminal experience—one that serves as an initiation into a dark-

---

less clearly differentiated and often interchangeable. A social occasion might combine
elements of disguising, dancing, and tournament-style combat. I use the older spelling
"mask" on the basis of E. K. Chambers, who argues that Ben Jonson in the early
part of the seventeenth century first established our contemporary spelling "masque,"
The Elizabethan Stage, 4 vols., vol. 1 (Oxford: The Clarendon Press, 1923), 1.153.
For the fluidity of terminology during the period, see Sydney Anglo, "The Evolution
of the Tudor Disguising, Pageant and Masque," *Renaissance Drama* 1 (1968): 3–44.
More recently, scholars recognize that earlier Tudor use of the term *mask* in the
Revels almost always referred to court entertainment so much so that the first Master
of Revels, Sir Thomas Cawarden, was described as the Master of "revelles and
Maskes," see Chapter 13 "Terminology" in Meg Twycross and Sarah Carpenter, *Masks
and Masking in Medieval and Early Tudor England* (Aldershot: Ashgate, 2002) at p. 328.
[4] Many critics focus on Amoret's experience of the mask. For example, Kathleen
Williams argues that the experience is all Amoret's fancy, *Spenser's World of Glass; a
Reading of the Faerie Queene* (Berkeley: Univ. of California Press, 1966), pp. 26–27.
Thomas P. Roche, following the work of Janet Spens, reads the house of Busirane
as an objectification of Amoret's fear of sexual love in marriage in, *The Kindly Flame:
A Study of the Third and Fourth Books of Spenser's Faerie Queene* (Princeton, NJ: Princeton
Univ. Press, 1964); Janet Spens, *Spenser's Faerie Queene: An Interpretation* (London:
E. Arnold, 1934). For more on Amoret's perspective, which suggests what we see
is not so much her fear as Scudamore's attempt at "maistrye," see also A. Kent
Hieatt, "Scudamour's Practice of Maistrye Upon Amoret," *PMLA* 77, no. 4 (1962):
509–10; and *Chaucer, Spenser, Milton: Mythopoetic Continuities and Transformations* (Montreal:
McGill-Queens Univ. Press, 1975) esp. chapters 7 and 8. Harry Berger notes the
increasingly introverted nature of the mask in, "Busirane and the War between the
Sexes: An Interpretation of the *Faerie Queene* III.xi–xii," *English Literary Renaissance* 1,
no. 2 (1971): 99–121. Such critical focus on Amoret's perception of the mask side-
steps the fact that as readers we experience it only as Britomart sees it. Lauren
Silberman shifts the emphasis away from Amoret to note that "it is Britomart for
whom the Masque is not just a spectacle but the scene of battle in her quest to
liberate Amoret from *Amor* and define her own chastity," in, "The Hermaphrodite
and the Metamorphosis of Spenserian Allegory," *Early Literary Renaissance* 17 (1987):
207–23 at 18. This argument is more fully developed in Lauren Silberman, *Transforming Desire: Erotic Knowledge in Books III and IV of the Faerie Queene* (Berkeley: Univ.
of California Press, 1995). Julia Walker observes that in the house of Busirane,
Britomart begins to recognize external projections of her internal sexual fears,
"Spenser's Elizabeth Portrait and the Fiction of Dynastic Epic," *Modern Philology* 90,
no. 2 (1992):172–99. Elizabeth Porges Watson notes "Britomart's detachment is
strangely uncharacteristic. It demands explanation, whether she at once recognizes
the masque as being phantasmagoric, merely symptomatic of its true origin, or
because it expresses imaginings of her own that have to be brought under control
before constructive action is possible," in "Mr. Fox's Mottoes in the House of Busirane,"
Spenser Studies 13 (1999): 285–90 at 87. Other discussions of this episode include
Helen Gardner, "Some Reflections on the House of Busyrane," *Studies in English*

natured eroticism.[5] Significantly, Spenser indicates the liminal quality of Britomart's experience most spectacularly by the processional pageant of Busirane's mask itself—a quality, in turn, that can best be understood in context with other kinds of Renaissance public spectacles. In this essay I will be dealing, then, with the tradition of Tudor masks, triumphs, pageants and their liminality, a liminality that I explore with the help of Arnold van Gennep and Victor Turner. Once we understand how a tradition of public, ritualized spectacle informs Britomart's experience, we can ask what sort of experience that liminal encounter with the mask initiates her into. Cupid's mask represents a fulcrum in Britomart's quest. Here, alone in the heart of an enchanter's lair, she confronts the full cast of emotional horrors that had made her inwardly quake in Canto ii when she speaks of Artegall with Guyon (III.ii.5).

She sees the mask of Cupid at midnight in the second chamber of Busirane's hall. It begins with a loud "shrilling Trompet," a "hideous storme of winde . . . /With dreadfull thunder and lightning atwixt," and a "direfull stench of smoke and sulphure mixt" (III.xii.1,2). Following this dramatic opening, the figure of *Ease* enters like one who introduces a play, "Yclad in costly garments, fit for tragicke Stage" (III.xii.3). A most "delitious harmony/In full straunge notes" of sweet melody accompanies the maskers as they march forth "in trim aray" (III.xii.6). *Fancy* as a "louely boy" leads the troupe, followed by *Desyre* (III.xii.7). After *Fancy* the mask figures become more grim and troubling: *Doubt* who looks "askew with his mistrufull eyes,"

Literature 34, no. 136 (1983): 402–13; Mark Bruhn, "Approaching Busyrane: Episodic Patterning in the *Faerie Queene*," *Studies in Philology* 92, no. 3 (1995): 275–90; James W. Broaddus, *Spenser's Allegory of Love: Social Vision in Books III, IV, and V of the Faerie Queene* (Cranbury: Fairleigh Dickinson Univ. Press, 1995), and Elizabeth Story Donno, "The Triumph of Cupid: Spenser's Legend of Chastity," *Year in English Studies* 4 (1974): 37–48. Critics such as Gardner (1983) and Bruhn (1995) fault explicators for the use of Book IV to explain Book III because this strategy blurs Book III's narrative logic and detracts from Britomart's rescue of Amoret as a discrete climax. However, I believe in situating the episode within the larger context of Britomart's quest, a quest that does not end in Book III as conclusively as does those of the earlier heroes, the Redcrosse Knight or Sir Guyon.

[5] I follow Victor Turner's definition and use of the term "liminal" (a definition itself influenced by Arnold van Gennep). Transition lies at the heart of the idea and stems from the Latin *limen* "threshold." Liminal rites were central to a culture's staging of various rites of passage and range from marriage rites to initiation rituals. Turner expanded and developed his concept of the "liminal" over a period of years. The most relevant texts for my discussion are: *The Forest of Symbols: Aspects of Ndembu Ritual* (Ithaca: Cornell Univ. Press, 1967), pp. 93–111; *The Ritual Process:*

Daunger who bears a net and rusty blade, *Feare, Dissemblance, Suspect, Griefe, Fury, Displeasure,* and *Pleasance* (III.xii.10–18). At the center of the mask Amoret, with a naked, wounded breast, "her feeble feet did moue" (III.xii.19). Her heart has been ripped from her chest, and transfixed "with a deadly dart," it is borne before her in a "siluer basin" (III.xii.21). The "winged God himselfe" follows with his blindfold unbound so that he can survey his "goodly company" (III.xii.22,23). After him follows more maskers, a rabble of "phantasies/In wauering wemens wit" of "paines in loue" (III.xii.26). They march three times around the room and disappear into the inner room. Behind them the door slams, "fast locked" and "driuen with that stormy blast" (III.xii.27).

Busirane's mask, his statue, and his tapestries show Cupid's spoils won at great cost to the victims. This Cupid is not the playful winged boy but a tyrant of love. The passions of love and specifically, eroticism defined as the amatory—sexual aspects of love figured in Amoret's wounded breast and bleeding heart at the mask's center—lie at the core of this liminal encounter. Spenser's portrayal of Britomart suggests a volatile eroticism that she never quite masters—and perhaps never can, or should. The mask of Cupid marks a liminal threshold for Spenser's exploration of chastity—a complex, multiple perspectival vision of chastity that I argue might be better understood in light of Georges Bataille's insights into erotic experience. Reading the mask through the social theory of van Gennep and Turner on ritual rites of passage and the erotic theory of Bataille helps make sense of its ties to public spectacle and its private, psychological consequences for Britomart, her destined union, and the frightening and alluring nature of eroticism. It leaves us with a Britomart who may not fully encompass virtuous desire and who may not be as chaste of a heroine as we might like to believe.

Structure and Anti-Structure, *Lewis Henry Morgan Lectures; 1966* (Chicago: Aldine Pub. Co., 1969), p. 95; and Victor Witter and Edith Turner, "Religious Celebrations," in *Celebration: Studies in Festivity and Ritual,* ed. Victor Witter Turner (Washington, DC: Smithsonian Institution Press, 1982). While much of Turner's work around ritual studies "primitive" tribal groups, his later work exhibits a shift toward complex industrial societies in the modern world. Realizing that the liminality of Ndembu ritual differs from the quasi-liminal character of modern cultural pageants like theatre and other leisure activities, Turner introduces the term "liminoid" phenomena that he suggests offer critiques on existing social practices. See Victor Witter Turner, *From Ritual to Theatre: The Human Seriousness of Play,* vol. 1 (New York: Performing Arts Journal Publications, 1982).

Just what happens to Britomart in Busirane's hall puzzles readers in part because Spenser fosters confusion through the "monstrous formes" that he asks his readers to examine (III.xi.51). As a mask, Busirane's entertainment has links to a Tudor court fascinated by spectacles. As part of a narrative within his epic poem, Busirane's mask draws on a literary tradition of allegorical triumphs of love. What makes this mask so incongruous is that Spenser fuses these two Renaissance pageant contexts—public productions of masks with the emblematic triumph tradition of continental humanists such as Petrarch and Du Bartas—along with two aspects of Cupid, the benign and the malignant. Cupid bore complex and often contradictory meanings during the Renaissance so that at times he is benign, a figure for positive and civilizing love as we will see in some Tudor masks. But at others he is malignant, a negative tyrant who champions erotic passion over all human endeavor just as Petrarch had imagined him to be in the *Trionfi*.[6] Busirane's mask of Cupid begins as if it were "on the ready flore/Of some Theatre," which suggests it is modeled on contemporary mask performances (III.xii.3). While the fact that there is no audience (except for the hidden Britomart) makes the production of such a mask strange and quite pointless—there is nothing to celebrate and no one to dance the concluding dance—Spenser later tells us in Book IV that Busirane's mask also played at the wedding feast for Amoret and Scudamor: "Amidst the bridale feast" when all the guests were "surcharg'd with wine" that "same vile Enchauntour *Busyran*" "Brought in that mask of loue which late was showen" (IV.i.3). This latter context provides some explanation for what the mask is meant to celebrate—the formal consummation of a courtship. However, if Spenser does faithfully model Tudor spectacle in Busirane's mask, he makes bewildering deviations by placing the Cupid of emblematic fame as the chief figure in a nuptial mask.

Although much critical discussion explores the later masque tradition that reaches its zenith under Ben Jonson and Inigo Jones early in the seventeenth century, less attention has been drawn to the earlier forms of these entertainments, what George Puttenham in his 1589

---

[6] The Renaissance view of Cupid is diverse and cannot be reduced to a simple "good" and "bad" figure; however, as Thomas Hyde has argued, the Busyrane episode is a dense blending of many strands of Spenser's "theodicy of Cupid," *The Poetic Theology of Love: Cupid in Renaissance Literature* (Newark: Univ. of Delaware Press, 1986), pp. 160–79. It is that blending that I explore.

The Arte of English Poesie discusses as "poeticall rejoysings" or "triumphs."[7]
Puttenham writes that these early "triumphs" primarily marked
moments of public celebration, "& the chiefe was for the publike
peace of a countrie."[8] They highlighted events of transitional importance such as royal entries, victory over an enemy, great occasions
of state, or the alliance of nobility through dynastic marriage. Because
these "triumphs" were often performed to celebrate transitional, ceremonial moments in the lives of the aristocracy and the court, they
figure as the kinds of liminal rites that van Gennep and Turner
describe. Tudor masks were liminal entertainments that celebrated
rites of cultural significance, marking transitions from battle to victory, from singleness to alliance, from old monarch to new, from
courtship to consummation.

This last context, the use of masks to celebrate nuptials, has the
most relevance for my reading of Busirane's mask. Sarah Carpenter
and Meg Twycross in *Masks and Masking in Medieval and Early Tudor
England* argue for a kind of subgenre of Tudor masks, what they call
"amorous masking," that carried with it a certain erotic charge and
encouraged flirtation while at the same time codifying the impulse
of an erotic encounter.[9] This variety of masking became popular
with Henry VIII's elaborate courtship spectacles for Katherine of
Aragorn where the disguises were linked with erotic arousal. They
continued to be popular throughout Elizabeth's reign. In 1566 Queen
Elizabeth attended at least two wedding masks; in 1573 there was
"A mask showen at Grenewitche after the marriage of William Drurye
esquire" and in 1595 Arthur Throgmorton makes use of a mask to
regain favor at the wedding of William Earl of Derby to Lady
Elizabeth Vere.[10] Although few extant textual and visual representations of them exist in England, continental examples describe public pageants and nuptial, amatory masks that influenced the English
celebrations.[11] We can guess at the nature of English performances

---

[7] George Puttenham, *The Arte of English Poesie* (Cambridge: Cambridge Univ. Press, 1970), p. 46.

[8] Ibid., pp. 46–7.

[9] Carpenter, *Masks and Masking in Medieval and Early Tudor England*, pp. 169–83.

[10] For accounts of these see Chambers, *The Elizabethan Stage*, I. 162,68; Mary Susan Steele, *Plays & Masques at Court During the Reigns of Elizabeth, James and Charles* (New Haven: Yale Univ. Press, 1926).

[11] Roy Strong includes a calendar of major festival events and publications from 1491–1641 that took place on the continent and in England. Among these are fourteen wedding festivals before the year 1600. Of these fourteen, seven include

by following Privy Council minutes and the detailed instructions for the triumphs surrounding the arrival, entry, and wedding ceremony given in Richard Pynson's pamphlet, *The Tradition and Marriage of the Princesse*, for Prince Arthur and Katherine's nuptials in 1501. They tell us that many masks performed at English weddings promoted the harmony of love, with Cupid figuring in his more benign aspects. The elaborate entertainments were presented to "to amplify and increase the royalty of this noble and solemn" occasion.[12] The pageant-master for the nuptials of Arthur and Katherine turned to the *Le Trosne d'honneur* of Jean Molinet for inspiration and borrowed heavily from its tropes of Platonic apotheosis as well as its astrological and classical motifs.[13] The wedding ceremony itself included disguisings and a series of elaborate pageant cars designed by William Cornish, containing allegorical figures such as a "Fountain of the Three Worthies" that illustrated the united realms of England, France, and Spain. Another pageant contained the Knights of the Mount of Love who won the Castle of Ladies, showing how a "Castle" or "Castile" might capitulate to Knights of Love, or to "London." Within these various pageants what becomes salient are the manners appropriate to lovers and the overriding symbolism of political union. According to Skiles Howard, the ordered proceedings of these earlier masks promoted equilibrium and eliminated destructive depictions of eroticism; the pageants' dancing rehearsed the move of the "heterosexual couples" toward the signification of matrimony.[14] Notably, at least in this dynastic wedding, erotic tableaux are suppressed in

---

descriptions of the event published at the time, and of these seven, three were also illustrated in *Art and Power: Renaissance Festivals, 1450–1650* (Woodbridge, Suffolk: Boydell Press, 1984), pp. 175–79. If Gordon Kipling is right, we can assume that the form might have been similar for the English weddings that have no surviving descriptions as he traces the transmission of Burgundian marriage ceremonies to England, *The Triumph of Honour: Burgundian Origins of the Elizabethan Renaissance* (The Hague: Published for the Sir Thomas Browne Institute by Leiden Univ. Press, 1977). For an example of what one of these ceremonies might have looked like, James Saslow provides documentation for the Medici wedding of 1589, *The Medici Wedding of 1589: Florentine Festival as Theatrum Mundi* (New Haven: Yale Univ. Press, 1996).

[12] Reprint of the descriptions of the wedding celebrations from Harleian MS 69, fols. 29–31 in Paul Reyher, *Les Masques Anglais; Étude Sur Les Ballets Et La Vie De Cour En Angleterre (1512–1640)* (New York: B. Blom, 1964), pp. 500–02.

[13] For a full account, see A. H. Thomas and I. D. Thornley, ed., *The Great Chronicle of London* (London: Printed by G. W. Jones at the sign of the Dolphin, 1938), p. 310.

[14] Skiles Howard, *The Politics of Courtly Dancing in Early Modern England* (Amherst: Univ. of Massachusetts Press, 1998), p. 40.

favor of motifs furthering hierarchical political ends. Masking and marriage coded the erotic impulse into acceptable social outlets of formalized dance and ceremony.

One painting from the period may serve to illustrate this point visually (Figure 1). Representing the principal stages of Sir Henry Unton's life, death, and burial, one prominent tableau features him presiding over a banquet and mask—probably that of his wedding. The portrait was finished after his death, but was commissioned sometime around 1580 and offers, therefore, a glimpse into the performance of early amatory masks. Sir Henry sits at the table's center with his wife at the right end. The maskers enter led by a green-clad huntsman, who addresses Lady Unton. The ten torchbearers look to be naked children, in black and white pairs, most likely representing the Cupids of Night and Day. Mercury, with Diana and six Nymphs' take central roles, bearing garlands. The mask takes place in a great chamber or hall with two tables of guests. The foreground depicts an ascending and descending staircase around a group of musicians. Moving in a clockwise manner, the maskers circle with a drummer, with a trunchman holding a paper—most likely to provide topical meaning and interpretation to the maskers' disguises—and with the Cupids bearing torches.[15] The maskers wear rich, silver-colored costumes with sprays of red flowers in green leaves; their headdresses are also silver and garlanded, and masks of red cover their faces. The procession appears graceful, orderly, decorous, balanced and above all, harmonious. The figures move in pairs, and the dark and light Cupids, wearing trailing headdresses of red and white, suggest a balance between the powers of night and day. These Cupid figures resemble more the Italian *putto*, the small winged boy, than the cruel, lecherously leering unmasked Cupid of Busirane's mask. The Cupid who appeared in nuptial masks would most likely have resembled those at Unton's feast. These Cupids do not invoke eroticism or sexual appetite, but instead code an eroticism carefully checked by the mask's circular rhythm and stately pace. The lighter Cupids, their decorous environment, and the harmonious pairing of black with white contain the darker figures and the more chaotic night and eroticism they evoke.

In the larger painting, the mask scene represents one stage in the narrative of Henry Unton's life. We also see him as a baby, as a

---

[15] The OED lists "trunchman" as an interpreter. The trunchmen were often present at masks to offer glosses on the performance.

Figure 1. The Life and Death of Sir Henry Unton ca. 1596

soldier and ambassador abroad, as a sick man on his deathbed, and, finally, in effigy being visited by his widow. Occupying a prominent space in the viewer's right-hand side of the frame, the mask occurs in the central chamber of his house. To the right we see him being nursed and to the left we see his funeral procession winding out from the bottom of the house and ending in the church. The mask's placement suggests that like birth and death, it marks a socially significant, ritual passage. It is a liminal rite that changes and confirms Unton's place in the public sphere. For Arnold van Gennep, "liminality" marks an important transitional moment in an individual's place within the larger culture; it marks moments of change from childhood to adulthood, from being single to being married, changes of the kind that we see represented in Unton's portrait. The liminal rites (in this case, the mask) perform an important transitional ceremony that ushers the participants from one social stage into another. Typically, because the rites are about transition, there is an implied momentary pause or suspension between the two stages, a gap that van Gennep and Turner read as a space of "other," outside the modes of usual social action. Liminal rituals scrutinize a culture's central values and axioms because of their unique position as in-between moments. Characters or entities that are liminal are neither what they were nor what they will be; they are "betwixt and between" categories of past and future social existence.[16] Amatory masks, then,

---

[16] Arnold van Gennep, Monika Vizedom, and Solon Toothaker Kimball, *The Rites of Passage* (Chicago: Univ. of Chicago Press, 1960).

served as liminal rites to prepare the individual to move between social categories. They were an important symbolic representation of love's order in maintaining society. As Skiles Howard argues, wedding masks, pageants, and triumphs were designed to perform details of rank, gender, and political ideology subsumed under the harmony of political union, noble alliance, and dynastic marriage—not to promote the consuming heat, male appetite, and destructive passions of love.[17] Erotic tableaux featuring the kind of Cupid we might see in Morley's *Trionfi* of Petrarch typically do not figure in these ceremonies, as the evidence that we do have favors the representation of a more benign Cupid presiding at masks such as we see at Henry Unton's feast. When Spenser tells us in Book IV that Cupid's mask was also a wedding mask for Amoret and Scudamor, his revision of the mask tradition is conspicuous. Seeing a wedding mask that stages the Cupid of emblematic triumph tradition instead of the harmonious figures of Unton's mask, evokes certain expectations only to undercut them. The idealized world typically portrayed by such celebrations undergoes a rude parody in Busirane's halls.

Considering the cultural function that masks could perform as markers of liminal rites of passage, Busirane's amatory mask suggests the important public symbolism of dynastic marriage operative in Spenser's narrative of Britomart and Artegall as founders of a dynastic line. In my reading, Cupid's mask becomes an important liminal rite of passage not only for Amoret's consummation of courtship with Scudamor, but also for Britomart. After all, it is her culminating battle and experience that punctuate Spenser's third book. The mask's status as a liminal rite parallels and reinforces Britomart's identity as a liminal figure, especially in terms of her sexuality. As Turner notes, liminal entities are often coded through images of wilderness and bisexuality. During liminal passages the ritual subject's identity becomes temporarily fluid; that is, normal social hierarchical distinctions such as class and gender oscillate and are even often momentarily suspended. Ambiguity looms large in the liminal process. Alone in the enchanted halls Britomart does indeed seem to be in a strange kind of wilderness and as a maiden appointed

---

[17] *The Politics of Courtly Dancing in Early Modern England*, p. 40. For more on traditions of civic pageantry, see also David Moore Bergeron, *English Civic Pageantry, 1558–1642*, rev. ed. (Tempe: Arizona Center for Medieval and Renaissance Studies, 2003); and *Practicing Renaissance Scholarship: Plays and Pageants, Patrons and Politics* (Pittsburgh: Duquesne Univ. Press, 2000).

with armor and shield, she presents an ambiguous, double-gendered figure. She is "betwixt and between" as she rides as a maid disguised as a knight. As a maiden she loves, fears, and desires Artegall. As a knight she moves through the halls of Busirane with "welpointed weapons" and boldly passes through the rooms, to rescue the trembling Amoret.[18] At the same time as she participates in both genders, she is strangely neither. Although she dresses as a knight and wields a sword, she remains underneath the armor female. But, she is not yet a woman (she has not been penetrated), neither is she a maid without desire. Her encounter with Cupid's mask serves as a moment of ritual passage for her—a moment when she can question the nature of eroticism and its socially sanctioned fulfillment in marriage. The ambiguities of her nature as a maid, but also as a fierce and able knight, raise questions about what her identity will be. Merlin tells her that she will not be remembered for her heroic feats as a knight, but as a womb, famous for "fruits of matrimoniall bowre," a mother of kings (III.iii.3). The nature of the quest itself, a quest of desire, love, marriage, and dynastic foundation, comes under pressure during Cupid's mask. The liminal quality of the passage through the halls encourages her to address the threat and allure of eroticism to her identity as a chaste heroine and future dynastic founder.

Busirane's mask carries the connotations with it of a public celebration resonant with cultural symbolism that marks the passage of a woman from one state into another—from virgin to matron. This passage was supposed to happen to Amoret with Scudamor (and ultimately to Britomart with Artegall). However, as Spenser tells us, it is all too liminal for Amoret. She remains imperiled on the threshold, unable to escape and unable to progress. Britomart, on the other hand, passes boldly, but then turns back her eye in dismay at the decay wrought by her success, and emerges to continue wandering. The rite of passage does not conclude in the matrimonial bower for Britomart. In fact, she still has not even glimpsed her knight in the flesh. Spenser presents us with a disfigured rite of passage, one that

---

[18] For the importance that gender plays in this incident see Maureen Quilligan, *Milton's Spenser: The Politics of Reading* (Ithaca: Cornell Univ. Press, 1983); Susanne Wofford, "Gendering Allegory: Spenser's Bold Reader and the Emergence of Character in the *Faerie Queene* III," *Criticism* 30, no. 1 (1988): 1–21. For more on Britomart's playing the masculine see Donald Stump, "Fashioning Gender: Cross-Dressing in Spenser's Legend of Britomart and Artegall," *Spenser Studies* 15 (2001): 95–119.

resembles a Tudor amatory mask, but one that warps the cultural values it is supposed to promote. Britomart's successful passage through the mask (what many have read as her defeat of its twisted erotic fantasies) should solicit some troubling questions about the nature of the chastity she represents.

Her progress through Busirane's halls follows what Victor Turner describes as one of the major aspects of a liminal rite involving three steps—exhibitition, ludic play or action, and finally, re-integration and instruction into the community. In the first stage (exhibition), initiates see a communication of symbolically resonant objects that pertain to their passage and that instruct them how to progress. For Britomart, the exhibition hall of tapestries serves a similar function. She sees a parade of erotic images showing Cupid's sport wrecking havoc on classical figures—Europa, Helle, Danae, Leda, Semelee— who are accosted by different forms of a shape-shifting Jove. In the second stage of Turner's liminal rite (ludic play/action), the initiate encounters a ludic recombination of images from the first phase that encourages reflection on those former symbolic objects. The reflection culminates in the initiate's action and passage. Masks, distorted images, bizarre configurations often confront the liminal subjects to disrupt accustomed ways of thought and encourage speculation. Busirane's mask with its strange troupe who "moue a comely pace" and in its horror "shewd a seemely grace" (III.xii.19) seems just such a recon-figuration of the harmonious amatory mask and Renaissance pageants it parodies. According to Turner, after reflection the initiate is expected to know how to act to successfully move through to the final stage in the rite of passage. The final stage, instruction and return to the community, erodes distinctions of previous status and enhances knowl-edge about how things work.[19] In other words, having seen and determined how to act, the figure returns to the community with a greater understanding of his or her new place. The public performance and ritual texture of liminality in Cupid's mask harks back to Tudor traditions of masking and registers an important context for reading Britomart's experience in Busirane's halls. It suggests what *should* happen—the mask ushers in a harmonious dynastic union and return to community after consummation. In Britomart's case, her rite of passage suggests an initiation into eroticism and the sexual knowledge it connotes without the sanctity of marriage.

---

[19] Turner, "Religious Celebrations," pp. 203–06.

While thus far I have been stressing the public ideal harmony that wedding masks were meant to promote (as Unton's decorous mask depicts) and that Spenser retools by featuring the darker Cupid of the emblematic tradition, George Puttenham records that wedding masks, in addition to affirming the harmony and concord of love, have another function, one that comes closer to justifying Amoret's fear at her own bridal feast, and one that Spenser pulls from the background into the foreground. While outwardly masks encode erotic harmony, behind the decorous façade lurks a darker purpose. According to Puttenham, wedding celebrations were divided into several sections. The first section celebrated the moment when the woman and her husband were brought to the bedroom chamber threshold. In the antechamber to that bridal room would be a large number of ladies and gentlemen who would perform the celebration in "tunes" that "were very loude and shrill" so that those without would not hear what happened in the next room: "to the intent there might be noo noise be hard out of the bed chamber by the skreeking & outcry of the young damosell feeling the first forces of her stiffe & rigorous young man, the being as all virgins tender & weake, & unexpert in those maner of affairs" up until around "midnight or one of the clocke."[20] The "skreeking" of the "young damosell" drowned out by the celebratory noise recalls the plight of Amoret who is bound to a "brasen pillour" (III.xii.30) with her "hart" "seeming transfixed with a cruell dart" (31) while the guests continued "bent to mirth" (IV.i.3). Her fear of crossing the threshold literally binds her in the form of Busirane's torments as she writhes bound to his bronze pillar. On the one hand, then, the public pageant of wedding masks idealizes the harmony of love. Such idealization glosses over the kinds of fears that Puttenham describes and that immobilize Amoret and that threaten Britomart. Amatory masks disguise the underlying sexual threat to the "young damosell" by her "stiffe & rigorous young man." They hide the psychological (as well as physical) trauma of sexual love from the virgin bride. Britomart, however, experiences this darker side in her rite of passage through the explicit erotic display of Busirane's mask.

Critics often remark on the strangeness of Britomart's solitary encounter with Cupid's mask and ask just where the mask of love happens: Is the phantasmagoric hall and mask a convoluted and

---

[20] Puttenham, *The Arte of English Poesie*, pp. 51–2.

parodic interior vision of the political and social celebrations normally associated with marriage? Is it simply an illusion or, more crit-
ically, Britomart's self-delusion?[21] During the mask's performance at
her wedding feast, by a sleight of hand, or "by way of sport, as oft
in maskes is knowen," Amoret is "Conueyed quite away to liuing
wight unknowen" (IV.i.3). Spenser's language here is as slippery as
Busirane himself as Alastair Fowler pointed out long ago. The gram-
mar allows for two possible interpretations; first, Busirane ferrets
Amoret away without the wedding guests noticing; second, Amoret
experiences Busirane's enchantments "internally, without anyone
knowing."[22] The second reading implies that a strong internal psychological dimension also drives this episode. Moreover, beyond
Fowler's point, these same two interpretations must apply to Britomart,
through whose gaze we watch the pageant.[23] Amoret's experience
shows Britomart's peril. Van Gennep and Turner's theory details
both a cultural and psychological aspect to liminal rituals. With the
example of amatory Tudor masks, we have a template for what
kinds of cultural rites Busirane's mask should perform. But we also
have a template for the kinds of psychological change that a liminal ritual enacts on the initiates. It prepares them psychologically
for a change of station and identity.

The mask's links to the literary tradition of allegorical triumphs
supply another angle for reading its psychological consequences for
Britomart. It is in understanding this second, private, narrative context for the mask that we move into the erotic territory mapped out
by George Bataille in *Eroticism: Death and Sensuality*.[24] Bataille is often
identified with a kind of perverse eroticism, one that finds delight in
the darker recesses of Cupid's wings where voyeurism, fetishism, and
sadomasochism recall the cruelest Cupid of Petrarch. For Bataille,
eroticism goes beyond sexual appetite and the reproductive drive. It

---

[21] The formulation comes from the A. C. Hamilton, *The Spenser Encyclopedia*
(Toronto: Univ. of Toronto Press, 1990), pp. 459–60.

[22] Alastair Fowler, *Triumphal Forms: Structural Patterns in Elizabethan Poetry* (Cambridge:
Cambridge Univ. Press, 1970), p. 51.

[23] While I agree with Judith Anderson's point that the representation of this site
"is finally the poet's as are all the figures within it," the fact that we see the representation of that site through Britomart suggests its special pertinence for her as
the major figure of Book III. Judith Anderson, "Busirane's Place: *The House of
Rhetoric*," *Spenser Studies* 17 (2003): 133–50 at 33.

[24] Georges Bataille, *Eroticism*, trans. Mary Dalwood (San Francisco: City Lights,
1986). All quotations are taken from this translation and cited by page number.

is a psychological state bound up with transgression, emotions of fear, hate, loss of self-identity, and aching desire. He lingers over the darker aspects of sexuality to provide a way of reading how integral these emotions are to a complete erotic experience. In Bataille's theory, the erotic experience ushers the initiate into the essence of what it means to be human—an encompassing of both the beautiful and the terrible. For him an individual can only be fully realized through an erotic understanding, which invokes the best and worst of human nature. It is in the erotic frame that the individual most strongly feels all the conflict of identity as both private and public, separate and part of a larger social tapestry. To read Britomart's passage through Busirane's halls as a liminal rite of passage into eroticism suggests that she cannot simply reject the destructive, distorted views of love that she sees there.

Many readers have noted that while Cupid's mask is remarkably orderly and hierarchical (Spenser himself does say that it was a company "In manner of a maske, enranged orderly"), the figures themselves parody order and are more in line with a Jonsonian antimasque troupe than a harmonious procession such as we see in Unton's wedding mask.[25] Like the triumphs of love in Francesco Colonna's *Hypnerotomachia Poliphili* (part of which was printed and translated in England in 1592), the mask figures evoke a Bataillean vision of chaotic eroticism and conjure the tyrant Cupid. Spenser's Cupid in Busirane's mask recalls the Cupid of emblematic fame that Geoffrey Whitney represents in his emblem reproducing Andreas Alciati's *Potentissimus affectus, amor* (Figure 2). In this vision of a Cupid triumphant, we see not the *putto* Cupid of Unton's wedding mask, but Cupid seated in a chariot flogging a pair of lions who draw his chariot forward.[26] This lion-whipping Cupid embodies an erotic mastery

---

[25] E. B. Fowler argues the mask combines both the Renaissance triumph and medieval processional form of the court of love, *Spenser and the System of Courtly Love* (New York: Phaeton Press, 1968). Roche in *The Kindly Flame* (1964) notes that the first six couples represent an allegorical courtship progression (78). Alastair Fowler (1970) discusses the numerical significance of the figures and notes that the total of 33 "symbolizes false chastity" (52).

[26] For more on the significance of the emblem see Arthur F. Marotti, "Animal Symbolism in the *Faerie Queene*: Tradition and the Poetic Context," *Studies in English Literature* 5 (1965): 69–86. Laurel Hendrix argues that Spenser plays with the emblem tradition, reversing two separate paradigms of love to counter moral commonplaces in the pursuit of a poetics of deferral, "*Pulchritudo Vincit?*: Emblematic Reversals in Spenser's House of Busirane," *Spenser Studies* 16 (2002): 23–54.

Potentiſſimus affeÄus, amor.   63

T H E Lions grimme, behoulde, doe not reſiſte,
   But yealde them ſelues, and Cupiddes chariot drawe,
And with one hande, he guydes them where he liſte,
With th'other hande, he keepes them ſtill in awe:
   Theye couche, and drawe, and dó the whippe abide,
   And laie theire fierce and crewell mindes aſide.

If Cupid then, bee of ſuch mightie force,
That creatures fierce, and brutiſhe kinde he tames:
Oh mightie I o v e, vouchſafe to ſhowe remorſe,
Helpe feeble man, and pittie tender dames:
   Let Africke wilde, this tyrauntes force indure,
   If not alas, howe can poore man bee ſure.

Quem non mille feræ, quem non Stheneleïus hoſtis,   Ouid. Epiſt. 9.
   Non potuit Iuno vincere, vincit amor.

Quæ

Figure 2. Whitney, *A Choice of Emblems*, 1586

that Spenser describes earlier in canto vi: a "winged boy" who with "spoiles and cruelty/Ransackt the world" and "Of many wretches set his triumphes hye" (III.vi.49). The text below Whitney's emblem describes a similar vision of violence where the lions are kept in awe: "They couche, and draw, and do the whippe abide."[27] In Busirane's vision, Cupid follows after the tortured Amoret, "riding on a Lion rauenous" with his eyes unbound that he might look on his "proud spoyle" (III.xii.22). Fancy, Desyre, Doubt, Daunger, Feare, Hope, Dissemblance, Suspect, Griefe, Fury, Displeasure, Pleasance, Despight, and Cruelty pass by in front of Britomart, each awarded an emblematic description paralleling the emblematic triumph tradition not only in Petrarch and Colonna, but also in popular emblem images such as those of Whitney. *Griefe* wears sorrowful sable and holds a "paire of Pincers" with which he "pinched people to the hart"; *Fury* appears in rags, and tears her garments and hair while tossing a firebrand; *Cruelty* looks like a "dreary Spright" who is "Cald by strong charmes out of eternall night" and who figures "deathes owne image" in her face; a confused rout of others follow from "Lewd Losse of time" to "Consuming Riotise." Concluding the masked procession of figures is "death with infamie" (III.xii.16,17,19,25).

These figures present the darker "night" aspect of Cupid without the balance of "day" that Unton's mask provides. They are the coercive and aggressive side to the armed Cupid who shakes his darts, and "clapt on hie his coulourd winges" and makes all his train to quake, the Cupid who is carefully excised from actual Tudor masks and triumphs (III.xii.23). Bataille's insights into erotic experience matter here because he argues that truly to experience the erotic means to engage the kinds of grotesque perversions we see in Busirane's hall. As Bataille writes, "the stirrings within us have their own fearfull excesses; the excesses show which way these stirrings would take us."[28] The excess of emotion and mutation of form that Britomart sees in the hall and in the mask suggest where her own desire might lead. Since she identifies as a martial maid, the suggestion that her desire for Artegall might end only in "death with infamie" would be anathema. Busirane's tortures are not simply a demonic parody of real love, but also they reveal something about the nature of love

---

[27] Geffrey Whitney, *A Choice of Emblemes* (New York: B. Blom, 1967), p. 63.
[28] Bataille, *Eroticism*, p. 19.

itself.[29] As Jon Quitslund notes, this episode "suggests that something
in the dynamic of true love brings its demonic Other into play, in
the lover's imagination if not at the heart of desire itself."[30] Pushing
Quitslund's point further, I argue that these perversions *are* the erotic
and this is one of the things that Britomart learns. She sees Busirane's
maskers are a necessary component for the kind of self-awareness
and ultimately self-dissolution (a return to the community in Turner's
passage) that an erotic liminal rite can enact. For Georges Bataille,
eroticism entails not simple sexual activity, but also a psychological
quest for identity. The fundamental impulse of the erotic seeks to
break down individual identity: "the whole business of eroticism is
to destroy the self-contained character of the participators."[31] Britomart's
quest is to find the knight she saw in the mirror, to ultimately lose
her identity as the "warlike mayde" and become the founder of a
dynasty. Bataille suggests that dissolution of selfhood and coalescence
with another cannot happen without violence. Britomart can discover more about her own sexuality and move forward through the
liminal passage only by taking on all of Busirane's horrors.

The first phase follows her wandering through the tapestry hall
with its amorous exploits and fulfills the "exhibition" stage of Turner's
liminal ritual of passage where the initiate sees symbolic representations that reveal the nature of inscrutable experiences such as love.
The woven images in the tapestries nearly overwhelm Britomart:
"That wondrous sight faire *Britomart* amazed/Ne seeing could her
wonder satisfie/But euermore and more upon it gazed,/The while
the passing brightnes her sences dazed" (III.xi.49). In this stage of
the ritual, the liminal figure becomes a kind of voyeur. Turner's
exhibition stage calls for a kind of intense scrutiny that parallels
Bataille's description of the voyeuristic gaze, the first phase of an
erotic encounter. Britomart needs to gaze with "busie eye," to read
what the images tell her, and understand what they portend in order

---

[29] Angus Fletcher considers Busirane's tortures to be a demonic parody and
Robert Wood argues that despite the vividness of this episode it represents a relatively early moment in Britomart's adventures and that the "specter of a destructive conflict between the sexes [has] been banished before the Britomart-Artegall
romance begins," "Britomart at the House of Busyrane," *South Atlantic Bulletin* 43,
no. 2 (1978): 5–11 at 11. Angus Fletcher, *The Prophetic Moment; an Essay on Spenser*
(Chicago: Univ. of Chicago Press, 1971).
[30] Jon A. Quitslund, *Spenser's Supreme Fiction: Platonic Natural Philosophy and the Faerie
Queene* (Toronto: Univ. of Toronto Press, 2001), p. 162.
[31] Bataille, *Eroticism*, p. 17.

to act (III.xi.50). Britomart gazes at the frozen moments of the classical figures' tormented love depicted in the tapestries and of the loathsome figures in the mask procession. She sees revealing myths about the nature of love and eroticism among the classical gods. From these images, Britomart might well conclude that indifference (Europa) and even repulsion of love (Danae who keeps "the'yron dore fast bard") make no difference in the outcome of an erotic encounter (III.xi.31). Neither strategy keeps the pillages of love at bay. But if she were to look carefully, she might also note how Leda seems complicit in desire as "She slept, yet twixt her eyelids closely spyde" the onrushing swan (III.xi.32). These woven images show the ravages of eroticism, but they also suggest a connivance that Britomart recognizes and later engages in herself when she fights by sleight, rather than by might. They also hint that there might be some complicity on the part of Britomart as she spies the onrushing Busirane later. It is her voyeurism that teaches her how to act and rescue Amoret. It also implicates her in Busirane's erotic vision.

Because she has often been understood only to look (rather than to act), Britomart is believed to gain interpretive distance. A detached overseer, she stands at the threshold of the exhibition put on by Busirane. It is this sense of interpretive distance that has led many critics to believe that Britomart remains unaware of the implications of what passes before her—she remains, in a word, chaste, uninfected by Busirane's visions of a cruel, dominating Cupid spurring on his lions and leaving in his wake a train of chaotic emotions and pierced, mangled flesh. The argument runs that because she stands separate, removed, she vanquishes Busirane and emerges a stronger representative of chastity.[32] I want to suggest a different reading. Reading Britomart not as only a passive spectator, but also as a voyeur gives her paradoxically a more active role.[33] As Bataille details, a voyeur does not just watch; the sexual acts she sees stimulate her

---

[32] Joanna Thompson admits that the "wholeness" of Britomart stems in part from her "refusal to deny her sexuality," but argues that Britomart ultimately can be aligned with Protestant models of chaste marital love. By implication, Britomart rejects Cupid and his destructive, distorted notions of love: "Encompassing the virtue of chaste desire, Britomart displays a God-given sexual impulse bound by temperance that is quite distinct from the lustful carnality capable of expression through courtly love," *The Character of Britomart in Spenser's The Faerie Queene* (Lewiston: Edwin Mellen Press, 2001), pp. 126–33 at p. 32.

[33] The problems of vision and "gazing" in Spenser are a source of ongoing interest in Spenser studies, but of greatest relevance to the problems surrounding wedding feasts and lavish public display that encourages "the gaze," see Sheila T. Cavanagh,

own desire. A voyeur is never fully innocent or detached from that
which she looks at but becomes implicated in the process of gazing.
Gazing upon the erotic tableaux of the tapestries triggers Britomart's
own confusion about desire and she pauses to look harder. As William
Oram succinctly remarks, when Britomart passes through the wall
of flame, she slows down.[34] Stanza after stanza describe how "rich
metall lurked priuily,/as faining to be hid from enuious eye" that
"here, and there" would show itself as if by accident, "Like a dis-
colourd Snake, whose hidden snares/Through the greene gras his
long bright burnisht backe declares" (III.xi.28). Her fascination suggests danger. Not only has she slowed her forward pace, the simile
of the room's contents to a hidden snake connotes a sinister environment that calls for swift action and movement, not more looking and longer gazing; yet, for twenty-six stanzas Britomart (and the
reader) "lookt about" (III.xii.54). The more she looks, the more she
becomes implicated in what she sees. The Renaissance commonplace
that desire springs from the beams of the lover's eyes reminds us of
the interface between sight and the affect of desire. In *Astrophil and
Stella* Sidney writes that "what we call Cupid's dart / An image is,
which for ourselves we carve."[35] In other words, we bear responsibility for the image we see of love. Like the voyeur whose own
appetite is stimulated by what she sees, the tapestries mirror all of
Britomart's fears, desire and, possibly, her fantasies. As we know
from her lament by the sea, she keenly feels the torments of "Cupid's
dart" from the image that she saw in her father's mirror.

According to Bataille, the real danger for the voyeur, however, is
vertigo. As the voyeur gazes, and feels desire, it becomes difficult to
establish the boundaries between the object and the subjective emotions: the line between the external stimulus and internal emotion
breaks down, resulting in confusion and momentary loss of identity.
This loss of identity is also suggested by Turner's formulation of the
liminal subject's ambiguity in the first two phases of a rite of passage.

Wanton Eyes and Chaste Desires: Female Sexuality in the Faerie Queene (Bloomington: Indiana
Univ. Press, 1994); Kenneth Gross, *Spenserian Poetics: Idolatry, Iconoclasm, and Magic*
(Ithaca: Cornell Univ. Press, 1985); Theresa M. Krier, *Gazing on Secret Sights: Spenser,
Classical Imitation, and the Decorums of Vision* (Ithaca: Cornell Univ. Press, 1990), esp.
chapter 4.
    [34] "Spenserian Paralysis," *Studies in English Literature* 41, no. 1 (2001): 49–70 at 60.
    [35] Sonnet 5 from *Astrophil and Stella*. Katherine Duncan Jones, ed., *Sir Philip Sidney:
A Critical Edition of the Major Works* (New York: Oxford Univ. Press, 1989), p. 154.

Such confusion is what breeds Britomart's peril and imperils her crossing the threshold and completing her quest to rescue Amoret. All she has at this point in the narrative is an illusory image seen quite tellingly in a mirror, a site where normally all she would see would be her own reflection. Her subsequent very real, turbulent emotions stem from this reflection. For Britomart, who in the larger quest of Book III pursues a vision of Artegall—a vision based on the belief that the knight she saw in Merlin's mirror represents a real knight—there is a psychological and emotional stake in her erotic object's external existence. However, the sights in Busirane's palace seem arranged to arouse her awareness of the insubstantiality of erotic objects and throw into question her pursuit of what may be only deceptive desire. The tapestries, the statue, and the maskers all vanish leaving only the memory of their existence. Does Britomart see Busirane's vision or her own? Like Bataille's voyeur, the ability to determine what is outside (an external object of eroticism) and what inside (an internal, narcissistic projection) complicates Britomart's psychological quest. As she stands in the "solemne silence" of the hall looking at the "thousand monstrous formes" of love (III.xi.53/51), her fate as a "warlike Mayde" seems possibly foretold in the fallen warriors just mentioned who "wrought their owne decayes" (III.xi.53/52). As Britomart gazes on the spoil of these noble figures in love's thrall, she herself stands in the strange position between voyeur and heroic knight. During the mask itself she is described as "plast/In secret shade" where she sees both "first and last" (III.xii.27). She casts her "busie eye" to "search each secret" of the rooms and "did greatly wonder" and "ne could satisfie/Her greedy eyes with gazing a long space" (III.xi.50,53). Her behavior is reminiscent of Leda who "twixt her eyelids closely spyde" (III.xi.32). In this exhibition stage Britomart cannot just look. To look is to engage, moving her, I argue, into an erotic frame.[36]

Unlike the timid Amoret, who does not move beyond the role of a passive, horrified spectator and a victim, Britomart moves from the exhibition phase into action, the second step in Turner's liminal

[36] On the complex psychological allegory of this passage see Felicity A. Hughes, "Psychological Allegory in the *Faerie Queene* III.xi–xii," *Review of English Studies* 29 (1978) 129–46; Benjamin G. Lockerd, *The Sacred Marriage: Psychic Integration in the Faerie Queene* (Lewisburg, London: Bucknell Univ. Press, 1987); Shirley F. Staton, "Reading Spenser's *Faerie Queene* in a Different Voice," in *Ambiguous Realities*, ed. Carole Levine and Jeanie Watson (Detroit: Wayne State Univ. Press, 1987), pp. 145–62.

passage. It is Britomart's action that further complicates a straightforward moral reading of this passage. If already we view her as a
voyeur, complicit in what she sees, her action can be read as compromise and as the actions of one schooled in the arts of Busirane's
eroticism. After spending the first two days and nights as a voyeur
of Busirane's visions of love "wandering/And gazing on that Chambers
ornament" (III.xii.29), Britomart stands on the third night again
before the doorway with the inscription "*Be not too bold.*" At this crucial moment, the text becomes ambiguous. We know from the previous cantos that after the first showing of Cupid's mask, she "issewed
forth, and went unto the dore" but could not open it with even the
most "rigorous uprore" (III.xii.27). When she realizes that "force
might not auaile" she takes a page from Busirane's book: "there
sleights and art/She cast to use" (III.xii.28). She realizes that her
masculine disguise and power as a knight that had unhorsed so many
rivals avail nothing. She must fight guile with guile.

When Britomart first sees the masks of Cupid in the enchanted
chamber, the maskers "forth issewd" from beyond the "yron wicket"
(II.xii.3). After they have passed, she "issewed forth, and went unto
the dore" (III.xii.27). A. C. Hamilton proposes in his textual notes
that the chiasmus of "forth issewd" and "issewed forth" suggests
that Britomart plays a role in the mask.[37] The ambiguous pronoun
"her" from canto 29 reinforces this reading. We see "her" "cou-
rered with her sable vestiment" when the brazen door flies open at
midnight (III.xii.29). The pronoun is ambiguous because it can be
read as applying to "the second euening" or to Britomart (III.xii.29).
If the latter, then the text would seem to solidify the suggestion that
Britomart enacts a role in Cupid's pageant as she dons a mask costume, a "sable vestiment." When the door flies open, she enters into
the final room and finds the "woefull Ladie" Amoret and surprises
the "vile Enchaunter" who in his haste topples his wicked books
(III.xii.30,31). The combination of the implication that she fights
guile with guile and Busirane's surprise at her appearance in the
final chamber support the reading of Britomart entering the third
room not by masculine force but by sleight, a sleight I read as her
performance in the mask. Her performance as one of the maskers
disguises her entrance into the sorcerer's den. Britomart's voyeurism

---

[37] Textual note to stanza III.xii.27 in Hamilton, ed., *Spenser: The Faerie Queene.*

teaches her how to enact a role within Busirane's chaotic triumph of love, a role she has been schooled in while wandering about the outer chambers. The suggestion of chastity appearing as one of the maskers with Dissemblance, Suspect, Daunger, and Doubt for at least a moment makes her one of the horrors of Cupid's train. Her success relies on participation in the perversions of Busirane's mask— a participation that cannot but compromise her as a figure of venerated chastity since either she or the chastity she represents looks different when imagined as part of the darker eroticism represented by Busirane.

The vanishing of the maskers when she enters through the third door—leaving her to face Busirane—marks her move into the final stage of the liminal rite of passage. It is here that the initiate receives instructions and prepares for return to the community. In the nuptial mask, this moment would coincide with the tender bride encountering the stiff, rigorous groom as Puttenham so vividly notes. Britomart sees a perversion of this consummation: Amoret stands immobilized, her heart bleeding and pierced through, bound to a pillar. Britomart leaps from being a voyeur into action, striking the astounded Busirane. He struggles against her and turns his "murderous knife" from Amoret and "unwares it stroke" into Britomart's "snowie chest/That little drops empurpled her faire brest" (III.xii.33). In the mêlée, the sorcerer's knife penetrates *her* breast; she is literally penetrated by the sorcerer himself. The wound "were nothing deepe imprest" but it drives Britomart to a fury that overcomes her sense and she nearly slays the enchanter, except that Amoret speaks to remind her that only he can undo the spell (III.xii.33). While Britomart does not experience consummation at the end of this mask, she nonetheless has been penetrated. This penetration marks her move out of liminality because it labels her as a woman, a figure that can be penetrated rather than penetrating. She bears this wound, and this knowledge, with her as she leaves to return to the world outside the halls. Britomart's instruction in this final stage of eroticism pierces her physically and emotionally, pushing her to lose objectivity and to rage in fierce anger. The high passion of her engagement recalls the high dudgeon of Guyon as he razes the bower of bliss in the final trial of Book II. To have destroyed Busirane would have meant her failure as Amoret's release relies on Busirane's unwinding of the spell. And while Busirane does unbind the spell and release Amoret, his knife wound remains in Britomart's chest, suggesting the one substantial

act in this hall where everything else vanishes with reversal. It may
not be a mortal wound, but it draws chaste blood. What are we to
make of this liminal passage that concludes with a virgin rescued
and chastity pierced?

My argument thus far suggests two possibilities for Britomart's
behavior in the final canto of Book III. First, she loses interpretive
distance because of her voyeuristic gazing at the erotic show of
Cupid's mask, and by enacting a role in that mask she fails fully to
embody the virtue of chastity, just as Guyon's radical destruction of
the bower of bliss has often been read as a lapse of temperance.
Her pierced breast remains as a symbol of that failure, just as her
backward glance suggests regret at the destruction of Busirane's erotic
vision—a gesture that in itself evokes Lot's wife who turns back for
one last glimpse of her beloved city of Sodom and becomes a pillar of salt. Second, Britomart's voyeurism and ultimate engagement
in both the erotic and liminal aspects of Busirane's halls facilitate
her own struggle with desire and her quest for the knight in the
mirror. This second reading suggests that if we read this episode as
a liminal rite of passage into eroticism, we realize that once she
becomes aware of her own ambivalence toward desire, she can confront it. For Britomart to triumph over Busirane, she must engage
with his vision, and feel the erotic pull of desire as the absolute loss
of objective vision. Part of the liminal experience involves action and
Britomart acts by becoming a part of the mask spectacle, engaging
all her worst fears regarding the potentially destructive nature of
desire. She succeeds not because she is unaware of the implications
of what she sees, but because she is fully aware, sees the show and
dances in it. She is not seduced, but she does not ignore the danger
of eroticism; she sees it for what it is. Her liminal rite of passage
shows her doing what Milton says Spenser does best; he shows his
figures engaging temptation in order to triumph over it.

I think we need to hold both interpretations. The implication,
however, of reading both possibilities portrays a Britomart who paradoxically succeeds because she fails. She rescues Amoret; she binds
Busirane with his own "greate chaine" (III.xii.41); she completes the
quest and rite of passage as they exit the halls. But her dismay at
the decay of the "goodly roomes" shadows her triumph (III.xii.42).
She realizes that the halls, like the mask, were ultimately ephemeral.
The performance has ended, but the memory lingers in Britomart
and the audience. Britomart has pulled down the theater of perverse

desire, yet finds it somehow still calling to her. Her enacting a role in the mask affects her in a way that cannot simply be reversed, undone, and erased as Busirane "those same bloudy lines reherse[s]" (III.xii.36). As Busirane's charms "back to reuerse" and the house begins to quake, horror fills "the virgins hart" and her "faire locks up stared stiffe on end" (III.xii.36), but she cannot reverse her rite of passage nor erase the knowledge she gained. The erasure can never be fully complete as we as readers return again and again to the images presented in this passage and Britomart leaves the hall penetrated by the sorcerer's knife—both literally and metaphorically. Most perplexing of all perhaps is that despite her witness to the "full dreadfull things out of that balefull booke" of Busirane's violent vision of Cupid, she experiences an emotion of dismay when they vanish. This backward glance by the victorious Britomart suggests a complex paradoxical view of what has happened in the hall. Busirane's vision may be proved an illusory fraud, but the frantic intensity of it leaves a wound in Britomart's breast and carves an image that remains at the forefront of consciousness, compelling and seductive for all its energy. The dark vision of Busirane cannot be banished and Britomart's initiation through the liminal passage is just that, an initiation, not an exorcism.

Reading Busirane's mask as a liminal rite of passage into eroticism—something we can do only by recognizing its place within the tradition of Renaissance spectacles and pageantry—rather than as the culminating battle of Book III changes how we read Britomart's triumph. Unlike the Redcrosse Knight and Guyon from the first two books, Britomart's quest continues unresolved into successive books. She completes the liminal rite of passage, but she remains without her knight. Instead of seeing Busirane's halls and mask as something she battles, conquers, then leaves behind, if we read her encounter with Busirane as a liminal rite of passage it suggests that we look not at what she defeats, but what she carries with her on the rest of her quest. Tudor masks and the cultural vision they were designed to project show an idealized concord and dynastic stability. They suggest that through participation, the maskers and dancers enact a displaced eroticism where a gentler Cupid, Platonic hierarchy and political harmony rule. Britomart experiences a disfigured rite as we have seen by comparing Busirane's mask with Tudor amatory masks such as those accompanying Arthur and Katherine's nuptials or Sir Henry Unton's wedding banquet. Britomart experiences no true consummation nor finds concord at the conclusion of Cupid's mask. The seeming order of Cupid's train only enhances its individual disorderly figures, who disintegrate into a hurried confusion, breaking the mask's supposed harmony and its ability to bring about unity. There is only the anti-masque. At the beginning of Book IV both she and Amoret continue to wander. Britomart's participation in such a botched rite facilitates her passage, but her triumph, like the twisted mask, remains tainted. Britomart's own quest may be compromised suggesting why this will not be her final test—the conclusion to Book III prefigures further emotional chaos.[38] As Turner and van Gennep outline, moving out of a liminal stage involves loss. Britomart has lost innocence. She has been penetrated. Her loss of innocence and her penetrability serve to move her away from her identity as a warrior maiden impervious to the spear thrusts of other knights and toward the dynastic role Merlin foresaw. Britomart's dismay at the vanishing rooms signals a recognition that part of her is also vanishing without a replacement. It also suggests that there is some complicity on her part in those halls that she relished. There are no wedding bells, only a deeper knowledge of eroticism.

Britomart's backward glance once more at the marvels of Busirane's hall forces us as readers to always see a double vision of the erotic: Anteros can never fully banish or erase Eros; a darker understanding of erotic knowledge shadows her triumph as she continues her quest. Even as the episode works to extinguish the tormented vision of Busirane, it imaginatively amplifies it while deferring the harmonious vision of Britomart's marriage. Her liminal passage has marked her with a dark vision of the erotic that cannot simply be undone. Spenser's attempt to contain eroticism's darker force yields a double-natured *eros* fraught with potential negativity and danger even as it supposedly functions ultimately as a positive force for the marriage between Britomart and Artegall. There is no simple triumph.

---

[38] Mary Grellner also has read this as a foreshadowing of more trouble for Britomart, but does not read it, as I do, as also an indication of ambiguous triumph. Mary Adelaide Grellner, "Britomart's Quest for Maturity," *Studies in English Literature* 8, no. 1 (1968): 35–43 at 40.

SPECTACLE AND THE FANTASY OF IMMATERIALITY: AUTHORSHIP AND MAGIC IN *JOHN A KENT AND JOHN A CUMBER*

Nora Johnson*

For some time now, critics have been at pains to detail the tensions between modern authorship and early modern theatrical spectacle. Following Foucault's description of the author as a limiting figure, "the principle of thrift in the proliferation of meaning," scholars of early modern drama have emphasized the inappropriateness of such a notion in the theatrical milieu.[1] Spectacle is—or we have generally assumed it to be—collaborative, material, subject to the wayward energies of performance, governed by the exigencies of the body. Constructing the author in the realm of theatrical spectacle would require, then, a process of subordinating the material, the wayward, and the collaborative in order to locate a fantasy of control and/or origin in an individual figure. Such authorial fantasy has seemed alien to the early modern playing companies, which emphasized physical display, encouraged improvisation and actorial independence, often preferred collaborative writing arrangements, and manifested only intermittent interest in the opportunities presented by a burgeoning print culture.

But there are, here and there, figures who have articulated a relationship to the spectacle of the stage that we recognize as authorial. When Ben Jonson, a playwright known for his laureate ambitions, writes of the loathed stage, or when he quarrels with Inigo Jones over the primacy of the text over scenery and costume, he clearly is struggling to wield an authority that subordinates spectacle to personal genius.[2] Self-declared origin and controller, Jonson constructs

---

* I am grateful to Scott Black, Betsy Bolton, Claire Busse, Jane Hedley, Laura McGrane, Steve Newman, Julian Yates, and especially to Lauren Shohet for assistance with this essay that exceeds the scope of individual citation.
[1] Michel Foucault, "What is an Author?" in *The Foucault Reader*, ed. Paul Rabinow (New York: Pantheon Books, 1984) 118.
[2] D. J. Gordon, "Poet and Architect: The Intellectual Setting of the Quarrel between Ben Jonson and Inigo Jones," in *The Renaissance Imagination*, ed. Stephen

his role as author in a way that critics have found strikingly pre-
scient, observing protocols that are variously associated with absolutism, modern subjectivity, and property ownership. In preferring
the text/spirit of the masque to its "bodily part," in separating himself from the influence of patrons, in attempting to link the judgment of a paying audience to the price of admission, Jonson establishes
an apparent disregard for the material, the spectacular, and the
financial that resonates with our own investment in the author as a
controlling subject.[3] For all that Jonson's career is bound up with
staging, his efforts to transcend the materiality of performance read
to us as explicitly anti-theatrical.[4]

If we read Jonson as constructing theatrical authorship in and
through anti-theatricality, so too we have read Shakespeare's Prospero
as an author-figure who cannot wait to bid farewell to the insubstantial pageant of the stage. He fails as Duke of Milan, after all,
because he prefers private study to public engagement, and his return
to Milan will be the occasion of further seclusion as his "[e]very
third thought" will be of the grave.[5] In the famous lines from *The
Tempest* so often taken as Shakespeare's own farewell to theatrical
work, the emphasis upon the destruction of spectacle is clear:

> Our revels now are ended. These our actors,
> As I foretold you, were all spirits and
> Are melted into air, into thin air;
> And, like the baseless fabric of this vision,
> The cloud-capped towers, the gorgeous palaces,
> The solemn temples, the great globe itself,
> Yea, all which it inherit, shall dissolve,

Orgel (Berkeley: University of California Press, 1975) 77–101. For other constructions
of authorship in the theatrical milieu, see Nora Johnson, *The Actor as Playwright in
Early Modern Drama* (Cambridge: Cambridge University Press, 2003).

[3] *Masque of Blackness*, lines 71–2, in Stephen Orgel, *Ben Jonson: The Complete Masques*
(New Haven: Yale University Press, 1969) 50.

[4] For a path-breaking study, see Richard Helgerson, *Self-Crowned Laureates: Spenser,
Jonson, Milton and the Literary System* (Berkeley: University of California Press, 1983).
Helgerson's description of Jonson's double-bind is particularly useful: "So long as
the pressure to define himself remained strong, so long, that is, as the accurate con-
strual of his status remained in doubt, he could be a laureate poet in the theater
only by opposing the theater" (160). See also Jonas A. Barish, "Jonson and the
Loathèd Stage," in *A Celebration of Ben Jonson*, ed. William Blissett et al. (Toronto:
University of Toronto Press, 1973) 27–53.

[5] David Bevington, ed., *The Complete Works of Shakespeare*, fourth edition, (New
York: Harper Collins, 1992) 5.1.315. Further reference to *The Tempest* will be to
this edition and will appear parenthetically within the text.

And like this insubstantial pageant faded,
Leave not a rack behind. (4.1.148–56)

Though the tone here is of wistful regret rather than feisty antagonism, Prospero, like Jonson, builds something we have wanted to call "authorial" out of the impulse to diminish what we see before us on the stage.[6] Both Jonson and Prospero, of course, are taking positions that are deeply disingenuous, or at very least fraught with paradox. Prospero here is deriving authority both from his power to stage the masque of Ceres and from his clear-sightedness about the transience of the physical. He is, moreover, going to continue running things for another whole act; this speech is neither Prospero's nor Shakespeare's farewell to anything. Like Jonson, who surely gains prestige from the glamour of Inigo Jones's sets and from his courtly patronage, Prospero has his hand in the till, reaping the benefits of spectacular entertainment even while seeming to turn his back on it.[7]

It is tempting to want to argue that Jonson and Prospero stand out for us as anachronisms in the construction of theatrical authorship because the stances they take are related to nascent forms of absolutism, emphasizing personal sovereignty over text and performance

---

[6] Alvin B. Kernan reads the connection between Prospero and authorship as an expression of desire for "some pure theater of the imagination, free of the limitations of real actors, stages, and audiences" that represents "the full potential of the playwright's art" [*The Playwright as Magician: Shakespeare's Image of the Poet in the English Public Theater* (New Haven: Yale University Press, 1979) 135]. Later critics pursuing the play's representation of theatrical work have been more interested in the ways in which *The Tempest* resonates with the conditions of early modern playing. David M. Bergeron comments that Prospero's list of towers, palaces, and temples "sound[s] like an inventory of properties for recent pageants and masques. How fitting that he should recall them," Bergeron continues, "fixed as they must be in Jacobean theatrical imagination" (206) ["The Politics and Technology of Spectacle in the Late Plays," in Richard Dutton and Jean E. Howard, eds. *A Companion to Shakespeare's Works*, vol. 4, *The Poems, Problem Comedies, Late Plays* (Oxford: Blackwell Publishing Ltd., 2003) 194–215]. See Daniel Vitkus's essay in the same volume for a reading of Prospero as a figure whose authority is maintained in ways reminiscent of the contracts that bound players to companies ("'Meaner Ministers': Mastery, Bondage, and Theatrical Labor in *The Tempest*" 408–26). See also Douglas Bruster, "Local *Tempest*: Shakespeare and the Work of the Early Modern Playhouse" *Journal of Medieval and Renaissance Studies* (1995) 25:1. 33–53. For a reading of these lines in relation to the sexuality of staging, see Nora Johnson, "Body and Spirit, Stage and Sexuality in *The Tempest*" *ELH* 64 (1997) 683–701.

[7] Association with Shakespeare's Prospero would, of course, be anathema to Jonson, who implied his strong contempt for Shakespearean romance generally and for *The Tempest* in particular. The Induction to *Bartholomew Fair*, for instance, establishes Jonson's authorial eminence by way of direct critique both of Shakespeare and of the spectacular in the theater: "If there be never a servant-monster i' the

alike.[8] Indeed, Jeffrey Masten's half-playful suggestion that Prospero
stands for Jonson, essentially colonizing the early modern stage for
the modern author, will be deeply influential in the pages that follow.[9] The present study, however, will concentrate not upon the historical novelty of these figures—not upon their status as harbingers
of the modern—but upon their continuity with the past. Though
surely a narrative that describes dramatic authorship as an emergent
form, profoundly implicated in proto-capitalist forms of individualism and ownership, can tell us much, our rush to describe modernity costs us dearly to the extent that it flattens out our descriptions
of the past. Rather than search out the glimmering horizons of the
modern, this essay will focus on a relatively banal figure who stands
in the background behind Prospero: the tried-and-true crowd-pleasing
magician figure of early modern drama, trotted out by Peele, Greene,
Marlowe, and others, as well as by Munday, and trotted out again
by Shakespeare in *The Tempest*.[10] In fact, lending weight to the power
of particular descriptions rather than sweeping historical narratives,
this essay will focus narrowly on a single magician play, Anthony
Munday's *John a Kent and John a Cumber*. Written some twenty years
before *The Tempest* by a hack writer—Jonson called him "Antonio

---

Fair, who can help it? he says; nor a nest of antics? He is loth to make nature
afraid in his plays, like those that beget Tales, Tempests, and such-like drolleries, to
mix his head with other men's heels, let the concupiscence of jigs and dances reign
as strong as it will amongst you" [ed. Eugene M. Waith, in *The Yale Ben Jonson*, ed.
Alvin B. Kernan and Richard B. Young (New Haven: Yale University Press, 1963)
lines 113–18]. See also Barbara Traister on Jonson's debunking of magic and his
subordination of it to the power of the poet [*Heavenly Necromancers: The Magician in
English Renaissance Drama* (Columbia: University of Missouri Press, 1984) 163–7].
   [8] See, for instance, Kurt Tetzeli von Rosador, who traces a "half-latent, half-
overt rivalry between the royal magic of the monarchy and the magician's art and
its representation in Elizabethan times and drama" ["The Power of Magic: From
Endimion to *The Tempest*" *Shakespeare Survey* 43 (1991) 1–13] 2.
   [9] Masten rejects this reading, of course, in the interests of understanding the play
as "registering—in a way that is neither coherent allegory nor decipherable intention—a number of the tensions and places of fracture in the new discourse of
author/ity only beginning to emerge within the theatre" (112). Nor should the current study be understood as embracing an allegorical or intentional reading. I do,
however, recognize forms of authority grounded in performance that have a long
history on stage, rather than seeing the figure of the author as essentially an import
from outside the theater. Jeffrey Masten, *Textual Intercourse: Collaboration, Authorship,
and Sexualities in Renaissance Drama* (Cambridge: Cambridge University Press, 1997).
See especially chapter 3, "Representing Authority: Patriarchalism, Absolutism, and
the Author On Stage" 63–112.
   [10] Barbara Traister outlines the traditions of magical representation on stage in
this period (*Heavenly Necromancers*, esp. chapter two, "The Magician in Minor Tudor
and Stuart Drama," 33–64).

Balladino"—Munday's play provides a rich and intriguing prehistory for Shakespeare's work and for Jonson's self-constructions.[11] Rather than linking Prospero and Jonson as Masten does, through their shared task of representing the future of authorship, this essay will offer its own, possibly mischievous, suggestion: that Shakespeare constructed his author-ruler out of the ordinary tools of the popular theatrical tradition, and that Jonson, too, owes some of his ideas about sovereignty to the run-of-the-mill entertainments of the early modern stage. When Jonson proclaims his superiority to actors, audiences, scenery, patrons and peers, in other words, he is not simply resonating with the logic of absolutism. He is also basing this performance upon something he saw in the theater: if not the literal magic display scripted by Munday, then a thousand other moments of spectacular authority negotiated with candid pleasure in the theatrical milieu. The fantasy of controlling spectacle is a deeply theatrical one, even if the material circumstances of playing would seem inimical to its construction. The candid pleasure of negotiation, moreover, constitutes a shared heritage for Prospero and Jonson that works to undercut their assumptions of sovereign authority.

In some ways, reading *John a Kent and John a Cumber* as a pre-text for the innovations of Jonson or Prospero might yield precisely the narrative of emergence that this essay is meant to work against. Even a brief sketch of the plot reveals a profound concern with Kent's ability to triumph over competitors and patrons while producing supremely enjoyable theatrical shows. The play begins with Sir Griffin Meriddock and Jeffrey Lord Powesse grieving because their beloveds

---

[11] See Robert R. Reed, Jr., on the relations between *The Tempest* and Munday's play ["The Probable Origin of Ariel," *Shakespeare Quarterly* 11:1 (Winter, 1960) 61–5]. For additional connections between *The Tempest* and Munday's work, see Gary Schmidgall, "*The Tempest* and *Primaleon*: A New Source," *Shakespeare Quarterly* 37:4 (Winter, 1986) 423–39. See Helen Moore regarding the likely association between Munday and Jonson as writers for Henslowe and as writers of pageants: "Jonson's satire against Munday is directed . . . at his motivation (to please the masses), his system of patronage (indiscriminate), his subject matter and style (hackneyed) and his popularity (considerable)" (152). Moore also suggests that one of the things Jonson disliked most about Munday was his influence on other writers ("Jonson, Dekker, and the Discourse of Chivalry," *Medieval and Renaissance Drama in England* 12 (1999) 121–65. See esp. 148–52. As Tracey Hill points out, "'Hackdom' has become a kind of prison both for Munday and for critics: the common assumption is that we do not have to explore the works of a writer such as Munday because we already 'know' what they are like—they are not worth exploring" [*Anthony Munday and Civic Culture: Theatre, History and Power in Early Modern London 1580–1633* (Manchester and New York: Manchester University Press, 2004) 2].

Sidanen and Marian are affianced to Morton and Pembroke, respectively, at the insistence of the women's fathers. Sir Gosselin Denvyle
offers them the assistance of the great magician John a Kent, who
is bound to him by an unspecified relationship of patronage. Kent
is easily able to deliver the women, but feels unsatisfied that the task
has been completed with so little effort. Morton and Pembroke enlist
the aid of a competing magician, John a Cumber, who is able to
deceive the Denvyle party and capture the women back. Having
been defeated, Kent nevertheless asks Cumber to give him another
chance, which Cumber grants out of what can only be described as
an excess of sportsmanship. In this round of the contest, the two
magicians battle through plots and counterplots that hinge on the
use of spirit actors, much like Prospero's.

Badly defeated by Kent and sorely humiliated, Cumber persuades
Kent to give the women back and let him try again. At least initially,
the lovers consent to this bizarre request; apparently they are more
invested in the fun magic shows at this point in the play than they
are in their own marriages. When Griffin does manage to register
an objection after the fact, is it surprisingly mild:

> would any man but you have beene so fond
> to yeeld the Ladyes, when we might have kept them?
> poor soules, with what unwillingness they went,
> pray God this rashness all we not repent.[12]

The ladies, like the men, had in fact said nothing but "we doo" en
masse when asked whether they accepted the terms of the latest Kent
and Cumber contest. Kent, and the play as a whole, offer virtually
no explanation for the strange sidetracking of the play's love plot:

> ffeare you, hope you, for my parte, Ile doo neither,
> but track his steppes that treades the way before,
> to doo the thing he can undoo no more. (1532–4)

Though the final pages of the manuscript are badly damaged, it
appears that Kent triumphs again, causing a great mist to surround
the abbey where the women are waiting to be married, so that
Cumber mistakenly admits Griffin and Powesse to the ceremony

[12] Arthur Emmet Pennell, *An Edition of Anthony Munday's* John a Kent and John
a Cumber (University Microfilms, Ann Arbor, Michigan, 1958) 1520–23. Further
references to Munday's play are to this edition, and through line numbers appear
parenthetically within the text. I have silently modernized u/v and i/j throughout.

instead of Morton and Pembroke. Of course the point here is to establish Kent's dominance, to tie the play's candidly excessive fondness for magic display to the cultivation of the Kent mystique; "If this [the final conquering of the brides] I doo not ere two hourse be spent," says John, neatly conflating the time of the play with the time of the audience, "Never let me be calld more John a Kent" (1568–9). Locating the play's spectacular pleasures in one controlling figure does in fact involve a systematic deployment of some forms of personal authority that are hallmarks of Jonson's career.

As for Jonson, patrons are handy suppliers of legitimacy for John a Kent and John a Cumber, but only the abjected characters in Munday's play are really subject to their influence. As part of the (ultimately thwarted) marriage celebrations, for instance, the Morton/Pembroke party is entertained by a troupe of "clowns," strongly reminiscent of the "rude mechanicals" in *Midsummer Night's Dream*.[13] If in serving their patrons the magicians perform a romantic comedy, the clowns enact the rituals of patronage as farce. In a display of idiocy that is profoundly connected to the play's larger concerns, the rustics are able only to act out the names of Morton and Pembroke using the coarsest of semiotic systems. "Morton" is represented by a Moor carrying a tun, "Pembroke" by a pen in water. This the rustics perform only after we have seen them vie with one another, in what seems a parody of the Kent and Cumber contest, for the position of star performer. Though Turnop wins, Hugh the Sexton is suggested because Sexton is "an office of retoritie" (344). If Kent's mastery of representation allows him a certain distance from the needs of his employers, surely the clown-players, looking for their own rhetorical authority, strengthen the suggestion that real theatrical power—Kent's kind—involves some mysterious ability to transcend the economic relations that underlie theatrical production. Their failure to go beyond uttering the names of the nearest aristocrats is met by a decisive humiliation, as the lords' putatively gracious response falls far short of the clowns' expectations:

> Oswen: My Lordes, my father's tennants, after their homely guyse,
>   Welcome ye with their countrey merriment:
>   How bad so ere, yet must ye needs accept it.

---

[13] See Note 20 below for a discussion of the likelihood that Munday's play was written in the late 1580s. *Midsummer Night's Dream* was written sometime in 1594–5 (Bevington, *Complete Works*, 147).

> Pembroke: Else, Oswen, were we very much to blame.—
>   Thankes, gentle freendes: here, drinke this for my
>   sake. (389–93)

The lords depart, leaving Turnop to call after them, "Before you go, in name of all this trayne,/Turnop accepts your golde, and thankes you for your payne" (400–1). Barely able to hold the nobility's attention long enough to thank them for their (apparently diffident) show of generosity, that is, Turnop and his crew represent the lowest possible form of the staging that Kent does so impressively. In the main plot, Kent makes the nobility do his bidding; in the clown performance Turnop and his peers have to be content with representing their patrons and escaping censure. As in Jonson's career, that is, there are two shows being put on: one in which patrons can be used to advance the status of the author and one in which patronage is at least potentially a debilitating form of subjection.[14]

The crude materiality of the clowns' performance here, however, "how bad so ere," is more complicated than it might seem. The Moor/tun Pen/brook display is clearly designed to set the players up as low, bumbling stagers. But the central conceit is not in fact so very far away from what we might consider proper aristocratic spectacle. Ben Jonson himself, for instance, describes the following gem of concretization for the Haddington masque: "The scene to this masque was a high, steep, red cliff advancing itself into the clouds, figuring the place from whence (as I have been, not fabulously, informed) the honorable family of the Radcliffes first took their name (a clivo rubro)."[15] The inspiration for the image comes apparently from the honorable history of the Radcliffes themselves, but Jonson's insistence that his sources are "not fabulous" may betray some mild anxiety about the quality of that inspiration. Julian Yates has, similarly, detailed the complex cultural work done by the Harrington family's impresa: a hare, with a ring, on a tun, atop the magnificent fountain that graced the estate at Kelston.[16] Surely some of the humor in

---

[14] See Joseph Loewenstein, *Ben Jonson and Possessive Authorship*, for a careful discussion of the ambivalence with which Jonson sought (and sought to control) patronage (Cambridge: Cambridge University Press, 2002); see especially pp. 160–67.

[15] Orgel, *Ben Jonson*, lines 20–23.

[16] "Under the Sign of (A)Jax; or The Smell of History," chapter three of *Error, Misuse, Failure: Object Lessons from the English Renaissance* (Minneapolis: University of Minnesota Press, 2003) 67–100; see especially p. 75.

Munday's scene must come from the inept delivery practiced by Turnop and his peers, but the fact that they wield representational tools no less inherently unsophisticated than Jonson's suggests that a complex attitude toward material display obtains here.

In this as in many other moments, contempt for the physical seems absolute, but at the same time, somehow, it seems merely tactical. When Cumber wins the first match with Kent, for instance, by disguising himself as Kent to lure the ladies back to Morton and Pembroke, Kent uses a language of shadow and substance to lessen the glory of Cumber's conquest: "under my shaddowe [i.e. in disguise as me]," says John a Kent, "have you done all this,/much greater cunning had it been thine owne" (964–5). Apparently, material realities are to be preferred over illusions, and apparently the obviousness of this preference renders Cumber's triumph so hollow that he consents to a rematch. But Cumber's plan for the next round, Kent learns, is to put on a play, performed "by the shaddowes of the Lordes and Ladyes" to disgrace Kent (1015). If Cumber doesn't seem to have learned the lessons of round one (substances are better than shadows), neither does John a Kent; "But his intent to deal with shaddowes only," muses Kent, "I meane to alter, weele have the substances" (1090–91). This time, though, "having the substance" turns out to mean "disguising myself as John a Cumber," which is how Kent triumphs in round two. This strategy is of course the opposite of the one practiced by Kent initially, when he ridiculed Cumber for disguising himself as Kent. In the exchange that follows, Cumber-disguised-as-Kent plots to humiliate the real Kent by deploying spirit actors in the roles of Morton, Pembroke, and their allies. The real Kent foils this plan by disguising himself as Cumber, employing the real Morton and Pembroke to humiliate Cumber-disguised-as-Kent, whom they believe to be the actual Kent. The Morton/Pembroke ally Llwellen sums up the strategy perfectly when he responds to Cumber's expression of shock:

> Cumber.   how now? whats this? my shaddowes taught to speak,
>   that to my face, they should unto my foe?
> Llwellen.   Shaddowes proove substance, John, thou art too weak,
>   then like a sillie fellowe, pack and goe. (1277–80).

Alas for Llwellen. His confident boast over "Kent" is actually his own humiliation, since "Kent" here is really Cumber-disguised-as-Kent. Both Llwellen and Cumber are trapped and defeated by Kent's confusing deployment of both shadow and substance. At virtually every turn, in fact, John a Kent manages to establish that the real is superior to the illusory, and yet we are never sure what the real or the physical might be. Is an actor in disguise real, or does he only become real in relation to an actor "dressed" as a spirit-actor? As if to confess this confusion, Kent enters the final round of tricks with a determination to be done once and for all with child's play: "Tu<sh> weele no shapes, nor none of these disguysings,/they <h t>ofore serv'd *bothe his turne and myne*" (1558–9; emphasis added). Disguises and illusions are decidedly inferior to reality (or at least to a stage-play reality). Having eschewed them, however, Kent adopts what everyone recognizes to be the lowest form of magic illusion, causing a heavy mist to confuse John a Cumber. Kent himself confesses that this is a cheap trick:

> O rare Magitian that hast not the power,
> to beat asyde a sillie dazeling mist,
> which a mere abce scholler in the arte,
> can doo it with the least facillitie. (1612–15)

In a wonderfully ironic triumph of the material, the manuscript of the play becomes virtually unreadable at this point, allowing us only a hint about John a Cumber's dismay: "Alas, alas, hath cunning John </no wiser way than this to f < . . ." (1624–5). These are Cumber's last words.

The play's ambivalence about materiality is instructive about the place of theatrical spectacle in the construction of theatrical authorship. Mastery is clearly of the utmost importance in the instances above, and the suggestion is made repeatedly that having the "right" attitude toward the shadow/substance debate is the key to the contest of dominance. Mostly Kent wins these moments; mostly he and his allies taunt John a Cumber for relying on silly shadows. But this supremacy is utterly fictional, dropped by Kent whenever expediency (in the form of pleasurable theatrical display) requires him to deal in shadows or mists. In our willingness to identify the anti-spectacular logic of a Jonson or a Prospero with the construction of theatrical authorship, we have lost track of the fact that such anti-theatrical performances are also tactical. Jonson too could condemn the loathed stage or the mere body of the masque without ceasing to appropriate the power of display as a form of authority. Reading a minor work like *John a Kent and John a Cumber* reminds us of the delighted ambivalence that Jonson inherits from theatrical practice itself: a love of contest, a love of mastery, and a love of spectacle that renders any one stance of mastery a momentary pleasure, to be dropped as soon as possible in the interests of producing another show.

Richly contradictory forms of mastery are by no means restricted to the question of substance and shadow, however, any more than Jonson's efforts at self-presentation are restricted to transcending the effects of Inigo Jones's scenery. John a Kent's strongest moments of self-construction are remarkable for their candid complexity about matters of audience and patronage. Kent is, for instance, notably uninterested in fulfilling the task to which Sir Gosselin Denvyle has set him. After winning Sidanen and Marian back from Morton and Pembroke, Kent speaks a soliloquy that feels much like a Vice-style address to the audience:

> Heer's loove and loove, Good Lord, was nere the lyke,
> but must these joyes so quickly be concluded?
> Must the first Scene make absolute a play?
> no crosse? no chaunge? what? no varietie?
> One brunt is past, alas, whats that in loove? (528–32)

Speaking in part for his own reputation as an entertainer and in part for the interests of the spectators, Kent seems to conflate a sense of generic exhaustion with a reflection on the empty pleasures of serving a master. Comic theater's stock in trade, the love match, is implicitly identified with subordination to patronage and discarded as joyless. This speech occurs just one hundred and fifty lines or so after we have seen the clowns Turnop and company bid ineptly for the favor of Morton and Pembroke. Just as the impresa was made to look clumsy in the hands of rustics, romantic comedy here looks like a hollow pleasure. Kent is surely correct about generic convention; it would indeed be boring to watch a comedy that wrapped up its love-obstructions in an act or two. As in *Othello*, such a prompt wooing would leave the play nothing to do but torture the poor married Desdemona. Like historical narratives, in other words, comic plots ask for disturbances, ask to be resisted.

As Kent has informed us in his first soliloquy, such disturbance will be the stuff of the John a Kent legend:

> But John a Kent what talkest thou<
> rather minde thou the pleasing joyes < >e.
> And since so good a subject they present,
> uppon these loovers practise thou thy wit.

> help, hinder, give, take back, turne, overturne,
> deceive, bestowe, breed pleasure, discontent.
> yet comickly conclude, like John a Kent. (130–36)

Kent constructs himself by rejecting comic form ("loove and loove"),
but he does so in the name of another comic pleasure, the hin-
drance. Playing one audience expectation off another, the romantic
conclusion off the comic delay, Kent manages to imply that he is
achieving something like artistic autonomy. Distancing himself from
the desires of his patron Denvyle as Jonson implicitly distanced himself from a career's worth of patrons, Kent comes remarkably close
to admitting that he has substituted the play's paying audience for
his fictional aristocratic employer.[17] And yet he presents this trading
of patronage for paying audiences as a triumphant act of self-display.
Speaking for and even anticipating the audience's desires, Kent will
somehow become comedy, concluding comedy as a way of concluding
himself. Locating the pleasure of the play in himself, that is, Kent
makes his connection to the audience seem as though it is also a
singular form of self-declaration.

Such singularity in multiplicity is also characteristic of the match
of wits between the play's two magicians. As with the contest between
shadow and substance, the distinction between Kent and Cumber is
all-important even while it is subject to being forgotten. When Kent
prepares the "silly mist" that will mark his final triumph (and thus,
as we have seen, the completion of his self-construction), he worries
aloud about what his actions will mean for John a Cumber's reputation:

> And for the blame shall not relye alone,
> on poore John Cumber, when the faulte is spyed,
> albeit his skill will be the lesse therby:
> The Prince Llwellen, and the Earle of Chester,
> shall bothe be by, and graunt as much as he. (1561–5)

As noted above, too, Cumber's final words express some kind of
interest in Kent's stature: "Alas, alas, hath cunning John </no wiser
way than this [?]" (1624–5). On a deeper level, much of the play's
unexplained causality has to do with the ways that the two Johns

---

[17] See Kathleen E. McLuskie regarding the tensions and opportunities produced
by overlapping systems of aristocratic patronage and commodification before an
audience in the drama of this period ["The Poets' Royal Exchange: Patronage and
Commerce in Early Modern Drama," in *Patronage, Politics, and Literary Traditions in
England 1558–1658* ed. Cedric C. Brown (Detroit: Wayne State University Press,
1993) 125–34].

identify with one another. When John a Kent first meditates on the play's too-hasty achievement of love and love, he virtually calls John a Cumber into being as an aspect of himself:

> O that I had some other lyke my selfe,
> to drive me to sound pollicyes indeed.
> Thers one in Scotland, tearmed John a Cumber,
> that overreachte the devill by his skill,
> had Moorton brought him to have sped his loove,
> I would have tryde which should the maister proove.
> But since my selfe must pastime wth my selfe,
> Ile anger them, bee't but to please my selfe. (541–48)

Upon discovering that John a Kent has stolen Sidanen and Marian, Morton does in fact think to send for John a Cumber. But Cumber has already, mysteriously, appeared among the members of the Morton/Pembroke party. He is present on stage at that very moment, on the slimmest pretense of dramatic causality, as though he had heard John a Kent's soliloquy and had been summoned by some mystical sense of connection. Hearing Morton vow to send for him, Cumber steps forward and reveals himself:

> Ile save my Lord that labour. Heers John a Cumber,
> entiste to England by the wundrous fame,
> that every where is spread of John a Kent.
> And seeing occasion falleth out so well,
> I may doo service to My Lord heerby:
> I make him my protectour in this case. (714–19)

For John a Cumber, service to Morton is a mere by-product of a strong affinity for John a Kent. If the vividness of the one-on-one contest has faded some by the time it reaches Prospero and Jonson, it survives in the form of Prospero's need to do combat with a range of figures, from Sycorax to Antonio to Ariel and Caliban. And of course it survives in Jonson's determination to square off against virtually everyone. What Kent and Cumber remind us is that the goal is contest, not victory. To fight with Inigo Jones is to seem more important than the scenery; to establish the superiority of text over spectacle too absolutely would mean doing without the masque form altogether.

Joseph Loewenstein has recently done much to counter the narrative of Jonsonian exceptionality that I query here.[18] Tracing with

---

[18] Loewenstein, *Ben Jonson*, and *The Author's Due: Printing and the Prehistory of Copyright* (Chicago: University of Chicago Press, 2002). See also Douglas A. Brooks, *From*

great nuance the worlds of printing, of literary imitation, of theatrical entrepreneurship in which Jonson worked, Loewenstein has made
it clear that Jonson's authorial ambitions grow out of a larger context of evolving rights in intellectual property negotiated between
theater and print culture. As critics, however, we remain more willing to establish the locus of authorial fantasy in the *prefaces* to printed
plays and in the practices of the printing house—perhaps in part
because we are anxious not to identify with the "Prospero as
Shakespeare" school of criticism?—than we are to talk about the
fantasies of mastery actually being performed on stage day after day
in early modern England.[19] This essay has endeavored, then, to
demonstrate that the stuff in the plays—the performers, the spectacles,
the conventions even of minor theatrical modes like the magician
play—are bound up with what we consider to be authorship, with
questions about control and origin, patronage, audience and autonomy,
materiality and transcendence. To explore the place of theater in
authorship fully, we must reach beyond terms like "residual" and
"emergent," terms that underlie much of our current thinking about
how the stage and the author are connected. True, something that
will become the modern author is in a nascent form in early modern
England, awaiting copyright, possessive individualism, and even
romantic interiority as cementing ideologies. At the same time,
however, to think of authorship as emergent in this period, while
collaboration, materiality, or the pleasure of the audience are understood to matter only insofar as they are increasingly subject to authorial disavowal, is inevitably to be reductive. There are of necessity
many forms of authorship, many counter-ideologies of the modern
itself. Even Jonson—even Prospero—should be regarded as complex
and self-contradictory. Such sovereignty as they construct is in the
end no more coherent, and no less evanescent, than the magic contest
produced by Munday and his players.

The point is not to deny that modernity is more characteristically
individualistic than pre-modernity, or that authorship can be bound
up in that move toward individualism. Nor would I suggest that
identifying Prospero as a "traditional" figure on the early modern

---

Playhouse to Printing House: Drama and Authorship in Early Modern England (Cambridge:
Cambridge University Press, 2000) esp. chapter one.
   [19] The comments of James P. Bednarz are useful here: "Print was important for
Jonson, but his drive for fame began on the stage" [*Shakespeare and The Poets' War*
(New York: Columbia University Press, 2001) 14].

stage means that *The Tempest* does not register subtle historical changes. But I am asking for more room in our narratives of historical change, more sense that a given moment or text will contain multiple constructs not fully accounted for by the terms "residual" and "emergent." If the relational authority imagined in this essay is more characteristic of—or more enthusiastically celebrated in—early modern England, it nevertheless remains an active possibility right through modernity. To argue that Munday's version of authority is residual in the late 1580s is to imagine a possibility fading from view as we move forward in time, and thus perhaps inevitably to limit the meanings we can read into later engagements with physical spectacle and patronage.[20] To stress historical continuity and literary borrowing over time is, on the other hand, to insist that these later figures, and the institution of dramatic authorship they help configure, remain actively open to collaboration, embodied spectacle, and audience pleasure.[21]

I propose, then, that we consider dramatic convention as a kind of drag against historical narrative, that we read the striking innovations of proto-authors like Prospero and Jonson alongside the relatively banal figure of the theatrical magician as produced by a hack writer. This is to acknowledge that theater has its own institutional calendar, not fully reducible to developments in property rights or political theory. As Heather Hirschfeld has argued, the theater in this period comes to be "a self-sustaining entertainment industry that, growing out of both popular and aristocratic troupe traditions and reliant on both royal patronage and popular acclaim, cannot be explained strictly in terms of economic, social, or political determinants."[22] Such

---

[20] Pennell dates the play to the late 1580s if not slightly earlier (*An Edition*, 44). William B. Long accepts Shapiro's argument that the playbook dates to 1590 (not 1595 or 1596, as was long believed) [William B. Long, "*John a Kent and John a Cumber*: An Elizabethan Playbook and Its Implications," in W. R. Elton and William B. Long, eds., *Shakespeare and Dramatic Tradition: Essays in Honor of S. F. Johnson* (Delaware: University of Delaware Press, 1989) 141; I. A. Shapiro, "The Significance of a Date," *Shakespeare Survey* 8, ed. Allardyce Nicoll (Cambridge: Cambridge University Press, 1955) 100–108].

[21] It is worth remembering in this context that Munday's play itself is grounded in older traditions of the ballad and the outlaw tale, as well as in conventional elements of the drama. These connections are detailed in J. W. Ashton, "Revision in Munday's *John a Kent and John a Cumber*" [*Modern Language Notes* 48:8 (1933), 531–37] and "Conventional Material in Munday's *John a Kent and John a Cumber*" [*PMLA* 49:3 (1934) 752–61]; see also Meredith Skura, "Anthony Munday's 'Gentrification' of Robin Hood," *English Literary Renaissance* 33:2 (2003), 155–80.

[22] Heather Anne Hirschfeld, *Joint Enterprises: Collaborative Drama and the Institutionalization of the English Renaissance Theater* (Amherst: University of Massachusetts Press, 2004) 6. I am grateful to Julian Yates for the suggestion that theatrical tradition constitutes

an observation may be particularly suited to magic comedy.[23] As has
long been established, and as even John a Kent has suggested above,
comedy is devoted to delay, to the forestalling of the inevitable, to
denial of historical causality.[24] Can we say the same about the relation
of spectacle to plot? *The Tempest*, after all, observes the unity of time
even while emphasizing the dilatory pleasures of its masques, its banquets, and its harpies. Ariel takes time to dress like a water-nymph,
and to show Prospero that he has done so, even though he is supposed
to be invisible when he performs that role.[25] Prospero "forgets" the
plot of Caliban while producing the masque of Juno and Ceres.
When Prospero labels that forgetting for us as preface to the "revels
are ended" speech ("I had forgot that foul conspiracy" 4.1.139), when
he calls attention to his power to suspend time in the moment of
spectacular performance, Prospero solidifies his authority before an
audience. In a similar way, John a Kent establishes his power over
the stage by making Sidanen and Marian, Griffin and Powesse, consent to postpone their own marriages. Handing the women back so
he can put on one more magic show, Kent asserts the priority of
spectacle over time. Perhaps the construction of authorship on the
early modern stage is announcing the hour of modernity, keeping
pace with something new. But comedies like Munday's insist that
this charismatic figure, who is after all famous because he produces
novelties, nevertheless coheres, concludes "like John a Kent," in part
because his thrilling innovations postpone forward movement. If
authorship comes to have a place on the early modern stage, it does
so in part because it resonates with forms of authority that have
their roots in the long traditions of popular entertainment.

---

a kind of alternative calendar in the theatrical realm, however strongly that realm
may be influenced by other cultural forces.

[23] Scott McMillin and Sally-Beth MacLean suggest tantalizingly that a tradition
of essentially anti-necromantic magic plays were part of the Queen's Men's response
to Marlowe's successes [*The Queen's Men and their Plays* (Cambridge: Cambridge
University Press, 1998) 157–8].

[24] Susan Snyder has outlined the dilatory pleasures of comedy and romance as
theatergoers in the 1580s would have known them [*The Comic Matrix of Shakespeare's
Tragedies:* Romeo and Juliet, Hamlet, Othello, *and* King Lear (Princeton: Princeton
University Press, 1979) esp. 36–8].

[25] Jonathan Goldberg, *Sodometries: Renaissance Texts, Modern Sexualities* (Stanford:
Stanford University Press, 1992) 143.

THE PLAY OF VOICE
ACKNOWLEDGMENT, KNOWLEDGE AND
SELF-KNOWLEDGE IN *MEASURE FOR MEASURE*

Sarah Beckwith

To the inhabitants of Shakespeare's work, it can seem that there's no art to find the mind's construction in the face. We can't reach the mind or thoughts or feelings of others; they lie behind, or beyond a surface appearance that screens and veils them. The characters in Shakespeare's plays don't simply find it hard to read and understand each other, they are liable to become fundamentally unknowable both to themselves and to others. In the often quoted words of Hamlet:

> ... I have that within which passeth show[1]

Shakespeare gives us an image of the human as in exile from his own body and expression. The inner man recedes as we try to get past the show of his behaviour to discover it and disappears from us as we seek urgently and ardently to move behind the mask of "mere" outer-ness. We might say, when the outer man disappears, the inner inexorably follows. In the process our words don't reach to the things they are supposed to reach to; they constantly fall short, miss the mark.

Often we see Shakespeare's characters bemoaning the divorce of words and thoughts. Here's Claudius trying to pray: "My words fly up, my thoughts remain below."[2] And here's Angelo: "heaven hath my empty words,/Whilst my invention, hearing not my tongue,/Anchors on Isabel."[3] Sometimes this divorce is because of a conscious deception as in *Macbeth*: "look like the innocent flower/But be the serpent under't,"[4] as seeming becomes necessary to maintain

---

[1] *Hamlet* 1.ii.85. All quotations are taken from *The Norton Shakespeare* edited by Stephen Greenblatt, (New York and London: W. W. Norton & Company, 1997).
[2] *Hamlet* 3.iii.97.
[3] *Measure for Measure* 2.iv.2–4.
[4] *Macbeth* 1.v.63–4. The face as visor to the heart is Macbeth at 3.ii.35–6:

a certain appearance, the face a visor to the heart. "Seeming! Seeming!" exclaims Isabella when she finally understands the full measure of Angelo's designs on her.[5] But in Shakespeare this duplicitous cultivation of appearances is not restricted to the strategic manipulations of a few evil characters who plot and devise, and theatricalise. Theatricality seems to have taken over our relations with others and we find ourselves no longer in our words; our expressions no longer express us.

It hardly describes, or begins to sound the depth, the resourcefulness or the profundity of Shakespeare's theater to describe him as celebrating the "fact" (the discovery?) that all the world is a stage.[6] Shakespeare's endeavour was to use theatre to rescue us from theatricality, and in the process to return us to our own words, to our expressions, and our bodies as the only access we have to each other. Such a return will be to the chronic, ubiquitous and daily disappointments of our relations with others and to the difficult, daunting, sometimes impossible responsibilities for everything that comes between us, to the realities of the separateness from each that is our human condition. Shakespeare wants to rescue (even redeem) us from the emptiness of our words, from the modes of play-acting that make us either emptily conformist or chronically unknown to ourselves and others. Our separateness will no longer be reassuringly metaphysical, but returned to our quite ordinary dealings with each other.

In Stanley Cavell's extraordinary analysis of skepticism, Shakespeare's theater was crucial. His two seminal works, *Must We Mean What We Say?* and *The Claim of Reason* both end with stunning analyses of Shakespearean tragedy, the seminal analysis of *King Lear* in "The Avoidance of Love" which ends *Must We Mean What We Say?* and the reading of Othello's self and world destroying doubt about Desdemona's fidelity which constitutes the devastating and moving finale of *The Claim of Reason*.[7] These analyses are never merely illus-

---

"we/Must lave our honours in these flattering streams/And make our faces visors to our hearts/Disguising what they are."

[5] *Measure for Measure* 2.iv.150.

[6] "All the world's a stage" is from Jaques' speech in *As You Like It* 2.vii.138. This expression has of course become a mantra of new historicist criticism that does not make a distinction between theater and theatricality and thereby misses the depth of Shakespeare's encounter with skepticism. For further comments on this theme, see below.

[7] "The Avoidance of Love" was first published in *Must We Mean What We Say?*

trative of concepts worked out prior to the readings; they are the prompts and sponsors to the very understanding (and transformation of skepticism's self-understanding) that the rest of these magnificent books divulge and explore. Both the CR and MWM develop unique, original, and fascinating readings of the later Wittgenstein in which Wittgenstein is shown to be obsessed with false pictures of privacy, of the inner/outer relation. Cavell's Wittgenstein sees skepticism as "the site in which we abdicate such responsibilities as we have over words, unleashing them from our criteria . . ., coming to feel that our criteria limit rather than constitute our access to the world."[8] Shakespeare's texts diagnose and account for the skepticism that besets our public and intimate relations with each other. In envisaging skepticism in the shapes of grief, of mourning, of doubt and jealousy, of isolation and inheritance rather than in a purely intellectual epistemology, Shakespeare can also diagnose the extent to which epistemology itself becomes a cover for the more haunting and intractable terrain of our relations with each other, the "practical difficulties" rather than the metaphysical impossibilities of knowing another and knowing oneself. Cavell himself has concentrated on the tragedies, and on *The Winter's Tale* in his examination of skepticism.

In this paper I will be concentrating on a play that has come to be awkwardly designated a "problem play." Though it "reads like a workshop for the tragedies written after it"[9]—a succession of plays only broken by the highly experimental romance *Pericles*—and though

---

(Cambridge: Cambridge University Press, 1969) and in an updated edition in 2002. The essay was reprinted in Cavell's collection on Shakespeare, *Disowning Knowledge in Seven Plays of Shakespeare* (Cambridge: Cambridge University Press, 1987) and in an updated edition in 2003. All subsequent quotations from this essay will be from the updated edition of *Must We Mean What we Say?* (henceforth MWM). The treatment of *Othello* occupies pp. 481–496 of *The Claim of Reason: Wittgenstein, Skepticism, Morality, and Tragedy* (Oxford: Oxford University Press, 1979), reprinted with a new introduction, 1999. All subsequent quotations are form the latter edition (henceforth CR). Cavell traces and enacts the centrality of Shakespeare to his analysis on p. 476ff. in his elucidation of tragedy as the "public form of skepticism with respect to other minds," a problem "largely undiscovered for philosophy" but traced out in Shakespearean tragedy.

   [8] This is Cavell's formulation in *Conditions Handsome and Unhandsome: The Constitution of Emersonian Perfectionism* (Chicago: University of Chicago Press, 1990), p. 22.

   [9] Kenneth Gross, in a fine essay on *Measure for Measure* in *Shakespeare's Noise* (Chicago: University of Chicago Press, 2001), p. 68.

it is placed in the first folio with the comedies, it is neither comedy
nor tragedy though it rehearses the conditions of both.

Like the tragedies, it is a play concerned with knowledge, self-
knowledge and judgment; like the comedies, it thinks about forgiveness, the necessary mode of romantic comedy's ending. *Measure for
Measure* makes judgment remorselessly reflexive. "Judge not, that ye
be not judged. For with what measure ye mete, it shall be measured
unto you again" is the Matthean text that haunts the play and gives
it its title.[10] It is a highly demanding text from Jesus's Sermon on
the Mount, a sermon which carries our responsibility not just to our
words and our deeds but our very thoughts, seen by numerous
exegetes as Christianity's internalization of the law. Since the reflexivity
of our words is a central dimension of the Cavellian concept of
"acknowledgment" (of which more later), I believe *Measure for Measure*
is a play that can illuminate that insight as that insight can illuminate it. In this play no judgment is made that does not implicate,
judge its maker. Even, or perhaps especially, words backed by the
confident legitimacy of the law come to seem vulnerable, exposed,
and intimately bound up with the desires and wishes, evasions and
self-pictures of the utterer. It is a play concerned with confession
and its absences and with the silences we come to, with forms of
self-silencing and speechlessness, with play-acting and theatricality,
the acting out of roles scripted for us by others.

I want to begin by tracing in this play the fate of the three characters for whom escape from, response to, and responsibility in one's
words seems most pressing, the history of three reachers after perfection and their history with words: Isabella, Angelo and Duke
Vincentio. All three of these characters are purists who carry cher-
ished pictures (the play calls them "figures") of themselves. This
picture of themselves is precious to them. Its preservation and its
loss are costly.

---

[10] Matthew 7.1–2. But Paul's epistle to the Romans on judgment is in the background too, Romans, 1.2: "Therefore, thou art inexcusable, O man, whosoever
thou art that judgest: for wherein thou judgest another, thou condemnest thyself;
for thou that judgest doest the same things."

Isabella

We hear of Isabella first through the hope her brother places in her as he's led off to prison and to death. His very life is invested in her eloquence. This is how Claudio sees his sister as he suggests to Lucio that she beg Angelo for remission of his punishment:

> in her youth
> There is a prone and speechless dialect,
> Such as move men; beside, she hath prosperous art
> When she will play with reason and discourse,
> And well she can persuade. (I.ii.160–164)

Her eloquence here does not lie in her speech—(and her ending in speechlessness in the last scene comes to be central). Claudio knows her skill, her "prosperous art" in reason and discourse, but this is introduced as "play." When she decides to play that game, she's good at it. What is paramount is less her skill in reason than her "prone and speechless dialect." It is not her words, but her youth, her prone-ness that might move men. When we meet her in I.iv through Lucio's mock annunciation ("Hail, virgin, if you be" (I.iv.16)) she prompts a new directness in him: he will not "tongue far from heart," jest with her as he might with other maids (I.iv.32). When Lucio makes his plea and invitation, she is assailed first by the thought of her inability to do him good. "Alas What poor/Ability's in me to do him good.?" (I.iv.73–4) And then by the thought, the possibility, provoked by him of the "power" she may have: "Assay the power you have." (I.iv.75)

So when she goes about her task of persuasion, we might have it in mind that her agreeing to the conversation at all is a kind of test (for herself) of a power she doubts she has. In this swift scene, then, she is moving from a desire for greater restraint in the regulation of the nunnery she is about to enter ("And have you nuns no further privileges?" [I.iv.1]) to a question about her own power and ability in the world as moved by and in her words.

In the first of her great conversations with Angelo (2.ii) her suasion is halted by the sheer fact of her abhorrence for Claudio's act. She loves her brother; but she hates what he's done and so she must explain that she is "at war twixt will and will not." (2.ii.33) She begins by depicting the vice she abhors and this is so much the focus of her mind that it is not clear, given how fervently she thinks such

a vice should meet the "blow of justice," how much she thinks her
brother should be saved at all. She seems under the force of a twin
compulsion—she must plead for him, and yet she must not. Her
brother fades out of the picture, so concerned and conflicted is she
in her own abhorrence, and she decides to separate the actor and
the fault. With obscene haste her brother becomes past tense. The
law is severe but just: "I had a brother then." (2.ii.43) At Lucio's
urging, she persists.

In her next thought, something of her brother's fate and less of
her own abhorrence seems to enter her words and she now wants
to plead against necessity: "Must he needs die?" (2.ii.48) Does it have
to be this way? Is there any other way out? Are there other possibilities to imagine? Is this the only compulsory route? Is it that
Angelo cannot reverse his edict to save her brother or that he will
not do it? She persists, undoing necessity and so locating her brother's
death as the word, will and responsibility of Angelo. Now with the
attention fixed on him and his intransigence rather than the just
fixity of the law, she can contemplate and wish for his potency: "I
would to heaven I had your potency/And you were Isabel!" (2.ii.69–70)
And this thought leads to the imagination of what it might mean to
trade places—for her to trade places with him, and for him to trade
places with her brother, to imagine himself in his place: "If he had
been as you, and you as he/You would have slipp'd like him, but
he, like you,/Would not have been so stern." (2.ii.67–8)

It's important to remember in this conversation that Isabella has
an audience to her powers. Lucio and the Provost are there not simply to urge her on but to witness her eloquence and she is so fired
up by their reception of her words ("Ay touch him; there's the vein,"
"Ay, well said". . . . "O him, to him, wench! He will relent," [2.ii.73,
92, 127]) that she produces some of the play's most moving words
on mercy and authority. She leaves the first meeting with a sense
that she's nearly done it, nearly won him around. "I'll bribe you"
(2.ii.149) is confident of her maiden prayers and powers and she
takes her invitation to return as hope of victory as does Lucio ["Go
to; tis well." (2.ii.160)]

By the time of the second conversation (2.iv) Angelo's "sense" has
bred with hers in that complex word that Empson analysed so brilliantly in this scene.[11] He has indeed knocked at his own bosom and

---

[11] William Empson's work on "sense" in *Measure for Measure* is first published in

found, not the same thing that Claudio feels for Juliet, but an over-whelming appetite in himself that he had not known he had. She has awakened a self-knowledge in him that he would have preferred never to have encountered, and it will be one used to entrap her not into a saintly and triumphant redemption of her brother, the act of brilliant intercession she has envisaged for herself, but into the very act she most abhors.

In the second conversation with Angelo she is on the back leg. Her own words seem to be taken in ways she has not intended, con-stantly sexualized by Angelo. "I am come to know your pleasure" becomes "That you might know it, would much better please me." (2.iv.31, 32.) And yet her persistent innocence of Angelo's designs means that he has to spell out in the most explicit of terms what he wants to do and what he wants her to do. She will not so quickly catch on to his meaning as to spare him the trouble of articulating his designs in detail. Once the nasty bargain is spelt out, Isabella has to take back her words in plea for Claudio. "You seemed of late," says Angelo, "to make the law a tyrant/And rather proved the sliding of your brother/A merriment than a vice." (2.iv.115–7) If you think fornication is such a small thing that you think he shouldn't be punished for it, why not submit to it yourself? It is an unkind, even feeble move, one that Claudio will try again in a slightly different tack, but she eats her words: "It oft falls out/To have what we would have, we speak not what we mean." (2.iv.118–9) She's thrown back on her own abhorrence of Claudio's act by the situation she's been manoeuvered into. And though he equivocates that heaven will hardly hold her accountable for a compelled sin, in fact he desires not sim-ply her inert subjection but her consent: "Fit thy consent to my sharp appetite,/Lay by all nicety and prolixious blushes/That ban-ish what they sue for" (2.iv.161–3.) Now, she has not only had to retract her words, she has had to admit she has not meant them. Meanwhile, Angelo is pressing his words home against her attempts to let him off the hook of them: "Believe me, on mine honour. My words express my purpose." (2.iv.148–9) Her eloquent, speechifying words on "man, proud man,/Dress'd in a little brief authority" (2.ii.120) start to dawn on her and all the horror of the realization

---

The Structure of Complex Words (London: Chatto and Windus, 1951), and reprinted in *Shakespeare: Measure for Measure, A Casebook* edited by C. K. Stead (London and Basingstoke: Macmillan, 1971).

that this authority who holds life and death in his hands, whose words are law, is himself a lie, a travesty of justice. Proud men are not what they seem and now she is loosed into the world in which no authority can be trusted.

What are her choices? Firstly, she will call it out, tell it how it is: "I will proclaim thee, Angelo." (2.iv.151) But she soon comes to see, as Angelo is quick to observe, that her words, truthful as they are, would not be believed in the face of that massive trust in Angelo's authority. In this world "my false o'erweighs your true" (2.iv.170) In a world of her word against his, hers stands no chance. She will "stifle in her own report." (2.iv.158) Now the only hope she can hold out is that her brother's reaction will relieve her of the horror of her situation. For he will so share her disgust at Angelo and be so protective of her honor that he will not allow her even to contemplate Angelo's wish, let alone enact it.

Things go wildly wrong in her conversation with Claudio. The Duke, disguised as friar, has brought him, but only apparently, to a readiness to die. Only apparently, because the vapid stoicism of his speech, (3.i.5–41), which pictures a life so hateful anyone would be happy to leave it behind, lacks all conviction. But in Claudio's passionate desire to live, to continue, to love, to see his child, all the loveliness of life, of *his* life, comes rushing back in. It is the "sensible warm motion" and the "dilated spirit" that he wants to go on inhabiting. (3.i.121) He wants this nearly as ardently as he fears death itself. It is this felt fear, this love of life with which Isabella is confronted and she can only say, "Alas, alas!" (3.i.133) But then, with the thought that it is indeed in her power to grant him life now, he asks her for that life, as simply and as directly as a man can: "Sweet sister, let me live." (3.i.134) This direct plea in the face of her response, makes her his killer not his savior. Allow me to live, my life is in your hands. He has not relieved her of her dreadful responsibility. Her disappointment is so bitter that he had better be sent off to die as quickly as possible. Now even if all she had to do would be to bend her knee to save him, she would rather pray for his death:

> Might but my bending down
> Reprieve thee from thy fate, it should proceed.
> I'll pray a thousand prayers for thy death,
> No word to save thee. (3.i.145–148)

This is chilling. Here is the lovely intercessor, the one addressed as the quasi-virgin Mary herself in Lucio's mock-annunciation, the sweet sister asked for mercy. She's hurrying on his death with her prayers.

When the mock friar comes along to offer her a "remedy," a solution that will allow her to save her brother and keep her honor intact, please the duke, do a poor lady a merited benefit at the cost of a simple substitution, a little play-acting, the thing "appears not foul in the truth of her spirit." (3.1.204) She puts her trust in his authority in the matter of the bed-trick. The bed-trick fails. Once he's slept with her as he thinks, it becomes even more urgent for Angelo to get rid of Claudio lest he be discovered. Again, the Duke as friar makes more promises, hints at greater solutions to be revealed, and she is asked to perform her part in the declamation of Angelo. She agrees to be directed by him though she is loathe "to speak so indirectly." (4.vi.14) She is asked to declaim Angelo as if she had really performed the bargain he proposed, thereby to denounce herself in denouncing him. "Reveal yourself to him" says the Duke. (5.i.28) Ask for justice from the very perpetrator of injustice. She understands that this makes her seem mad, and she risks that rebuff. But the Duke appears to side with Angelo: and she is left with her desperate, utterly bereft words: "And is this all?" (5.i.114)

When her brother is brought on, not dead but alive, all the words between them hang in the air. The last time he saw her, she wished death upon him. Now she has just pleaded for his murderer as less guilty than the man who at least did the thing he died for. How will she greet him? How he her? What new and dreadful self-knowledge has his release from death afforded her? She might have learnt how to plead for the life of a man for the sake of a sister mocked with a husband. But she still has to face the man she wished to die. And now to face herself, to understand herself as the woman who uttered those words.

Her speechlessness is often read as astonishment in the face of the Duke's unexpected proposal. And critics have rushed to give words to her speechlessness.[12] Her friar is apparently her prince but he also

---

[12] Most brilliantly in Philip C. McGuire's chapter on *Measure for Measure* in *Speechless Dialect: Shakespeare's Open Silences* (Berkeley: University of California Press, 1985), an immensely detailed and dense reading of five alternative stagings of this silence. Of

had other thoughts about her all along. But her silence might be a silence too in the face of a new knowledge of who she is, of what she is capable. Her words have not had the potency she desired, but they have had other effects. Here they fail her. She CAN say nothing. She cannot face her brother without acknowledging her relation to him. So she's brought to feel the weight of her words in new ways and they hang heavy in her speechlessness.

Angelo

Angelo like Isabella "has no tongue but one." We are to understand that he has never felt what other men feel until he desires Isabella. But this new knowledge of himself is not a leveler. It helps him understand other men, all flesh and blood like him, not one little jot better because it fails in any way to make him common with them.[13] Because he has always been better than other men, he will now be that much the worse. (The last thing he will be is LIKE them. God forbid.) Whether saintly or depraved, he still counts himself in exile from his fellow men.

Whatever other men think of his attempt to live exempt from his body, Angelo has, until his encounter with Isabella, apparently lived a life unpunctured by desire. And as a model of perfection, he regards himself as exemplary for other men. He will measure other men by himself and because he's so perfect he can hold them to the highest of standards. In the unlikely scenario of his own temptation and fall, he too will suffer the necessary and deserved punishment. ["You may not so extenuate his offence/For I have had such faults; but rather tell me,/When I that censure him do so offend,/Let mine own judgment pattern out my death/And nothing come in partial." (2.i.27–31)]. Isabella seems to concede his perfection when she says

---

course, it is not merely Isabella's silence that is striking but the silences of Angelo, Barnardine, Claudio, Juliet, and Marianna, showing starkly against Lucio's endlessly interrupting wittering and the Duke's theatrical assumption of all voice to himself.

[13] This is partly of course because he can only understand, only conceive of his lust (though he once calls it love) as depraved and can only imagine a dark, coercive place for it. Since his very thoughts render him evil, he has crashed from sainthood directly to damnation.

"We cannot weigh our brother with ourself." (2.ii.129) But his lust for Isabella shakes his state of man and renders him powerfully unknowable to himself. Angelo's self-picture has been so utterly wedded to the picture of his perfection that the revelation of imperfection is utterly shattering. He embarks on a course in which all his actions are there to preserve an utterly hollow public picture that he fully knows to be sham. But the point is that this public picture has not been sham until now—it has been who he is. And without it he is nothing. He never thinks of embarking on a path of anything other than preservation of this public image. And he cannot survive its sundering. Now even his most private words have been emptied out of their meaning: "heaven hath my empty words/Whilst my invention, hearing not my tongue,/Anchors on Isabel, Heaven in my mouth/As if I did but only chew his name,/And in my heart the strong and swelling evil/Of my conception. (2.iv.2–7.) With this new knowledge comes a scorn for all those he has taken and is taking in, and he might even thus include himself who has believed so entirely in his own perfection: "O place, O form,/How often dost thou with thy case, thy habit,/Wrench awe from fools and tie the wiser souls/To thy false seeming." (2.iv.12–15) It is as if the entirety of the man has become a shell to himself as well as to others, but without this, he is nothing. He has imagined himself "undiscernible." But once "discerned," he can not bear the trial of his shame and can only wish to die, a wish I do not see undone by the Duke's "Methinks I see a quickening in his eye." (5.i.489)): "Then, good prince,/No longer session hold upon my shame,/But let my trial be mine own confession/Immediate sentence then, and sequent death,/Is all the grace I beg." (5.i.363–6) His plea is for the Duke's word as punishment to replace his "own confession." It's interesting here that Angelo's discourse for confession is entirely legal and bound up with punishment, not forgiveness and self-knowledge. In the latter model, confession would involve being open to one's own weakness and repentance would bring about metanoia or radical transformation. Death is far preferable to Angelo than acceptance of frailty and failure. It's not simply, then, that by his own lights he understands himself to be deserving of this, but that the utterance of a confession is impossible to him. His picture of himself dies in his own eyes with his desire to ravish Isabella, but he cannot live with himself as he is, absent his public image. For him, there really is nothing beyond seeming.

The Duke

The Duke of dark corners also has "a complete bosom" and cannot imagine that the "dribbling dart of love" can pierce it. (1.iii.2–3)
In him theatricality is most developed, most entwined with power
and governance, most connected with the ability to know others,
and to manage a self-revelation that is strictly controlled and scripted.
Indeed the Duke's capacity to reduce all relations with others to
ones of knowledge, and to manage his own image in relation to that
of others, is deeply bound up with his theatricality. Unlike Angelo
who identifies himself with the image of perfection he seems in the
eyes of others, the Duke finds his subjection to the eyes of others a
torment. Indeed his image is rather of one who is held in, consti-
tuted by the idle dreams of a thousand wits, and he feels himself to
be racked with, tortured by their fancies. (4.ii.56–61) Not being quite
perfect, he's wary of the opinions and words of others and sees them
as confinement and subjection, a prison-house of language.

His surrogation of Angelo is from the beginning bound up with
a retreat from the consequences of his own actions, with a refusal
to take responsibility for his own actions and words. In his confession to the real friar, this is complexly seen under the guise of the
assumption of responsibility. One reason he puts Angelo in the role
is to see if he's really as perfect as he appears to be. But it is also
a brilliant administrative ruse. It seems the Duke can hardly go
wrong. If Angelo succeeds, he will have put into practice the laws
that would make the Duke look like a tyrant; if he fails, it will be
Angelo's responsibility, not his. It's a win-win situation, a conventional administrative ploy. Either way he can take the credit and re-
stage himself as the returning redeemer. It is striking that what he
wishes to avoid is the accusation or imputation of tyranny:

> Sith 'twas my fault to give the people scope,
> 'Twould be my tyranny, to strike and gall them
> For what I bid them do. (1.iii.35)

During the course of the play, he'll solicit the confessions of others
and it is his tactic here systematically to convert this discourse of
self-knowledge and transformation into the acquiring of information.
Utterly hidden himself, and so incapable of being known by others,
he can, so he thinks, discover them in the truth of the confessional.
The confessional is for him a form of effective espionage. It brings

knowledge about others that he can then use in his theatre. He also has no compunction whatsoever in quite casually breaking the seal of the confession: "I have confess'd her," he says to Lord Angelo of Marianna, and "I know her virtue." (5.i.520) He lies to Claudio that he has confessed Lord Angelo and "knows" that he is only testing Isabella his sister. (3.i.168) Indeed everything is subject to his knowledge and he imagines that all difficulties "are but easy when they are known." (4.ii.188–9)

In the last scene, as critics have often acknowledged, everything becomes subordinate to the Duke's theatre. The language of pardon and forgiveness is now staged as a one-way donation, something granted exclusively by the Duke who imagines that it is solely his to dispense. In the swift culmination of the scene, the Duke dispenses pardons alike to the guilty and the guiltless—to Escalus, Isabella, the unrepentant Barnadine, Claudio, the Provost and to Angelo, "I find an apt remission in myself." (5.i.492) In the very last words of the play the Duke invites everyone to his palace and promises to tell them "What's yet behind that's meet you all should know." (5.i.532)

The scene ends with a variety of marriages. But what kind of marriages are these? *Measure for Measure* is the last comedy because these marriages are so problematic. Romantic comedy's marriages are the very image of the ability to go on. In Northrop Frye's terms, marriage is the means by which the individual and the social are recognised in each other.

In the history of the sacrament of marriage, as of the sacrament of confession, consent is absolutely vital. Medieval canon law did not recognize a marriage as valid without the consent of the parties involved. Church canonists understood the essence of marriage to lie in the intention of the couple entering the marriage and not in the sacerdotal blessing.[14] In the sacrament of confession too it is the

---

[14] I develop this point and the subsequent point about contrition/volition in the sacrament of confession in more historical directions in "Handling Sin in *Measure for Measure*: Shakespeare and the Performance of Penance" in *Reading the Medieval in the Early Modern* edited by Gordon MacMullan (Cambridge University Press, 2006). There is a huge literature on the marriage contracts in *Measure or Measure* since the distinction between Angelo, whose marriage to Marianna is contracted in words *de futuro* and Claudio's *de presenti*, is crucial to how we judge the judgment of Claudio by Angelo. Words of present consent are understood to constitute a fully legal

voluntary movement of the heart known as contrition that is seen as an absolutely, efficacious, and incontestable part of the sacrament. But in the last scene of *Measure for Measure*, the Duke's voice has taken over all others. Their wills are no longer important in this theatre of discovery where all revelations are made by virtue of his staged "uncoverings." He has turned the very institutions of confession inside out in order to stage his own redeeming ministry. The political name for this is tyranny, the very injunction that he has sought so hard to avoid in the first instance.[15] Both confession and marriage, former sacraments whose histories are deeply bound up with questions of the will, of intent and consent, are appropriated by the state and thoroughly theatricalised in this play and this theatricalization is bound up with "tyranny," itself conventionally understood as the unboundedness of a sovereign will. And theatricality is both the method and mechanism in his staged public entry.[16] All modes of human relationship are subordinated to, subjected to the Duke's notion of *knowledge*. The Duke apparently *knows* these others; he knows them by virtue of his instrumentalizing of their self-revelation in confession amongst other things. And his instrumentalizing of them in this way is deeply bound up with his own means of evad-

---

marriage; words of future consent can be cancelled by one or the other party but are rendered legal and permanently binding if followed by sexual intercourse, an act undertaken by Angelo when he sleeps with Marianna even though he thinks he is having intercourse with Isabella. A useful recent essay which gives a good account of the previous three decades worth of scholarship on this issue and makes some helpful suggestions of its own is Victoria Hayne, "Performing Social Practice: The Example of *Measure for Measure*" in *Shakespeare Quarterly*, Vol. 44, No. 1 (Spring, 1993), pp. 1–29. Much of the literature on marriage contracts becomes so obfuscatingly technical that the central point about the utter vitiation of the volition of the parties in the Duke's theatricalized solution becomes obscured as the question of marriage becomes re-defined as a legal legitimacy enforced and appropriated by the royal will at the end of the play. We are meant to be appalled, in my view, by the way the Duke makes the desires of his "subjects" both inoperable and unnecessary. This is also brilliantly Austinian territory because medieval canon law in fact allowed plenty of manoeuvre for the "welsher" and the "bigamist" because of its focus on intention. See here, *How to Do Things With Words* (Cambridge, Mass.: Harvard University Press, 1962), p. 10.

[15] 1.iv.35–6: "Sith twas my fault to give the people scope? 'Twould be my tyranny to strike and gall them/For what I bid them do." Angelo may operate "in the ambush" of his name and so protect his "nature" from slander. (1.iv.41–43).

[16] That the last act is a royal entry is made clear by the Duke at 4.iii.86–7: "by great injunctions I am bound to enter publically" and by Angelo and Escalus as they puzzle over the Duke's missive at 4.iv.4–9. This aspect of the proceedings is rendered strikingly clear in the version of the play filmed by the BBC.

ing self-knowledge through theatricality, a theatricality that has involved the most concerted exploitation of the innermost fears, wishes and fantasies of others.[17]

There is a strong sense of suppressed expression in the last act. It is as if, encouraged to give the claims and cries for justice, to reveal the inquities of the judges, those claims are then "stifled in their own report." (2.iv.158) Each claim brings shame and danger on the one who speaks it. In this play we are not, it seems, to be rescued from "enforced or stifled words, from enforced silence, from voices not our own, from falsifying accents, from the breath of words held too long."[18] Rather the costs of the repudiation of our own voices are shown painfully over and over again.

Have we not missed the point if we see the Duke's theater as resolving anything at all, as providing in that searching word of the play, a "remedy"?[19] For sure, we are asked to imagine, to engage in myriad substitutions and exchanges: Isabella for Marianna, Ragozine for Barnadine for Claudio, Angelo for Vincentio, a maidenhead for a brother's head, an eye for an eye and a tooth for a tooth. At myriad points, characters are exhorted to put themselves in the place of others and to measure others by themselves—["ask your heart what it doth know/That's like my brother's fault" says Isabella to Angelo (2.ii.140–1)]. And this might be seen as exploring the power of theatre in identification and empathy. But such forms of identification are useless without the acknowledgment of a *particular* relation to

---

[17] In Simon Mc Burnley's Theatre de Complicité dark production for the Royal National Theatre in the summer of 2004, the Duke, played by David Troughton, has manipulated and engineered all the proceedings to win Isabella for himself. To the utter bewilderment and horror of all on stage, the lights go up on the back-stage in which there lies a bedroom framed by bars like the prison that has dominated the set as he speaks the play's last words: "So bring us to our palace, where we'll show/What's yet behind that's meet you all should know."

[18] These words are from Cavell's fascinating essay, "Skepticism as Iconoclasm: The Saturation of the Shakespearean Text," in *Shakespeare and the Twentieth Century: The Selected Proceedings of the International Shakespeare Association World Congress, Los Angeles, 1996* edited by Jonathan Bate, Jill. L. Levenson, and Dieter Mehl (Newark: University of Delaware Press, 1998), p. 246.

[19] The idealization of the Duke is a surprisingly robust theme shared by Christian allegorists, cultural materialists and royalists alike. For a recent example, see Debra Shuger, *Political Theologies in Shakespeare's England: The Sacred and the State in Measure for Measure* (Houndsmills: Palgrave, 2001) who advances the Duke's disguise as a friar as a "gesture toward the sacerdotal nature of royal authority, and thus what it means to bear 'the sword of heaven'," p. 60.

the other. Angelo thinks his sin is exactly the same as Claudio's when he first understands himself to feel desire. This knowledge, though, takes him further into self-concealment, subterfuge and evasion. He would prefer to keep secret this awareness of himself. And Shakespeare, I think is making us take a very cold and hard look at the difficulties of acceding to knowledges we already have but wish to avoid.

So those avatars of inwardness—the nominally ascetic, crowd-hating Duke, the Puritanical Angelo and the novice nun, Isabella, all of whom pride themselves on a devotion to the truth about themselves, are seen as skilful evaders and avoiders. And this evasion and avoidance is of the demands for *action* made by their own self-knowledges.

If this is a moral play, it is also profoundly anti-moralistic. And this is because it throws us, as reader or audience, onto the difficult terrain of acknowledgment.

All three of the characters I've been exploring conceive themselves to be truth seekers and part of the truth they seek is about themselves. At the beginning of the play each displays a marked and sure complacency about the adequacy of their own access to themselves. The Duke imagines that he has "ever loved the life removed" (1.iii.8) but far from revealing his desire for contemplation this is understood as a concerted removal of his own life from the scrutiny of others, from its imbrication in the lives, words and opinions of others. Angelo thinks all beneath himself and yet holds all to his own lifeless and cold example. Isabella desires the greatest possible restraint in her own imagined novitiate. Before she's even begun the rigors of such a life, she imagines it as insufficiently rigorous (1.iv.1). During the course of the play, Angelo and Isabella certainly learn new things about themselves but it is fully arguable what such knowledge amounts to. In relation to others, knowledge takes you so far. It is what we do, how we respond to others that is the intractable and key terrain.

This is the terrain that Stanley Cavell has brilliantly termed "acknowledgment." The term takes us into the very heart of his exploration of the interrelationship between theatre and skepticism. In the essay "Knowing and Acknowledging," the companion piece to "The Avoidance of Love" in MWM, Cavell comes to read skepticism as the re-description of a metaphysical finitude (our human condition as knowers) as an *intellectual* lack.[20] Cavell is here working with two Wittgensteinian remarks. The first—"It can't be said of me at all (except perhaps as a joke) that I *know* I am in pain"—is meant to get at the thought that the role of observation and evidence work differently in the case of self-knowledge than in the knowledge of other minds.[21] (We would think someone rather odd if we heard them saying, "I'll just check to see whether I'm in pain"). The second remark is when Wittgenstein, approaching the thought of the failure of one person to know the other person's identical pain, will voice the following skeptical remark:"But surely another person can't have THIS pain!" as he strikes himself on the breast.[22] As Cavell explores these locutions and the situations in which they may or may not be given sense, he comes to the thought that, as Mulhall puts it: "although it is possible to be ignorant of the fact that someone is in pain, it is not possible simply to know that fact."[23]

"I know I am in pain" is not an expression of certainty, it is an expression of pain. "I know you are in pain" is not an expression of certainty, it is an expression of sympathy. Your suffering makes a claim on me and in the face of that, it is not enough that I know (am certain) you suffer—I must do or reveal something. I must acknowledge it, otherwise I do not know what your being in pain means.

In intellectualizing the problem of other minds, in making it a problem of knowledge and the limits of knowledge, this domain of response and responsibility is suppressed and evaded.

Theatricality is built into this understanding of skepticism because for Cavell, "I can't be known" and "I can't know others" present a picture of the world in which far from being expressive of mind, my body is a veil that hides and screens my thoughts from you. Our bodies are now masks and disguises that we can't get beyond. The whole world becomes a theatre because now our minds are

---

[20] The phrase "metaphysical finitude as an intellectual lack" comes from "Knowing and Acknowledging" in MWM, p. 263.

[21] Ludwig Wittgenstein, *Philosophical Investigations* translated by G. E. M. Anscombe (Oxford: Basil Blackwell & Mott, Ltd., 1958), Remark No. 246, p. 89.

[22] *Philosophical Investigations*, Remark No. 253, p. 91.

[23] Stephen Mulhall, *Stanley Cavell: Philosophy's Recounting of the Ordinary* (Oxford: Clarendon Press, 1994), p. 111.

metaphysically inaccessible; they can no longer express us and so we wander around trapped in our own deceiving bodies, craving, struggling to get beyond them. It is in this way that the world might be understood to be a stage for us. We will convert the world to a stage, the other to an actor, each time we withdraw the concept of the inner from his or her pain-behaviour because it is something that it is up to us to grant.

Now it is part of the depth of the Cavellian insight in "Knowing and Acknowledging," and part of the depth of Shakespearean theatre, that it rejects the Cartesian complacency that imagines that if we don't know others, we do know ourselves. Self-knowledge and the knowledge of others have to be found and found out; they can be lost.[24] They are never found once and for all. And this is because words do not so much come between, say, in the case of pain, the experience and the expression of it, as if words had to connect this thing, this inner object, to themselves, but rather *are* the response, the expression themselves, and they make a claim upon us to which we respond, to which we must respond, to which we do respond. (Evasion, ignorance, and avoidance are responses, not the absence of response. Sometimes, frequently, such claims are unbearable—this is why Cavell reads the Shakespearean diagnosis of skepticism as tragic.) And we can suppress our own words and expressions. Just as "I know you are in pain" can be an expression of sympathy and understanding rather than an assertion of the correctness of an identification, so "I know I am in pain" can be an expression not of an absurd or obvious sureness or transparency of one's own mind to oneself, but an acknowledgment of something. It can't be given a use, it can make no sense unless there is a context in which, a reason for which I wish to suppress the expression of pain.

A few years ago I went to the 50th birthday party of a friend who had multiple sclerosis. Her parents were at the party and my friend's guests were told not to tell them what we all knew—that

---

[24] The phrase "found out" and the notion of finding out are central in this play. The phrase is voiced in Isabella's words: "Why, all the souls that were were forfeit once,/And He that might the vantage best have took/*Found out* the remedy" (2.ii.75–8, my italics). The applicability of the terrain of acknowledgment to questions of self-knowledge is brilliantly explored in Richard Moran's *Authority and Estrangement: An Essay on Self-Knowledge* (Princeton and Oxford: Princeton University Press, 2001).

she had multiple sclerosis. She had not told her parents, wishing to spare them pain by pretending she had none. One could imagine them, saying to her: "We know you are in pain, you are walking slowly and with difficulty, you are having to touch the wall as you walk down that corridor. You seem depressed. We know something is wrong. Please tell us what is wrong with you. Surely you are in pain. Why won't you admit it?" And she, eventually seeing she had spared them nothing, might say in reluctant, rueful acknowledgment. "Yes, I know I am in pain. I know it better than anyone. I've had this disease for five years and I suppose this is now obvious to you. I think I am now ready to bear your responses." In this example it is possible to see that "I know I am in pain" includes the knowledge of pain; it is not an alternative to it. But the acknowledgment includes the arena of response, or recognition that what comes with this knowledge is the unavoidability of her parents' pain and response, that this will now be part of what binds and comes between them. To concentrate exclusively on the impossibility of knowing your mind for certain will spare us this uncompromisingly painful arena of our embodiedness and of the absolute inevitability of another's response. In the case of mental phenomena, Cavell says, at the end of the essay on "Knowing and Acknowledging: "when you have twisted or covered your expressions far or long enough, or haven't yet found the words which give the phenomenon expression, I may know better than you how it is with you."[25] I may know you better than you know yourself. But what you won't know about yourself or about me will not be blankness or absence—it will be the presence of something—"a confusion, an indifference, a callousness, an exhaustion, a coldness."[26] To say that our behaviour is expressive does not necessitate the expression of our behaviour—but in order not to express our behaviour, we will have to suppress it. Cavell says "if he twists it far or often enough, he may lose possession of the region of the mind which that behaviour is expressing."[27]

Skepticism's understanding of acknowledgment as certainty, as knowing THAT or this for sure and its fixation upon the limits of that knowledge as when we say "we only know, we can only know

[25] "Knowing and Acknowledging," *MWM*, p. 266.
[26] "Knowing and Acknowledging," *MWM*, p. 264.
[27] "Knowing and Acknowledging," *MWM*, p. 264.

the feelings of others from their behaviour" suggests that there is
some other, alternative and better way of knowing. To this extent
it is a denial of our embodiedness, including our existential, actual
separation from each other, and it is also, for Cavell, a denial of
our own expressions as ours. (And if they are not ours, we are either
not in them because we feel too lost to be found in them, or we
are chronic conformists, reading our inherited scripts, in short, actors.)
Craving a God's eye view, we then deny the only form in which
we can communicate, know or acknowledge at all. Cavell says, it is
skepticism about other minds (rather than about the external world)
that is primary, and from our daily dealings and relations, there is
no study, like Hume's, to walk out of. We can and do relieve ourselves of the skepticism in relation to the external world, sometimes
as soon as we give up philosophy. Now in the case of our relations
with others, there is no way of blocking the threat of skepticism
because there are no criteria, as Cavell puts it, for existence, only
for identity. We can know that what you are expressing is called
pain, but not whether it is pain you are feeling, or merely pretending
to feel. It is not that your body stops me from seeing what is really
inside you, but that there is simply no human way of distinguishing
that something is, rather than *what* something is.[28]

Part of *Measure for Measure's* brilliance, as I see it, concerns the
ways in which it links acknowledgment, and self-acknowledgment in
and through our history with words. For Cavell, dramas of acknowledgment are played out in Shakespearean tragedy and comedy—
which would have to be comedies of forgiveness, the kinds of forgiveness that might allow us to go on, to marry each other, to conceive
of ourselves as social and not private beings. This play does just
about end in marriage, but, as in the play which may be regarded
as its companion piece, all is not well that ends well. The marriages
are co-erced, performed under compulsion and with no consent. This
is more than the shadow that falls across the earlier comedies—
Marcade's announcement of the death of the Princess's father at
the very end of *Love's Labours Lost*, Beatrice's chilling "kill Claudio,"
Malvolio's humiliated, vindictive, historically prophetic, "I'll be revenged

---

[28] This region of Cavell's thought is elaborated in Part One of *The Claim of Reason*
in the discussion of criteria.

upon the whole pack of you." Here it is only legitimacy that is preserved in marriage, and there is nothing in it of individual joy, volition, desire, futurity and possibility that assures us that this human group will be able to go on and converse with each other. There are many one-way pardons, but nothing that looks like forgiveness which never changes but always transforms the past, always blessedly releases us from the consequences of our passions and actions, frees us from estrangement, hurt and betrayal, in short, human damage.

Coda

It is the common story told by critics when they chart the history of theater from the Middle Ages to Shakespeare (a terrain that until 20 or so years ago was entirely subsumed under the concept of "pre-Shakespearean theatre" as if everything had to be judged in terms of its triumphant supercession in the bard) that Shakespeare discovers inwardness. Now it is surely irrefutable that in the words he gives to his characters he has developed his poetic drama to such an extent that we can chart the very thoughts of his characters as they think them. Nothing quite precedes this and only with a great deal of critical labor can anything truthfully be said to anticipate it. But this is often presented as a discovery of inwardness itself, as if no one had inner thoughts until Shakespeare discovered them, revealed them or showed us we had them. At the same time, it is commonly asserted that what Shakespeare reveals is that all the world is a stage, that appearances always conceal, that the reality of other minds is veiled, that we are chronically unknown, unknowable perhaps, to the world of others. What we have within passes show but this just renders everything show. A most recent and sophisticated version of this reading goes something like this: once people had religion, now they have theatre. Religion duped everyone, dressed priests up in robes, used disguises to pry people's innermost secrets, lifted a little biscuit up in the air and said it was the body of Christ, the same one on every altar in Christendom. Now theatre has taken on the resources of religion but to disenchant and not enchant. So now, we will no longer be duped. We will now be able to see that "the official position of the church" is emptied out; "the forlorn hope of an impossible redemption persists" but it is "drained of its institutional and doc-trinal significance, empty and vain," but "ineradicable."[29] Religion pretended it was real, but theatre knows it is not, so illusion is revealed and not continued. The veil of the temple is torn. So Shakespeare will help us not ever to be fooled, not to trust in words which can only be empty. On the reading I have advanced here, motivated by my readings of Wittgenstein and Cavell, this would put Shakespeare fully inside a conventional skeptical position. Yet, what Shakespeare, like Wittgenstein, might be seen to be obsessed with, is precisely false pictures of the inner and outer which render us powerless and impotent in the face of our own words. In failing to remember the normal and normative ways in which words and world are in relation, the fundamental community that underlies our agreements and disagreements is denied. Hence what comes with the picture of inaccessible inwardness is an eradication of the inher-ence of that inner life in the life and community with others. This picture everywhere models the constitutive relation of the "early mod-ern" to the medieval period, but it might also, and more fruitfully begin to sound the *peculiarity* of Shakespeare's relation to the Middle Ages in relation to his contemporary playwrights. For the return to our words as ours, out of theatricality and isolation, and to a rec-onciled community is co-incident, not divergent. Shakespeare tracked and charted our alienation from our own expressions, which meant from the imbrication of our inner lives in the language, the thoughts of others. This is why the distinction between theatre and theatri-cality is so important and so frequently elided by critics.[30] Like

---

[29] Compare the different spirits of Cavell's phrase "theater's competition with religion" and Greenblatt's discussion of these same questions in *Shakespearean Negotiations* (Berkeley: University of California Press, 1988) and *Hamlet in Purgatory* (Princeton: Princeton Univ. Press, 2001). [The words quoted above, are of course, from Greenblatt's justly famous essay on Harsnett and *Lear*. See Cavell's response in "Skepticism as Iconoclasm" *Shakespeare and the Twentieth Century* (Newark: University of Delaware Press, 1998), p. 246].

[30] Although Cavell is widely quoted and admired by Shakespeare critics, he might be said to be not "available" to them in the sense he gives this word in his own essay "The Availability of Wittgenstein's Philosophy" in *MWM*. In the preface to the revised edition of *Disowning Knowledge*, Cavell confesses his reluctance to publish a collection on Shakespeare in isolation from the philosophical questions in which the original analyses were embedded: ". . . . excising the philosophy takes the heart out of what drove the composing of the text," p. xiv. His fear has proved prophetic and one motivation of this essay is to make available a just response to Cavell's insights in relation to that philosophy. See however Richard Halpern's unpublished

Wittgenstein, Shakespeare might be understood to be deeply fearful of losing our inner life, which meant for him losing our connection with others and with our bodies and words. In the works succeeding the great tragedies he will find his way back to the possibility of restoration and forgiveness through theatre, notably through the more and more concerted pursuit of medieval source stories. But he will do so, can do so, only by virtue of so thoroughly understanding the necessities, inevitabilities of evasion and avoidance in our life with words. To do this we must be able to distinguish, or be shown ways in which we do and can distinguish—not finally, once and for all, but habitually and in specific contexts and situations—between sincerity and hypocrisy, between lies and truth, between theatre and theatricality.

paper "Intimate Histories: Stanley Cavell on, and as, King Lear," delivered at the Shakespeare Association of America conference in New Orleans, April, 2004, and the forthcoming work of Larry Rhu, integrating Cavell's work on film with his work on Shakespeare in productive and innovative ways. I thank both authors for allowing me to read their work in advance of publication.

SPECTACLE AND EQUIVOCATION IN *MACBETH*

Richard C. McCoy

In *Macbeth*'s last act, Shakespeare seems intent on presenting a clear and conclusive moral spectacle, one that moves beyond the play's pervasive equivocations. As Macduff moves in for the kill, he threatens Macbeth with an ignominious and definitive fate:

> Then yield thee, coward,
> And live to be the show and gaze o'th'time:
> We'll have thee, as our rarer monsters are,
> Painted upon a pole, and underwrit,
> "Here may you see the tyrant." (5.10.23–27)[1]

Macduff wants to make Macbeth into an emblematic advertisement for treason's dire consequences, complete with a suitably lurid *pictura* and an "underwrit" *subscriptio*. This dramatic combination of the thing itself with word and image promises a vivid fusion of sign and signifier. Macbeth refuses to surrender, but Macduff defeats and decapitates him, and he returns with "Th'usurper's cursed head" (21) impaled on his sword. The flourishing of the old king's severed head is followed by the new king's invitation "to see us crowned at Scone" (5.9.41). In its harshly literal juxtaposition of these two heads of state, the play's climax thus presents a truncated tableau of the king's two bodies and dramatizes the traditional proclamation, "The king is dead, long live the king." Malcolm concludes by promising to govern "by the grace of grace" (5.10.38), invoking monarchy's divine right and sacred authority.

Nevertheless, there is something wrong with this picture. The spectacle it presents is not quite as clear as it seems and equivocation proves inescapable. For one thing, the play's last word is given to Malcolm, an unprepossessing figure who pales by comparison with the other characters. He is neither a brave and brutal warrior like

---

[1] William Shakespeare, *Macbeth* 5.10.23–27 in *The Complete Works*, eds., Stanley Wells and Gary Taylor (Oxford: Clarendon Press, 1986); all citations of the play are to this edition unless otherwise noted.

Macbeth or Macduff whom he manipulates to fight on his behalf. Nor is he a holy ruler like his "royal father ... a most sainted king" (4.3.109–110) or his ally and protector, Edward the Confessor. He is, moreover, a mere placeholder whose line will be supplanted by the ancestors of King James. *Macbeth* was evidently performed at Hampton Court for King James in 1606, and its "*show of eight kings*" and other spectacles are often seen as royal tributes.[2] Yet, as I have argued in *Alterations of State*, Shakespeare's attitude towards contemporary notions of sacred kingship and divine right is ambiguous.[3] After all, in *Hamlet*, he places the claim that "There's such divinity that doeth hedge a king/That treason can but peep to what it would" (4.5.122–3) in the mouth of a regicide and usurper. *Macbeth* presents even loftier visions of sacred kingship along with some of the ghastliest images of its violation and disturbing hints of its dissipation. After murdering Duncan, Macbeth himself declares, "Renown and grace is dead" (2.3.93) in Scotland. By contrast, grace abounds at the English court of the sainted Edward the Confessor. Edward heals the afflicted with his royal touch, and "sundry blessings hang about his throne/That speak him full of grace" (4.3.159–60). Malcolm, Duncan's oldest son, finds refuge there, but, given his shortcomings, his own state of grace is uncertain. In the play's longest, strangest, and to many, most tedious scene, Malcolm renounces all the "king-becoming graces" (4.3.92) and proclaims himself guilty of sins worse than Macbeth's. After driving Macduff to despair, he then proceeds to "Unspeak mine own detraction ... [and] abjure/The taints and blames I laid upon myself" (4.3.124–5), leaving those listening quite confused. All Macduff can say at this point is "Such welcome and unwelcome things at once/'Tis hard to reconcile" (4.3.139–40).

Malcolm resorts here and elsewhere to the equivocation that bedevils the entire play, and, for many, that insures a fall from grace.

---

[2] Henry N. Paul argues in *The Royal Play of Macbeth: When, Why, and How it was Written by Shakespeare* (New York: Macmillan, 1950) that it was a "royal play for court performance as a compliment to" King James I performed at Hampton Court in 1606 to honor Christian IV's visit to England that summer, 1606 (1). But see Michael Hawkings, "History, Politics and Macbeth," in *Focus on Macbeth*, ed. John Russell Brown (London: Routledge & Kegan Paul, 1982) who argues for the ambiguity of *Macbeth*'s royalism and disputes its status as a command performance (185).

[3] For a discussion of Shakespeare's ambivalence towards sacred kingship in *Hamlet*, see my *Alterations of State: Sacred Kingship in the English Reformation* (New York: Columbia University Press, 2002), xii–xiv and 56–85.

"Equivocation" is, of course, a major theme in *Macbeth*, surfacing explicitly in the Porter's speech (2.3.8–11) and again in Macbeth's recognition that the witches have misled him (5.5.40–42). Most critics think equivocation is always a bad thing, and several do not like Malcolm using such devious expedients to attain the throne. More recent critics find these stratagems inevitable and oddly reassuring because they expose the illegitimacy of all aspirations to power. Steven Mullaney says that Malcolm's prevarication taints him indelibly, exposing the "family resemblance between authority and its Other."[4] In his view, equivocation or "Amphibology marks an aspect of language that neither treason nor authority can control."[5] Mullaney chooses the weirder and more sinister synonym to emphasize the dangerous unruliness of language, and he sees Shakespeare's wordplay as a "*malignant* power" that threatens to reduce all to chaos.[6] A deconstructive emphasis on linguistic nihilism marks many other recent approaches. Malcolm Evans insists in *Signifying Nothing* that equivocation is "a condition of language" that precipitates a "crisis of the sign."[7]

There are parallels here with the larger argument made by Sarah Beckwith in *Signifying God*, her fascinating study of the Corpus Christi Plays. Beckwith contends that the Reformation replaced a vibrant "sacramental theater" with an anti-theatrical "theater of epistemological doubt."[8] Renaissance signs become "mere signs"; i.e., semblances and counterfeits, disguises and illusions. "The effect," Beckwith contends, "is at once a devastating erosion of trust in the shared, public nature of signs as the basis and product of our agreements and disagreements."[9] Thinkers from Weber onwards have blamed the Reformation for this distrust and disenchantment, and medievalists are not alone in lamenting it. Looking at this sad decline from the other, early modern end, Stephen Greenblatt charts a "transformation

---

[4] Steven Mullaney, *The Place of the Stage: License, Play and Power in Renaissance England* (Chicago: University of Chicago, 1988), 126.

[5] Mullaney, 125.

[6] Mullaney, 128.

[7] Malcolm Evans, *Signifying Nothing: Truth's True Contents in Shakespeare's Texts* (1986; Hemel Hempstead: Harvester Wheatsheaf, 1989), 116.

[8] Sarah Beckwith, *Signifying God: Social Relation and Symbolic Act in the York Corpus Christi Plays* (Chicago: University of Chicago Press, 2001), 152.

[9] Beckwith, 156.

of faith into bad faith" (113) in Renaissance England.[10] Desecration of the sign is inevitable for those who made iconoclasm, in the words of Eamon Duffy, "the central sacrament of . . . reform" (480).[11]

But, in fact, neither the Renaissance theater nor the Reformation church were so radically iconoclastic. A determination to salvage legitimate icons, customs, and ceremonies was the motive behind the determined search for a *via media*. Many reformers sought a liturgical compromise between what Theodore Beza calls "transubstantiation and a trope."[12] Beza's wonderful phrase caps a sophisticated critique of the false binary that emerged from the theological summit meeting between Martin Luther and Ulrich Zwingli at Marburg in 1529. Beza rejects what he sees as the literal-minded naiveté of consubstantiation on the one hand and arid abstraction on the other, arguing instead for the spiritual efficacy of signs. Similarly, Richard Hooker insists that sacraments should not be taken for "bare *resemblances* or memorials of thinges absent, neither for *naked signes* and testimonies assuringe us of grace received before, but (as they are in deed and in veritie) for meanes effectuall."[13] Several scholars, including me, have called attention to this sacramental pragmatism and have found a comparable force in the performative efficacy sustained by Renaissance drama. Anthony Dawson argues that Shakespeare's characters become something like a "virtual" rather than a "real presence" in their enduring vitality, and Jeffrey Knapp shows how audience "participation" acquires "specifically Eucharistic overtones."[14] Without explicitly representing miracles or mysteries, the romances can still provoke wonder and demand our faith. And, as I have argued elsewhere, without depicting the sorrowful sights of a passion

[10] Stephen Greenblatt, *Shakespearean Negotiations: The Circulation of Social Energy in the Renaissance* (Berkeley: University of California Press, 1988), 113

[11] Eamon Duffy, *The Stripping of the Altars: Traditional Religion in England, 1400–1580* (New Haven: Yale University Press, 1992), 480.

[12] Cited in Jaroslav Pelikan, *The Christian Tradition: A History of the Development of Doctrine; Reformation of Church and Dogma, 1300–1700*, 5 vols. (Chicago: University of Chicago Press, 1984), 4:201.

[13] Richard Hooker, *Of the Laws of Ecclesiastical Polity* (5.57.5), ed. W. Speed Hill, 7 vols. (Cambridge, MA: Harvard University Press, 1977), 2:247.

[14] Anthony B. Dawson, "Performance and Participation" in Anthony B. Dawson and Paul Yachnin, *The Culture of Playgoing in Shakespeare's England: A Collaborative Debate* (Cambridge: Cambridge University Press, 2001), pp. 24–26. Jeffrey Knapp, *Shakespeare's Tribe: Church, Nation, and Theater in Renaissance England* (Chicago: University of Chicago Press, 2002), p. 132.

play, the tragedies can still elicit an empathy and engagement that allows a potent but secular sense of communion.[15] Shakespeare's plays do so paradoxically by frequently emphasizing the contrast between sign and signifier and between presence and pretense. As Pauline Kiernan points out in *Shakespeare's Theory of Drama*, Shakespeare constantly reminds us "that what is being presented is not the truth, and that the characters are not real people, but fictional creations played by real people," but the result is, in her words, "a potent mix, not disturbing rupture."[16] *Macbeth* achieves comparably para-doxical results by foregrounding equivocation. As we have seen, equivocation in this play has generally been condemned for its cor-rosive impact on social trust, but I want to argue that, in Shakespeare's theater, it can be a force for good.

Macbeth himself thinks otherwise, concluding that "the equivoca-tion of the fiend,/. . . lies like truth" (5.5.41–42). The witches intended to deceive him from the start; they snared him first, as their leader, Hecate, says, "by the strength of their illusion," and then they draw "him on to confusion" (3.5.28–9). As he gradually realizes he's been deceived, he is almost unhinged by his disillusion. The witches, of course, promised him he was safe "Till Birnam wood remove to Dunsinane" (5.3.2) and said "No man that's born of woman/Shall e'er have power upon thee" (5.3.6–7). However, their assurances are full of figurative loopholes that mislead by creating a false sense of "security/. . . mortals' chiefest enemy" (3.5.32–3). Macbeth's confidence in Birnam wood's stability overlooks the possibility of synecdoche, a possibility realized when Malcolm's soldiers cut down its branches. Forgetting the lethal dangers of childbirth, he is shocked by Macduff's announcement that his adversary "was from his mother's womb/ Untimely ripp'd" (5.10.15–16). Macbeth attacks "these juggling fiends . . ./That palter with us in a double sense" (5.10.19–20), and his vulnerability to the witches' double-talk suggests that he was both naïve and literal-minded. He not only failed to see their evil inten-tions, but he was also oblivious to the ambiguities of their promis-sory language. Jan Blits points out that what "Macbeth calls paltering

---

[15] Richard C. McCoy, "'Look upon Me, Sir: Relationships in *King Lear*," *Representations*, 81 (2003 Winter), pp. 46–60.
[16] Pauline Kiernan, *Shakespeare's Theory of Drama* (Cambridge: Cambridge University Press, 1996), p. 11.

is, in fact, nothing but the Witches' figurative speech. Macbeth says that the Witches' prophecies 'lie like the truth' (5.5.44), but they do so only in the way that all metaphors do."[17] Donald Foster says, "Although his imagination spawns timeless metaphors, his dull brain is, nevertheless, all too literalistic."[18] The otherwise eloquently imaginative Macbeth is thus duped by figures of speech.

As his disillusion grows, Macbeth despairs of all signification and turns bitterly anti-theatrical. In his notoriously bleak soliloquy, life is an illusion doomed to pointless repetition: "Tomorrow, and tomorrow, and tomorrow,/Creeps in this petty pace from day to day/...And all our yesterdays have lighted fools/The way to dusty death" (5.5.18–22). When events initially confirmed both his hopes and the witches' prophecies, Macbeth saw them all "As happy prologues to the swelling act/Of the imperial theme" (1.3.127–128). By the end, life becomes nothing more than "a walking shadow" (5.5.24). The terms are still theatrical, but his conception of his role and the performance is much grimmer. He is appalled at the prospect of becoming "a poor player,/That struts and frets his hour upon the stage" in "a tale/Told by an idiot, full of sound and fury,/Signifying nothing" (5.5.23–27). Behind this dark soliloquy is a recoil from the stage itself and all of its illusions. Anti-theatrical prejudice has a long history, as Jonas Barish shows in his classic study of the syndrome, flourishing among playwrights disenchanted with the stage as well as outright adversaries; Ben Jonson is perhaps the best-known example among Shakespeare's contemporaries.[19] Among modern playwrights, Antonin Artaud defiantly declared himself "the enemy of theater" and sought to create plays that moved beyond the ambiguous "language of words" to a more transparent "language of signs." For Artaud, a theater of cruelty was an attractive prospect because it was more "directly communicative."[20]

In some ways, *Macbeth*'s last act gravitates towards a theater of cruelty, but its codes are more complex. Macbeth himself describes

---

[17] Jan H. Blits *The Insufficiency of Virtue: Macbeth and the Natural Order* (Lanham, MD: Rowman and Littlefield, 1996), 193.

[18] Donald Foster, "Macbeth's War on Time," *English Literary Renaissance* 16 (1986), 337.

[19] Jonas Barish, *The Anti-Theatrical Prejudice* (Berkeley: University of California Press, 1981).

[20] Antonin Artaud, *The Theater and Its Double*, transl. Mary Caroline Richards (New York: Grove Press, 1958), 107.

his plight in terms that evoke the simple brutality of bear-baiting—
"they have tied me to a stake: I cannot fly,/But bear-like, I must
fight the course" (5.7.1–2) And Macduff's determination to make
Macbeth "the show and gaze o'th'time" anticipates fixing his significance in a rigid sign system. Yet such seemingly objective signs
induce a sense of *déjà vu* and confusion because we've seen it all
before, starting with the head of "the merciless Macdonwald" (1.2.9)
"fix'd upon our battlements" (23) by Macbeth himself. In Howard
Felperin's view, "the essential doubleness" of these images suffuses
the play's climax with a sense of "radical equivocation" and per-
plexity, and Malcolm's denunciation of "this dead butcher, and
his fiend-like queen" (5.11.35) is merely an "ingenuous repetition of
convention."[21] I think this is interesting—and wrong. I readily concede that here and elsewhere, Malcolm engages in double-talk, but
it is far from vapid or naïve. Indeed, Malcolm is one of the play's
most astute equivocators—wary, self-conscious, and disingenuous—
and it is precisely because he equivocates that Malcolm is my hero.
Let me try to explain why.

Malcolm is on guard from the moment his father is murdered,
and he immediately sees through the duplicity of some of the mourn-
ers: "To show an unfelt sorrow is an office/Which the false man
does easy" (2.3.135–136). In his big scene with Macduff, he declares
his suspicions even more forcefully, warning that he will only believe
what he knows to be true (4.3.9) and responding cautiously to
Macduff's exhortations: "What you have spoke it may be so, per-
chance" (4.3.11). Malcolm is not mollified by Macduff's assurance
that "I am not treacherous" (4.3.18)—why should he be? Instead,
he insists on the need for defensive scrutiny:

> That which you are my thoughts cannot transpose:
> Angels are bright still, though the brightest fell:
> Though all things foul would wear the brows of grace.
> Yet grace must still look so (4.3.21–24).

Grace is repeatedly attributed to the play's good kings—Duncan and
Edward the Confessor—and hailed as the hallmark of their sanctity.
However here Malcolm forcefully redefines grace in terms that are

---

[21] Howard Felperin, *Shakespearean Representation: Mimesis and Modernity in Elizabethan Tragedy* (Princeton: Princeton University Press, 1977), 140–141 and 136.

more secular and worldly than religious. The syntax of lines 23 and 24 is particularly interesting because "grace" is both passive and active, and "look" both transitive and intransitive. On the one hand, grace *appears* constant and "looks *so*," appearing as it always should, amidst the dissimulations of "all things foul." On the other hand, by looking hard at "all things foul" and seeing through their dissimulations, grace "*looks* so" and acts against them. In this wonderfully equivocal formulation, grace shifts from an inherent but passive sanctity to a more aggressive hermeneutic strategy. Malcolm's "royal father/was a most sainted King" (4.3.109), but Duncan had "no art/To find the mind's construction in the face" (1.4.11–12). The son is more artful and discerning, determined to see through "the brows of grace." As a result, he regains the throne his father lost. His success is not attributable to sanctity; rather, he relies instead on a cunning stratagem of equivocation and careful scrutiny to test potential friends and adversaries alike. Malcolm aspires not to the God-given grace of sacred kingship. He aims instead for the shrewd poise—or grace—of Machiavelli's prince.

Malcolm then proceeds to test Macduff by lying about his own character. He claims all "particulars of vice" (4.3.52) with an imaginative exuberance for depravity that is increasingly alarming:

> . . . there's no bottom, none,
> In my voluptuousness: your wives, your daughters,
> Your matrons, and yours maids, could not fill up
> The cistern of my lust. (4.3.60–3)

It gets worse. He moves from threats of sexual rapine to warnings of "staunchless avarice" that will make him "cut off the nobles for their lands" (4.3.79–81). Macduff blanches at each of these disclosures but reluctantly accepts them. Perhaps they must be tolerated as the occupational hazards of monarchy. The third strike is too much for Macduff, though, and at this, the tipping point, Shakespeare alters his source. In Holinshed's *Chronicles of Scotland*, Malcolm's final admission is that he is "inclined to dissimulation . . . and all other kinds of deceit," and, for Macduff, this proves "the worst of all, and there I leaue thee." In the play, dissimulation is omitted and replaced by a comprehensive depravity. Malcolm excels, he says, "In the division of each several crime" (4.3.97). Why did Shakespeare replace dissimulation in the catalogue of Malcolm's offenses? He does so, I suspect, because it might be not only a necessary evil for a monarch

intent on retaining his throne, but because it is also the indispensable stock-in-trade of the player. As William O. Scott notes, it is
"the function of the player to lie like truth and of the audience to
believe what it knows to be equivocation."[22] In assuming the role of
a depraved tyrant, Malcolm "out-Herods Herod"—but it turns out
to be just an act.

Malcolm's equivocal performance gives him the upper hand. He
is able to force Macduff's hand by vowing to "Pour the sweet milk
of concord into Hell,/Uproar the universal peace, confound/All unity
on earth" (4.3.99–101) and he seems to confirm his turpitude by
adding, "I am as I have spoken" (4.3.103). For Macduff this is the
last straw, and he embraces a life of exile as his only recourse. But
as soon as Macduff reveals his true feelings, Malcolm abruptly reverses
course and proceeds to "Unspeak mine own detraction . . . My first
false-speaking/Was this upon myself" (4.3.124–132), reducing his
auditor to a stupefied silence. As he considers "each several crime,/*Acting*
it many ways" (4.3.96–97; my italics), Malcolm stands as a fascinating foil to Macbeth. Macbeth has difficulty reflecting on the horrors he undertakes—"I am afraid to think what I have done"
(2.2.49)—but he still must do what for him is unthinkable. By contrast, Malcolm relishes imagining the most heinous crimes without
ever having to commit them. In his exuberant description of his supposedly depraved appetites, he displays the same "gusto" that John
Keats ascribes to the "poetical character" whose contemplative attitude renders its amoral fantasies less menacing. "It does no harm
from its relish of the dark side of things any more than from its
taste for the bright one; because they both end in speculation."[23]
Malcolm has no need to act because he can manipulate others like
Macduff to act on his behalf. His power derives not from action but
"Acting" and equivocation.

In the play's final speech, Malcolm remains a subtle foil to Macbeth
in other ways. He asserts his new authority through a combination
of political cost-calculation and close attention to timing, telling his
nobles that "We shall not spend a large expense of time,/Before we

---

[22] William O. Scott, "Macbeth's—and Our—Self-Equivocations," *Shakespeare Quarterly*
37 (1986), 174.
[23] John Keats, "To Richard Woodhouse," (27 October 1818) in *Selected Poems and
Letters*, ed. Douglas Bush (Boston: Houghton Mifflin, 1959), 279.

reckon with your several loves,/And make us even with you"
(5.11.26–28). He bestows the new title of Earls upon his thanes,
insisting that these honors be distributed equally. Malcolm combines
a sense of urgency about the tasks awaiting him with a determined
composure. Included among his list of things "to do/Which would
be planted newly with the time" are the recall of "our exil'd friends
abroad/That fled the snares of watchful tyranny" and the punishment of those "cruel ministers" who served Macbeth (5.11.30–34).
Malcolm's metaphor for his plans recalls his father's earlier promise
to Macbeth with its scriptural allusion to Jeremiah: "I have begun
to plant thee and will labour/To make thee full of growing" (1.4.28–29).
Yet Malcolm's reference to new planting and new times reflects a
resilient awareness of altered circumstances. In contrast to Malcolm's
assurance, Macbeth's reflections on what he must do seem panicked
and desperate. When Macbeth thinks about killing Duncan, he stands
"here, upon this bank and shoal of time" and prepares to "jump
the life to come" (1.7.6–7), but he already anticipates the defeat of
his "Vaulting ambition, which o'erleaps itself/And falls on th'other"
(1.7.27–8). Shortly afterwards, Lady Macbeth harshly rebukes him
for his defeatism, which she links to bad timing. Previously, when
neither "time, nor place/Did then adhere . . . yet you would make
both" yield, but as soon as "They have made themselves" amenable
to his will, "their fitness now/Does unmake you" (1.7.51–4). Malcolm,
by contrast, can confidently assure himself and his audience in his
last speech that, whatever "needful else/That calls upon us, by the
grace of grace,/We will perform in measure, time, and place"
(5.11.37–9).

Malcolm's peculiar phrase, "the grace of grace" is, in my view,
his most intriguing equivocation. The words recall the traditional
proclamation of sovereignty's sacred authority "*Dei gratia*," and the
line is usually glossed accordingly; in his Oxford edition, Nicholas
Brooke explains it as "the grace of God, apostrophized as the essence
of graciousness."[24] Yet, the phrase's odd redundancy deviates from
the standard formula, and its repetition recalls the portentous doubling—"Double, double" (4.1.10)—of the witches' incantations. As
Gary Wills notes, "'doubling' was another word for equivocation"

---

[24] *The Tragedy of Macbeth*, ed. Nicholas Brooke (Oxford: Clarendon, 1990), 211.

or double-talk, and doubling the word certainly renders its meaning equivocal.[25] Grace can imply political favor and artful elegance as well as divine right. Since royalty was frequently addressed as "Your Grace," the phrase could also mean the grace or patronage of the monarch. *Macbeth* was indeed performed at court before King James I, and Malcolm's admission of his dependence on "the grace of grace" (5.2.38) may sound a note of deference to the play's most eminent spectator and the company's royal patron. The phrase could then stand as a final compliment by the player king to the real king and an implicit recognition of his own humbler, derivative status. Malcolm accepts his role as a stand-in and placeholder for the ruler whose reign was predicted in the fourth act.

In doing so, Malcolm also embraces the role of a "poor player/That struts and frets his hour upon the stage," a role that Macbeth frantically repudiated. When combined with attention to "measure, time and place," the phrase "grace of grace" certainly suggests a notion of grace more performative than religious. For some of Shakespeare's contemporaries, such theatrical and artistic grace was morally suspect, and theatrical double-talk only increased their suspicions. Doubling was a charge frequently leveled against actors by their adversaries. Men like John Stubbes attacked them as "double-dealing ambidexters" whose role-playing made them liars.[26] But those who love and understand the theater recognize that actors are, in words attributed to William Hazlitt, "the only honest hypocrites" because they frankly admit the artifice of their role and performance.[27] "Lying like truth" can thus acquire another less sinister and more positive significance because the equivalence implied cuts both ways. When properly understood, drama's equivocal dissimulations can permit us to see certain realities with greater clarity. In the words of the Chorus of *Henry V*, we can "sit and see;/Minding true things by what their mock'ries be" (4. *Chorus* 52–3). At the same time, the audience's

---

[25] Gary Wills, *Witches and Jesuits: Shakespeare's* Macbeth (New York: Oxford University Press, 1995), 97. See also Frank Kermode on Shakespeare's predilection for various forms of doubling in *Hamlet* (100–114) and its tendency to "introduce unease and mystery into an expression" (102) in *Shakespeare's Language* (New York: Farrar, Straus, Giroux, 2000).

[26] Cited in Evans, 135.

[27] Bert O. States, *Great Reckonings in Little Rooms: On the Phenomenology of Theater* (Berkeley: University of California Press, 1964), 200.

"imaginary puissance" enables its members to participate in the arduous fellowship projected here and elsewhere; Joel Altman has noted the Eucharistic undertones of solidarity in *Henry V*.[28] Malcolm's "thanks to all at once, and to each one" (5.11.40) restores a sense of grateful reciprocity and social communion shattered by Macbeth's reign. Hopes are revived that

> we may again
> Give to our tables meat, sleep to our nights,
> Free from our feasts and banquets bloody knives.
> Do faithful homage, and receive free honors,
> All which we pine for now. (3.6.33–37)

Malcolm's last notes of gratitude and humility resemble those sounded by the epilogue of another player-king and theatrical master of illusion. After posing as an almost omnipotent magus, Prospero also acknowledges the artifice of his illusions and his dependence as a player. Finally, Malcolm's version of an epilogue also offers a more inclusive contrast to the "happy prologues to the swelling act/Of the imperial theme" (1.3.127–128) performed almost entirely within Macbeth's mind. Even as he concedes the derivative qualities of his own "grace of grace," Malcolm renews a sense of connection to his fellow players and his audience.

---

[28] Joel Altman, "'Vile Participation': The Amplification of Violence in the Theater of *Henry V*." *Shakespeare Quarterly* 42 (1991): 1–32.

MAPPING SHAKESPEARE'S BRITAIN

Peter Holland

Late one evening, a farmer in Eastern Europe suddenly heard a knock at the door. Outside were overcoated officials from Russia and Poland. They explained that they were redrawing the boundary line, the border between the two countries, and the line went straight through the man's farm. 'You have a perfectly free choice', they explained, 'No pressure at all. You can either be in Poland or in Russia but we need an immediate answer.' 'That's easy: I'd like to be in Poland.' 'That's fine, no problem but, just out of curiosity, why did you pick Poland?' 'Oh, the winters are better there.'

History is written in the drawing of national borders and border lines are a visible manifestation of the politics of map-making, what Shakespeare contemptuously calls in *Troilus and Cressida* "mapp'ry" (1.2.205),[1] a word so rare *OED* can offer only this example before 1840. Whether they are straight lines that divide countries along lines of latitude or longitude or complex lines following the course of a river, the line is the central feature of human intervention in the political acts of cartography, a manifestation visible on the landscape only through the accompaniment of such symbolic acts, the barbed wire and border posts, the barriers and human presences that enunciate the language of nation as limited space and a nation's own sense of perimeter. On the map the habit of coloring for empires also demonstrates possession, the ownership of territory far removed from the nation at the heart of its colonialism.

National histories are defined through geographies, not the whole earth analysis that is the true province of geography but the partial mappings and explorations, the study of regionality that made up the new early modern discipline of chorography, not only the delineation on the map but also the description, the analytic account both of the landscape and the history of human interventions on that landscape, in towns and castles, villages and battlegrounds, the whole

---

[1] All quotations from Shakespeare are from *The Complete Works*, eds. Stanley Wells, Gary Taylor *et al.* (Oxford: The Clarendon Press, 1986).

course of human activity which is indivisible from that delineation.[2]
As William Cunningham defined it in 1559, as the word "chorography"
makes its entrance into English usage, in his book *The Cosmographical
Glasse*, there is already the beginnings of a definition of chorography
as a discipline separable from geography,

> For lyke as Cosmographie describeth the worlde, Geographie th'earth:
> in lyke sorte Chorographie, sheweth the partes of th'earth, divided in
> them selves. And severally describeth, the portes, Rivers, Havens,
> Fluddes, Hilles, Mountaynes, Cities, Villages, Buildinges, Fortresses,
> Walles, yea, and every particular thing, in that parte conteined. (6–7)

In Cunningham's sequence he moves from the natural to the human,
from rivers, havens and floods to cities, villages and buildings. As I
shall return to much later, the history of early modern English cartography to some extent recapitulates that sequence as the subsequent remappings, from Saxton to Norden to Speed, make increasingly
prominent the human over the natural, and the local over the regional.
Yet the natural is not impermeable to the human:

> See how this river comes me cranking in,
> And cuts me from the best of all my land,
> A huge half-moon, a monstrous cantle, out.
> I'll have the current in this place dammed up,
> And here the smug and silver Trent shall run,
> In a new channel fair and evenly. (*I Henry IV*, 3.1.95–100)

---

[2] On the rise of chorography, see Richard Helgerson, *Forms of Nationhood* (Chicago:
University of Chicago Press, 1992), esp. pp. 105–147. For its application to the
study of Shakespeare's English histories, though not his British ones, see especially
Michael Neill, "'The Exact Map or Discovery of Human Affairs': Shakespeare and
the Plotting of History" in *Putting History to the Question* (New York: Columbia University
Press, 2000), pp. 372–97 and Phyllis Rackin, *Stages of History* (London: Routledge,
1990), especially her now well-known comment that "[t]he movement from *Richard
II* to *Henry V* resembles the movement in Renaissance historiography from chronicle to chorography, from the history of royal dynasty to the maps and geographical descriptions that assembled a picture of national identity from the component
parts of the land" (p. 137). On mapping and Shakespeare see also especially John
Gillies, *Shakespeare and the Geography of Difference* (Cambridge: Cambridge University
Press, 1994); Bruce Avery, "Gelded Continents and Plenteous Rivers: Cartography
as Rhetoric in Shakespeare" in John Gillies and Virginia Mason Vaughan, eds.,
Playing the Globe: Genre and Geography in English Renaissance Drama (Madison: Fairleigh
Dickinson Press, 1998), pp. 46–62; Garrett A. Sullivan, Jr., *The Drama of Landscape*
(Stanford: Stanford University Press, 1998), pp. 92–158. See also Jess Edwards,
"How to Read an Early Modern Map: Between the Particular and the General,
the Material and the Abstract, Words and Mathematics," *Early Modern Literary Studies*
9.1 (May, 2003): 6.1–58 <URL: *http://purl.oclc.org/emls/09-1/edwamaps.html*>.

In the politics of maps we are of course aware of the two crucial examples in Shakespeare, the map of England being divided up and redivided here in Hotspur's irritation in *1 Henry IV* and the map of Britain being divided up in *King Lear*. Hotspur's refusal to accept the map as an account of the new political division will instead require a future new survey, of the kind that had been undertaken for the counties of England by Christopher Saxton between 1574 and 1579, so that the map can in future accurately represent the retrenched river. The local chorography would then reflect both the moved Trent and the political consequences of possession that would have caused the winding river to be even. The new survey would have recorded the history of division, mapping as a marking of history as well as geography.

It is immediately striking how comparatively infrequently maps appear on the early modern stage. Alan Dessen and Leslie Thomson, in their *Dictionary of Stage Directions in English Drama: 1580–1642* (Cambridge, 1999), list only two, neither of which are the examples from Shakespeare since, such is the nature of their work, there is no stage direction to refer to the maps and hence they cannot be indexed. The later example is in Middleton's *Anything for a Quiet Life* (performed around 1621) where, as Knavesby tries to persuade the Cressinghams to buy land in Clangibbon in Ireland, a map of the estates is produced for Sir Francis to consider: "'What's this, Marsh ground?' 'No, these are Boggs, but a little Cost will drain them'."[3] The map here is an example of by far the commonest form of early modern mapping, the delineation of an estate to mark out owner-ship, the map's extents equivalent to the limits of possession.

Dessen and Thomson's earlier example is the map that is brought on for the dying Tamburlaine to consider in Marlowe's play, a map across which he can chart his past and lament the absence of the future: "Here I began to martch towards *Persea*" but also "And shall I die, and this unconquered?"[4] Tamburlaine's map here is written over with his biography, just as, in Part 1, he proposed to redefine both the outline form of contemporary maps and their contents:

---

[3] Thomas Middleton, *Anything for a Quiet Life* (1662), sig. F1r.
[4] Christopher Marlowe, *The Complete Works*, vol. 5 ed. David Fuller and Edward J. Esche (Oxford: Clarendon Press, 1998), 5.3.127 and 151.

> I will confute those blind Geographers
> That make a triple region in the world,
> Excluding Regions which I mean to trace,
> And with this pen reduce them to a Map,
> Calling the Provinces, Citties and townes
> After my name and thine *Zenocrate*. (4.4.81–6)

The conventional triple pattern of the early form of universal maps, what are called T-O maps (that is, a world map centered on Jerusalem and divided into three regions, Europe, Africa and Asia), is insufficient for Tamburlaine's ambition and his sense of the geography of the world: there are regions that lie beyond the geographers' records, their construction of knowledge, and he will draw these spaces beyond the three continents and subject them—the word "reduce" comprises both possibilities—and, most significantly, rename them, leaving a different kind of recording of his geographical presence in the transformation of place-names, that activity of which, in the context of Ireland, Brian Friel has written so brilliantly in his play *Translations* (1981).

But it is remarkable that there are no more examples of maps on stage. Being suspicious of Dessen and Thomson's methodology I have checked the occurrences of the word 'map' and its cognates on the Literature On-line database for the period 1580–1620 and can find only two more occurrences that are as firmly unequivocal as these two and the two in Shakespeare. One I mention here: the anonymous play *The Puritan* was performed by the St Paul's boys company in 1606 and, since the 1607 quarto announced that it was written by "W.S.," it found itself added to the Shakespeare canon among the apocryphal plays included in the 1664 second issue of the Third Folio; at one moment in its frenetic action, George Pyeboard tries to occupy the Serjeants who come to arrest him with maps that are clearly present on stage but Serjeant Puttock is sceptical: "these Mappes are prittie painted things, but I could nere fancie 'em yet, mee thinkes they're too busie, and full of Circles and Coniurations, they say all the world's in one of them, but I could nere find the Counter in the Poultrie".[5] Puttock cannot find the one place that is most significant for him, the debtors' prison where he takes those he arrests. He cannot, that is, locate his own world on the map,

[5] *The Puritan* (1607), sig. E4r.

cannot find himself in relation to the "Circles and Conjurations," the quasi-magical forms of representations out of which maps are constructed. Raven, the other Serjeant, isn't surprised: "how could you finde it? For you know it stands behind the houses." Dogson, their yeoman, elaborates this sense in which the map ought to replicate the physical reality it signifies: "Masse, that's true, then we must looke ath' back-side fort; Sfoote here's nothing, all's bare." Turning the map over shows only the absence of its marks. But Puttock, though he finds maps overcrowded and busy, would still prefer them to be busier with a different kind of blurring between the real and the representational: "I should love these Maps out a crye now, if wee could see men peepe out of doore in em, oh wee might haue em in a morning to our Breake-fast so finely, and nere knocke our heeles to the ground a whole day for em." If work could be accomplished within the reality of the map rather than of that to which the map alludes, life would be easier for the workers.

Those missing markings, the absence of the people to whom the human geography of mapping alludes, are gaps that Puttock regrets. Their presence is of course at the same time a dense signifier of human histories, since few maps show only or primarily a nonhuman landscape, the ones in Michael Drayton's *Poly-Olbion* (1612) with their emphases on rivers and other natural features and representations of what are in effect the *genii loci*, the spirits of each place, being a marked exception. But, just as throughout the early modern period the making of maps was itself an assertion of a moment of history and the charting of histories, especially histories of ownership, so in *King Lear*, the play with which I shall be primarily concerned for its mapping of a particular concept of Britain, the map in the first scene functions powerfully in relation to histories of mapping as well as histories of ownership. In a brilliant passage in his autobiography, Ingmar Bergman describes *King Lear* as itself a continent:

> We equipped expeditions which with varying skill and success mapped a few heaths, a river, a few shores, a mountain, forests. All the countries of the world equipped expeditions; sometimes we came across one another on our wanderings and established in despair that what was an inland lake yesterday had turned into a mountain today. We drew our maps, commented and described, but nothing fitted.[6]

[6] See Ingmar Bergman, *The Magic Lantern* (London: Penguin Books, 1988), pp. 258–9. My thanks to Russell Jackson for pointing out this passage.

In this vision of a metamorphic landscape, Bergman marks the impossibility of mapping. Within the play itself the landscape has a certain stability but the action's re-mapping still hovers at the outermost edge of the possible.

My aim is to place that mapping of Britain at the opening of *King Lear* in a set of contexts, a series of adjacencies that function for me as ways of reading the map, a way of using context as thickening of meaning that also functions as a paradigm of this map in multiple histories, an early modern one and *King Lear*'s history. I shall move on to consider the map in stage and film versions of the play and the map in connection with Elizabethan and Jacobean mapping of England. I want, though, first to try to bring a group of other dramatic or performative works into relationship with *King Lear*, to create for a moment a different kind of density of dramatic presence from that which the play is usually given, to surround the play with other images of Britain.

The first three are plays that have centrally to do with the division of Britain. I mention briefly here a fourth but will not pursue it: *Gorboduc*, a play that, for all its interest in the consequence of the division of the kingdom, seems to me not to be particularly active in London by 1606. There had been no edition of *Gorboduc* since 1590[7] and no sign of a continuing performance presence in England, though there was an important performance in the Great Hall of Dublin Castle in September 1601 before Mountjoy, the Lord Deputy of Ireland who had perhaps chosen the play to define his position in relation to the rebellion by O'Neill, the Earl of Tyrone, and the imminent arrival of an invading Spanish force in Kinsale.[8] Of my three two are tied up with that company that has such a probably crucial presence in Shakespeare's life, the Queen's Men. Since Scott McMillin and Sally-Beth MacLean's brilliant and measured study, certainly the most outstanding exploration of an early modern theatre company we yet have, the case for Shakespeare's close knowledge of the Queen's Men's repertory seems to me conclusive.[9] Whether

---

[7] In 1590 it appeared as an addition to Lydgate's *The Serpent of Deuision* (STC 17029).

[8] See Christopher Morash, *A History of Irish Theatre, 1601–2000* (Cambridge: Cambridge University Press, 2001), pp. 2–3. My thanks to Kevin de Ornellas for pointing out this reference.

[9] Scott McMillin and Sally-Beth MacLean, *The Queen's Men and their Plays* (Cambridge: Cambridge University Press, 1998).

he joined them as an actor after the death of William Knell in Thame in 1587 does not matter. What is significant is his evident connection with their repertory, including, of course, the unpronounceable *King Leir*.[10]

One other play that may have been in the Queen's Men's repertory, the first of my three contextual plays, is *Locrine*, published in 1595, without a specific link to the Queen's Men on its title-page, by Thomas Creede who published a number of other Queen's Men's plays. Though McMillin and MacLean are typically careful in seeing no more than a possible case for its inclusion,[11] its links with *Selimus* strengthen the connection. More significant is Katherine Duncan-Jones's recent advocacy of the identity of the W.S. named on this title-page, like *The Puritan*, for *Locrine* is "Newly set foorth, overseene and corrected" by W.S. The play's author might well have been Charles Tilney who was helped out for the dumb shows by Sir George Buc, later Master of the Revels, according to a manuscript note in Buc's hand on a copy.[12] As Duncan-Jones puts it, "there is no good reason to doubt that [Shakespeare] was indeed the "overseer" of the text."[13] I would not go so far but I do not find it remotely improbable that Shakespeare knew the play.

Of course the action of *Locrine* is not the *Lear* narrative but its status as a triumphantly British drama, a narrative of national success for a nation that had once existed and would not begin to exist again until after James's accession in 1603, is intriguing. There are comparatively few Elizabethan plays on *British*, rather than English, history (and not much of a rash of them after 1603): we can add to *Gorboduc*, *King Leir* and *Locrine*, little else beyond the multi-authored Gray's Inn play *The Misfortunes of Arthur* (1587). *The Misfortunes of Arthur*, by the way, has a number of fascinating resonances with *King Lear*—though I should emphasise that I am not arguing for it as source, simply as a kind of dramatic context: its cast includes the Duke of Cornwall, the King of Albanie and Arthur "King of great

---

[10] The problem is, of course, to differentiate *Leir* from *Lear*, something no speaker seems able to do.

[11] Ibid., p. 92.

[12] W. W. Greg, 'Three Manuscript Notes by Sir George Buc' *The Library* 4th ser., 12 (1932), pp. 307–21.

[13] Katherine Duncan-Jones, *Ungentle Shakespeare* (London: The Arden Shakespeare, 2001), p. 42.

Brytain"[14] as well as a great battle at Dover between Arthur and
Mordred who is assisted by foreign princes and British earls (compare the French forces of Cordelia with the Earl of Kent) to whom
Mordred offers a division of the kingdom with one to receive "all
Brytish lands that lie/Betweene the floud of Humber, and the *Scottes*,"
one to have "The *Albane* Crowne" and one "The *Cornish* Dukedome"
(2.4.21–2, 33, 40). It is striking then that all four of these British
history plays concern the division of the kingdom. It was, in effect,
impossible to think dramatically of British history without also thinking of the mapping of division.

  In the case of *Locrine* the play is an account of the first division
of Britain, the turning of Brutus's united land into a divided one, a
necessary and pragmatic response both to Brutus's imminent death
and to the presence of the three sons, Locrine, Albanact and Camber.
Brutus's is not a full-scale division of the kingdom into thirds; Locrine
is to be "a captain to thy brethren" given "the regal crown" while
Camber is given "the South for thy dominion" and Albanact, "thy
father's only joy,/Youngest in years, but not the youngest in mind"
is told "Take thou the North for thy dominion."[15] Is it over-fanciful
to hear in those words to Albanact some kind of pre-echo of Lear's
words to Cordelia? Perhaps, but I also note that the division is, in
Locrine's case, as with Lear's daughters, bound up with marriage,
as Brutus arranges his son's marriage to the "peerless Guendoline"
(1.2.197). I also note at this point that there is no description offered
by Brutus of the country that is being divided up, except for his
comment that Albanact's northern share is "A country full of hills
and raggèd rocks,/Replenishèd with fierce untamèd beasts," a moment
of chorography whose significance is less regional than individual,
the country matching the individual's temperament: it is a country
"correspondent to thy martial thoughts" (1.2.208–10). These two lines
are conventional and therefore reasonably similar to—though I do
not want to argue an influence on—the only two lines of description in Lear's division: "With shadowy forests and with champaigns
riched,/With plenteous rivers and wide-skirted meads" (1.1.64–5).

---

[14] Brian Jay Corrigan, ed., *The Misfortunes of Arthur: A Critical, Old-Spelling Edition*
(New York: Garland Publishing, Inc., 1992), p. 73.
[15] *The Lamentable Tragedy of Locrine: A Critical Edition* ed. Jane Lytton Gooch (New
York: Garland Publishing Inc., 1981), 1.2.150, 189, 200, 204–7.

Brutus's division is rational, a strategy for controlling the kingdom with, as it were, a president and two vice-presidents, that fails only when, after Albanact's death, Locrine falls in love with his murderer's widow. Brutus in, for example, Holinshed creates three distinct nations, effectively named after his sons: Albania (Scotland), Cambria (Wales) and Loegria (England).[16] But the author of *Locrine* denies the completeness of this separation, instead both allowing the putative ruler of England a triumphant control over the others and relocating the geography of the drawing of the line: Camber rules the south, not the West, and Albanact's land is not explicitly coterminous with Scotland. The map is redrawn to accord with a hierarchical structure that early modern historiography had not anticipated. There is no hint of a critique of the division in the play—nor indeed is there in Holinshed's *Chronicles*—only of Locrine's irrational sexual desire. There is also no map.

But the second case that I want to place alongside *King Lear* is, similar to but far more troubling than the division in *Locrine*, supremely rational. *Thomas of Woodstock*, also often known as *Richard II Part 1*, is mostly familiar as a supposed source for Shakespeare's *Richard II*, narrating the events preceding Shakespeare's action. As such it seems to belong to an earlier date and an earlier period of Shakespeare's work. But recent work by Mac Jackson has produced a startlingly later re-dating for the play.[17] Jackson's investigation of vocabulary and of verse forms, among other characteristics, completely undermines the conventional claim for the play as coming from 1592–3. Instead Jackson's thoroughly convincing arguments place it some ten years later, in the first decade of the 17th century, and therefore written as a deliberate prequel to Shakespeare's *Richard II* and not a source.

The division of the kingdom in *Woodstock* is a terrifying scene. Tresilian reads the conditions: the four recipients "all jointly here stand bound to pay your majesty, or your deputy, wherever you remain, seven thousand pounds a month for this your kingdom."[18]

---

[16] See *Holinshed's Chronicles of England, Scotland, and Ireland* 6 vols., (London, 1807), 1:443–4.

[17] See Macd. P. Jackson, "Shakespeare's *Richard II* and the Anonymous *Thomas of Woodstock*," *MRDE* 4 (2002), 17–65.

[18] A. P. Rossiter, ed., *Woodstock: A Moral History* (London: Chatto and Windus, 1946), 4.1.182–4.

The legal document defines the handing over the kingdom, its leas-
ing out, in terms that might well have infuriated Shakespeare's Gaunt.
But when the king turns to the details of the division what is most
striking is the extraordinary weight of detail that it attracts. This
time there is a map (another that Dessen and Thomson cannot list).
Richard asks for it: "Reach me the map" (4.1.220)—again, and perhaps only driven by my major concern, I find a possible pre-echo
of *King Lear* "Give me the map there" (F 1.1.37), though how many
ways are there for a king to demand a map? He then moves on to
the division: "we may allot their portions, and part the realm amongst
them equally./You four shall here by us divide yourselves into the
nine-and-thirty shires and counties of my kingdom parted thus:—/
(Come stand by me and mark those shires assigned ye)" (4.1.220–5).
But as the five crowd round the map with four eagerly watching
what they will receive, Richard does not simply mark lines and speak
of them; instead he lists the 39 shires and counties he is handing
over. "Bagot, thy lot betwixt the Thames and sea thus lies: Kent, Surrey,
Sussex, Hampshire, Berkshire, Wiltshire, Dorsetshire, Somersetshire,
Devonshire, Cornwall, those parts are thine/As amply, Bagot, as the
crown is mine" (226–30). Bushy receives Wales "together with our
counties of Gloster, Wo'ster, Hereford, Shropshire, Staffordshire and
Cheshire: there's thy lot" (234–5); Scroope's land goes "From Trent
to Tweed" and includes "All Yorkshire, Derbyshire, Lancashire,
Cumberland, Westmoreland, and Northumberland" (238–40).
Mockingly, Richard turns last to Greene, by this point looking a
little peeved, "Now my Greene, what have I left for thee?" (242)

> I kept thee last to make thy part the greatest.
> See here sweet Greene:—
> Those shires are thine, even from the Thames to Trent:
> Thou here shalt lie, i' the middle of my land.

This erotics of this division is then completed by Greene's list, an extraordinary detailing of the remaining 17 shires in one single run: "Thou
hast London, Middlesex,/Essex, Suffolk, Norfolk, Cambridgeshire,/
Hertfordshire, Bedfordshire, Buckinghamshire,/Oxfordshire, Northamptonshire,/Rutlandshire, Leicestershire, Warwickshire, Huntingdon-
shire;/And Lincolnshire—there's your portion sir" (252–7).

   In a fine article, "The Scene of Cartography in *King Lear*," an
article that has provoked a great deal of my thinking in this paper,
John Gillies has rightly commented on the parallels here between

Greene and Cordelia, both placed structurally last, both especially favoured (Greene alone is identified as Richard's 'minion'), each given the richest piece of land.[19] But I am less happy with Gillies's assumption that the map must be a hand-prop simply because of "the sheer exhaustiveness of the geographical detail in the dialogue" (p. 113). Gillies finds something excessive about the passage where I find it powerful as a litany of space, a counting of the shires, an indexing of Richard's England that will be fully Richard's no more.

Shakespeare, if he did indeed know *Thomas of Woodstock*, must have seen it only a few years before writing *King Lear* (or seen a manuscript like the only version that survives). Its method of creating the account—or more properly the accounting—of the nation is a conscious and inimitable creation of the kinds of chorographical sequence that marked Elizabethan cartography and chorography. These projects can be seen first in Christopher Saxton's maps, engraved between 1574 and 1579 and brought together into a single volume atlas in 1579, "the earliest uniform national atlas produced by any country,"[20] and a twenty-sheet wall map in 1583; secondly in Camden's *Britannia*, first published in Latin in 1586 (going through six editions by 1607) and published in English in 1610 in Philemon Holland's translation, the 1607 Latin and 1610 English edition carrying maps based on Saxton and John Norden, drawn by William Kip, the inclusion of which Camden has planned as early as 1589;[21] thirdly, in the two parts of *Speculum Britanniae* covering Middlesex and Hertfordshire, the only completed segments of John Norden's project to be published,

---

[19] See John Gillies, "The Scene of Cartography in *King Lear*" in Andrew Gordon and Bernhard Klein, eds., *Literature, Mapping, and the Politics of Space in Early Modern Britain* (Cambridge: Cambridge University Press, 2001), pp. 109–37, esp. pp. 120–1. Klein has some brief comments on the play in Bernhard Klein, *Maps and the Writing of Space in Early Modern England and Ireland* (Basingstoke: Palgrave, 2001).

[20] John Goss, *The Mapmaker's Art* (Skokie, Illinois: Rand McNally, 1993), p. 161. On Saxton, see especially Sarah Tyacke and John Huddy, *Christopher Saxton and Tudor Map-making* (London: The British Library, 1980). For other work on Tudor maps see also Sarah Tyacke, ed., *English Map-making 1500–1650* (London: The British Library, 1983); P. D. A. Harvey, *Maps in Tudor England* (London: The Public Record Office and The British Library, 1993); and, for a longer vista, Catherine Delano-Smith and Roger J. P. Kain, *English Maps: A History* (London: The British Library, 1999), esp. pp. 49–111.

[21] See R. A. Skelton, *County Atlases of the British Isles 1579–1850: A Bibliography* (Folkestone: Wm Dawson and Sons, 1978), p. 26.

in 1593 and 1598 respectively, containing maps and extensive accompanying listings; and finally, a few years later, in John Speed's superb 1611 volume, *The Theatre of the Empire of Great Britaine*. All are part of the growing mass of Jacobean chorography. Camden's *Britannia* was first published in Latin in 1586 with the subtitle identifying it as *chorographica descriptio* while Holland's 1610 translation as *Britain, or A chorographicall description of the most flourishing kingdomes, England, Scotland, and Ireland, and the ilands adioyning, out of the depth of antiquitie*, brings the regionalism to the fore. These projects—Saxton, Camden, Norden and Speed—provide the chorological context for *King Lear* and I shall return to them later.

Shakespeare would rightly and inevitably chose a radically different method from *Thomas of Woodstock* in *King Lear*, a massive refusal of such detailing. In *1 Henry IV*, the lines are clear if not on the stage then at least to anyone with a rudimentary knowledge of English geography:

> The Archdeacon hath divided it
> Into three limits very equally.
> England from Trent and Severn hitherto
> By south and east is to my part assigned;
> All westward—Wales beyond the Severn shore
> And all the fertile land within that bound—
> To Owain Glyndŵr; and, dear coz, to you
> The remnant northward lying off from Trent. (3.1.69–76)

It has a precision mid-way between the deliberate exhaustiveness of the scene in *Thomas of Woodstock* and the equally deliberate imprecision of *King Lear*, "Of all these bounds even from this line to this ... this ample third ... A third more opulent" (1.1.63, 80, 86). *Thomas of Woodstock*, as a development of Shakespeare's method in *1 Henry IV*, marked the limit of that approach. In moving from a known England with its counties which had been the subject of such exhaustive, popular and prestigious study as in Camden's and others' work to a Britain that belonged to a historical past connected with but discontinuous from the present growing political reality of Great Britain— something that, for instance, would constitute Elizabethan cartographers' representations of particular kinds of national and local histories in their maps—Shakespeare shapes a vagueness that would pose its especial problems to directors having to show this map.

My third play in this group is, of course, *The True Chronicle History of King Leir and His Three Daughters*, first published in 1605. In a recent scholarly study, Richard Knowles has persuasively argued that the detailed evidence for Shakespeare's use of this source play shows that he was using the edition of 1605 and that there is no conclusive evidence for its influence on his earlier work derived from whatever contact he may have had with it in the Queen's Men's repertory. Shakespeare's choice to organize the opening of his play in marked contrast to *King Leir* had been prompted by reading an old play newly published.[22] It is worth remembering the action of the opening sequence in the play. It begins with the funeral of Leir's queen, a figure so typically suppressed in Shakespeare's version of the narrative. None of the daughters is married. Leir is thoughtfully and wisely advised by his sensible counsellors to marry his daughters to "some of your neighbour Kings,/Bordring within the bounds of Albion,/By whose united friendship, this our state/May be protected 'gainst all forrayne hate,"[23] a sense of the potential unity of the geographical unit of the island, Albion, set against the foreign threat of continental Europe. The love-test here is explicitly a stratagem, explained by Leir to his counsellors, to ensure that pressure can be put on Cordella, who, annoyingly, "vowes/No liking to a Monarch, vnlesse loue allowes" even though "She is solicited by diuers Peeres" (61–3); the love-test will make her agree to be matched "with a King of Brittany" (91), the word used here not to indicate a part of France but as a form of Britain that will rhyme with "policy." Gonorill will marry the *King* of Cornwall, Ragan the *King* of Cambria—and I note, incidentally, that the status of the suitors is, as the noble advised, of equal rank with Leir himself. Cordella's intended husband is the King of Hibernia, the Irish King, not self-evidently a monarch within the island but clearly conceived of as being within a concept of Albion as Britain. Significantly there is no sign of Scotland in the play. Given the westward bias of the two husbands of the elder sisters, it is significant too that the division is not predetermined; as Leir announces,

> My Kingdome I do equally deuide.
> Princes, draw lots, and take your chaunce as falles.
> *Then they draw lots.*
> These I resigne as freely vnto you,
> As earst by true succession they were mine.

---

[22] See Richard Knowles, "How Shakespeare Knew *King Leir*" *Shakespeare Survey 55* (Cambridge: Cambridge University Press, 2002), pp. 12–35.
[23] *The History of King Leir 1605*, ed. W. W. Greg (Oxford: Oxford University Press for the Malone Society, 1907), ll. 52–6.

> And here I do freely dispossesse my selfe,
> And make you two my true adopted heyres:
> My selfe will soiorne with my sonne of Cornwall,

[confusingly in view of Shakespeare's play, this means he will be staying with Gonorill]

> And take me to my prayers and my beades.
> I know, my daughter *Ragan* will be sorry,
> Because I do not spend my dayes with her:
> Would I were able to be with both at once;
> They are the kindest Gyrles in Christendome. (549–61)

Cornwall and Cambria had anticipated getting equal shares, halves, in a conversation earlier, each getting "The moity of halfe his Regiment" (441), with the same ambiguity about whether a moiety is a half which Shakespeare so cunningly pursues in the opening lines of his play "neither can make choice of either's moiety" (1.1.6). The arbitrary nature of the division here and the movement of the action eventually towards France mean that the division can stay unmapped, unlocated, dis-placed.

Cumulatively, the texts I have been looking at figure the dramatic possibilities of a divided Britain as Elizabethan dramatists, including Shakespeare himself, had explored the topos by the time *King Lear* was being written. But the second group of works I want to place briefly beside *King Lear* is a new and particular kind of outcropping of British performance after 1603 within the context of a newly emerging Jacobean Britain. Britain itself—or more properly, given the particular forms of representation, herself—appeared in Dekker's *The Magnificent Entertainment*, the performances at James's coronation procession through London on 15th March 1604. At the first of the seven gates of the spectacle, set up at Fenchurch, the design, not by Dekker but by Ben Jonson, showed at the top a figure Dekker called simply "*The Brittayne Monarchy*"[24] but which Jonson describes more fully. The theme of the first gate was London itself and was dominated by 'Monarchia Britannica' because London was "*camera regia*," the king's chamber. Jonson quotes Camden's *Britannia* here: London is "the epitome of the whole of Britain, the seat of the British Empire,

---

[24] Thomas Dekker, *The Dramatic Works*, ed. Fredson Bowers 4 vols. (Cambridge: Cambridge University Press, 1953–61), 2.260.

and of the kingdoms,"[25] Britain, "a woman, richly attyr'd," with the two crowns of England and Scotland above her throne and with "her hayre" symbolically "bound into foure severall points, descending from her crownes," becomes visible here, a Britain not yet Great but one whose position is unequivocal.

Something similar in making Britain present in spectacle was the major part of the pageant for the new Lord Mayor written by Anthony Munday and put on by the Merchant-Taylors Company on 29th October 1605, *The Triumphs of Re-United Britannia*. If, as is of course quite possibly the case, Shakespeare had never come across the play *Locrine*, let alone rewritten it, he could have seen the events of that division of the kingdom dramatised in Munday's pageant where Britannia, "a fayre and beautifull Nymph," tells Brutus that "his conquest of her virgine honour . . . she reckons to be the very best of her fortunes."[26] The children who perform the pageant narrate the history in the characters of Brutus, the three kingdoms he created, his three sons, Troia Nova (London, the city founded by Brutus) and the three great rivers, Thames, Severn and Humber, the last two being, as Munday's preface identifies, the initial boundaries between the three kingdoms, before "the limits of Loegria were enlarged" and the Tweed and the Solway became "the principal boundes betweene us and *Scotland*."[27]

The links and parallels, stopping far short of influence, between *King Lear* and Munday's pageant were well explored by Richard Dutton in an article in 1986.[28] Dutton points to the allusive nature of Munday's pageant, its assumptions of spectator knowledge of the early history of Britain and, in particular, to the leap of Gogmagog, a member of the indigenous population of "uncivill, monstrous huge men of stature, tearmed Giants"; Gogmagog was thrown off a cliff by Brutus's counselor Corineus, the father of Guendoline in *Locrine*, a leap "at a place beside *Dover*" as a result of which "*Brute* gave unto *Corineus* a part of his lande, which according to his name, was, and

[25] Ben Jonson, *Works*, ed. C. H. Herford and P. and E. Simpson 11 vols. (Oxford: The Clarendon Press, 1925–52), 7.84 (my translation).
[26] David M. Bergeron, ed., *Pageants and Entertainments of Anthony Munday: A Critical Edition* (New York: Garland Publishing, Inc., 1985), p. 6.
[27] Ibid., p. 4.
[28] Richard Dutton, "*King Lear, The Triumphs of Reunited Britannia* and 'The Matter of Britain'," *Literature and History*, 12 (1986), pp. 139–51.

yet is unto this day, called *Cornwall*."[29] The complex etymologies of place, like the naming of Britain itself on which Camden and others spend so much space, here link across the different narratives that lie behind *King Lear*: Cornwall, Corineus and a fall from a cliff near Dover.

For Dutton the significance of Dover lies not only in its presence in the Gloucester narrative but also in its placing as "one of the three supposed 'corners' of Britain,"[30] a space alluded to by Munday's placing his figures on "a Mount triangular, as the Island of *Britayne* it selfe is described to bee,"[31] and which in Holinshed and Camden (and many others) are located at the tip of Cornwall, at Dover and at Caithness in Scotland. As Dutton notes, "Shakespeare had invoked all three 'corners' of that triangle in his play, in the names of the characters," since he includes both Cornwall and Albany, from Holinshed, but, Dutton goes on,

> it was Shakespeare's own decision to make Lear's staunchest advisor the Earl of Kent and to concentrate so much of the action . . . near Dover. His is the only version of the Lear story to project the action so clearly against the traditional symbol of the three-cornered island.[32]

Though Dutton does not discuss it, the three-cornered island will be divided into three in *King Lear* which was performed before the person who is the true focus of Munday's pageant, James.[33] I do not want to consider the much-examined significance of the Boxing Day performance of *King Lear* before King James,[34] except to emphasise the possible presence there of two of the three dukes James had created, the only three dukes in Britain, the Dukes of Cornwall and Albany. As Andrew Gurr has recently reminded us, there were no dukes in England after Elizabeth had executed the Duke of Norfolk in 1571. The most senior rank was earl. But James had made Prince Henry Duke of Cornwall in 1605 and Henry's younger brother had

---

[29] Bergeron, p. 4.

[30] Dutton, p. 142.

[31] Bergeron, p. 4.

[32] Dutton, p. 143.

[33] Marie Axton suggests that James was present at Munday's pageant but there is no evidence that he was; see *The Queen's Two Bodies* (London: Royal Historical Society, 1977), p. 136.

[34] See, for instance, Leah Marcus, *Local Reading and its Discontents* (Berkeley: University of California Press, 1988), pp. 148–59.

been Duke of Albany since 1601, a fact which, as Gurr suggests, must have "prompt[ed] a *frisson* at the very outset of the performance":[35] "I had thought the King had more affected the Duke of Albany than Cornwall" (1.1.1–2).

This balance of king and dukes, strikingly unlike the status of the equivalent characters in *King Leir*, seems to me to matter. More than anyone has noted, *King Lear* is a play concerned about the status relationship of king to dukes, a relationship in part mirrored by the relationship of the *King* of France and the *Duke* of Burgundy, a figure whose historic equivalents were in continual conflict with the Kings of France, until Burgundy was annexed on the death of Charles the Bold in 1477, conflicts which were intensified not least by problems over marriages, as the rulers of Burgundy fought to maintain the independence of their territory which extended north across the Netherlands, making it as geographically proximate to Cordelia's share as France was.

The moment of this performance, as the title page of the quarto stated, on "*S. Stephans night,*"[36] that is, 26th December 1606, is the culmination of the play's accumulation of its own histories but its subsequent histories rethink its mappings. From the contexts of division and the early modern mapping of Britain, I want to turn to the play's performance histories, to see how the map has figured in particular productions. I suggested earlier that the map poses a problem for directors. I want to note four of their solutions, examining them for their mapping of the symbolic geography of each production's views of the play's politics.[37] In Michael Elliott's television version (1983), with Olivier as Lear, a massive map, backed by hides, is unrolled across the floor of the space in front of the king—little in the theatre is ever new: Jackie Bratton notes the same thing being done in 1923 in a production in Florence.[38] Before speaking, Goneril responds to a gesture from Lear and throws herself prostrate on the

---

[35] Andrew Gurr, "Headgear as a Paralinguistic Signifier in *King Lear*," *Shakespeare Survey 55* (Cambridge: Cambridge University Press, 2002), pp. 43–52, p. 45.

[36] Title-page of Q 1608.

[37] Kenneth Rothwell also considers them in his rather disappointing article, "In Search of Nothing: Mapping *King Lear*" in Lynda E.Boose and Richard Burt, eds., *Shakespeare the Movie* (London: Routledge, 1997), pp. 135–47.

[38] J. S. Bratton, ed., *King Lear: Plays in Performance* (Bristol: Bristol Classical Press, 1987), p. 65.

map, kissing it, saluting, as it were, the sign of nation. Regan, later, kneels before her father and, just as she is about to kiss his hand, kisses the map first, with a smile shared with her father, displaying herself as a daughter who has learned from her sister's example. This repeated emphasis on the map's potency makes it a symbol in some respects stronger than the crown itself: when this Lear confirms the redivision in two, "This coronet" (1.1.139)[39] is his own crown, not Cordelia's, and he throws it onto the map where it rolls across it with no respect for the boundaries Lear has drawn. But it is the drawing of the boundaries themselves that intrigues for, by the use of an overhead shot, Elliott makes clear who gets what: Olivier's sword marks the north for Goneril and the west for Regan, leaving for Cordelia a vast tract of England, even bigger than Greene's share in *Thomas of Woodstock*.

Unlike the very visible map in this version, the map in Peter Brook's 1971 film is only slowly revealed, a section uncovered as Goneril is given her share and then a third more when Regan has spoken. The map is not here a two-dimensional representation but a relief model that physicalises the presence of the kingdom as land-scape, moving from symbolic geography to something much more representational, as if the hills and rivers that had been seen on Christopher Saxton's Tudor maps have taken on a three-dimensional form more adequately to show the share of which "With shadowy forests and with champaigns riched,/With plenteous rivers and wide-skirted meads,/We make thee lady" (1.1.64–6). The division has been made with strings and pins, the three shares of this pie chart coming from a geographic centre, that imaginary midpoint of Britain (though, unlike Elliott's emphatic representation of the islands, noth-ing about Brook's map clearly shows that it is Britain that is being divided). Lear re-marks the division after the rejection of Cordelia, uprooting two pins and bisecting Cordelia's share, leaving the strings dangling over the relief's edge, the wedge that Cordelia's third had driven on one side of the land between the moieties of Cornwall and Albany now removed.

That the play is anxious about the potential rivalry between Albany and Cornwall is clear: Curan asks Edmond "Have you heard of no

---

[39] The Oxford edition reads "crownet" but, since Olivier says "coronet," I have retained his form.

likely wars towards twixt the Dukes of Cornwall and Albany?"
(2.1.10–11) and Kent tells the Gentleman of the "division,/Although
as yet the face of it is covered/With mutual cunning, 'twixt Albany
and Cornwall" (3.1.10–12). In Adrian Noble's RSC production in
1994, the map, in paper, spread across the entire stage-floor, later
being ripped apart as the production continued, so that the events
were played out across the divided kingdom, just as Kenneth Branagh's
Renaissance Theatre Company's production in 1990 had been played
across a stage-floor covered with red rubber fragments, initially
arranged within a template of the outline of Britain (and through
which Lear's stick could mark division) but scattered across the stage
as the actors moved through it in the course of the rest of the play.
But when Noble's Fool, gagged, drew the lines of the shares across
the stage-floor with a paintbrush, it became clear (especially if one
was not seated in the stalls) that the division had a political aim,
deliberately making Cordelia's share the one that prevented any contact at all between Albany and Cornwall, a means of separation of
the dangerous elements. The use by Anthony Ward, Noble's designer,
of the stage-floor map may owe something to Branagh's production
but it may also have been influenced by Chris Dyer's set for Cicely
Berry's brilliant production at The Other Place in 1988, one of the
finest, least-known and certainly least-studied recent productions of
King Lear. Dyer created a stone floor which was also a map of Britain
but which, at the start of the storm, had two wedges removed so
that it fell apart to leave jagged, awkward boulders across which the
rest of the action was played, making the break-up on the kingdom
brilliantly manifest.

The final example I want to add to this array is Grigori Kozintsev's
film (1970). Where Gielgud at the Old Vic in 1940 had snatched
the map from his chamberlain, crumpled it and hurled it to the
ground,[40] Yuri Yarvet's anger is even more extreme. This Lear's rage
is vented on the map that he pulls up, twists and turns, starts to
tear, throws, kicks and otherwise manhandles. As the map starts to
be destroyed the effect of the rage on the kingdom is anticipated (as
it will be soon when the peasants outside prostrate themselves at the
sight of the king on the battlements, unable to hear his invective

---

[40] See Terence Hawkes, "Lear's Maps" in *Meaning by Shakespeare* (London: Routledge,
1992), pp. 130–1.

against Cordelia). But Kent, often in productions associated with the
map from the start (as at the Old Vic in 1946[41] or in Jonathan
Miller's 1982 BBC Shakespeare version), here kneels to plead for
Cordelia but first straightening the distorted map at his feet, trying,
as it were, to repair the tear in the kingdom that the rejection of
Cordelia has created.

There are other possibilities and Marvin Rosenberg records some
of them: Reinhardt's Lear whose throne had a dome above it with
a painted map on it; Orson Welles who marked "divisions on a map
large enough for a man to walk through—and when he was angered,
he walked through it."[42] The map, if visible, need not represent
Britain at all, a Shakespeare performance group at UCLA used a
map of California, an image that, I was told by a student,

> worked because California really is a three part state, southern with
> the 'L.A.' lifestyle, central with a large agricultural based culture and
> large stretches of rural land, and the northern Californian/San
> Franciscans, with their own distinct lifestyles, who swear that they
> would love to dissassociate themselves from L.A.[43]

A Hungarian production in 1993, directed by János Ács in the "Új
Színház" (New Theatre in Budapest), showed Lear playing with a
heap of real soil on a table, drawing different shapes, forms and
patterns, though the audience could not really see what those patterns were, making the materiality of the land of Britain brilliantly
apparent.[44]

The map as sign of the kingdom functions as a chorography of
Britain; it is the King of Britain who disunites the kingdom. The
productions, in different ways, explore the symbolic potency of the
event. But the nature of the map itself still perplexes me. Brecht
recurrently saw the map as the central prop, the crucial part of the
scene's *gestus*. In *The Messingkauf Dialogues*, the Dramaturg's concern
to "show the feudal conditions" is taken up by the Actor:

> In that case you might as well take his division of his kingdom seri-
> ously and have an actual map torn up in the first scene. Lear could
> hand the pieces to his daughters . . . He could take the third piece, the

---

[41] Bratton, p. 59.
[42] Marvin Rosenberg, *The Masks of King Lear* (Berkeley: University of California
Press, 1972), p. 53.
[43] E-mail information from Brian Willis, to whom my thanks.
[44] E-mail information from Géza Kállay, to whom my thanks.

one meant for Cordelia, and tear that across once again to distribute to the others. That would be a particularly good way of making the audience stop and think.[45]

In the "Short Description of a New Technique of Acting" Brecht again saw the tearing of the map as a means of making

the act of division . . . alienated. Not only does it draw our attention to his kingdom, but by treating the kingdom so plainly as his own private property he throws some light on the basis of the feudal idea of the family.[46]

But Brecht's most acute perception of all links the map differently, connecting to the audience and to the nature of the emotional charge that the performance without A-effects created:

The spectators at the Globe theatre, who three centuries ago saw King Lear give away his kingdom, pitied honest Cordelia, who didn't get one of the pieces, not the thousands of people who were thus given away.[47]

It is with the relationship of the map to the people that I want to close.

As John Gillies has noted, the images created by Lear's limited description of Goneril's share are "entirely consistent with the rich pictorial ornamentation of Saxton's maps of England."[48] Saxton's mappings, the results of Thomas Seckford's aim of a national survey, show hills and rivers and the names of towns but the human spaces are distributed disconnectedly across the landscape. Copies of the maps owned by Lord Burghley list in their margins the names of leading families and where they lived; the map of Northamptonshire includes the names of justices. He also noted on the map of Devon lists of 'Dangerous places for landing of men' and the location of gunpowder stores, making the map a military resource. But Burghley is making up for Saxton's lack of such information. Human geography in Saxton's representational world shows communities, the

---

[45] Bertolt Brecht, *The Messingkauf Dialogues* (London: Eyre Methuen, 1965), p. 63.
[46] Bertolt Brecht, *Brecht on Theatre*, ed. John Willett (London: Methuen, 1964), p. 143.
[47] Quoted by Margot Heinemann, "How Brecht Read Shakespeare" in Jonathan Dollimore and Alan Sinfield, eds., *Political Shakespeare* (Manchester: Manchester University Press, 1985), pp. 202–30 (p. 216).
[48] Gillies, *Shakespeare and the Geography of Difference*, p. 46.

natural traces of aristocratic ownership (he shows the parks but not
the country houses to which they belonged), occasional bridges, a few
mineral deposits and a very few antiquities.

When John Norden created the fragments of his chorography,
Speculum Britanniae, (only two volumes were published by 1598), even
though his format was half the size of Saxton's, he recorded more
villages and parks (i.e. spaces of privately owned land), added many
roads to Saxton's landscape so that the towns and villages become
connected across the landscape, as well as marking some battlefield
sites, the divisions of hundreds within the county (the next level down
of administrative unit, rarely marked by Saxton) and, on some, a
plan of the county town as an inset. He differentiated "houses of
the Queen's" from "houses of nobility," noted chapels-of-ease—he
was the only cartographer to mark this ecclesiastical category—and,
for Cornwall, indicate the mineral deposits that his text urged King
James to exploit.[49] Norden's maps appear within a context of substantial documentation listing roads and gentry, churches, battles and
beacons, the material evidence of human presences and human
history. He also provided a grid system to enable readers to locate
names on the map that were referred to in his chorographical descriptions, "without which helpe a place unknown would be long to find
in the Mappe,"[50] something of which Norden was so proud that he
included mention of it on the title page of the first volume, "w[th]
direction spedelie to finde anie place desired in the mappe," a sign
of the map's engagement with human use, the act of searching and
locating.[51]

Norden's movement to the recording of human geography, or in
effect making the chorography a reflection of a human landscape,
accelerated with John Speed's *Theatre of the Empire of Great Britaine* in
1611. Speed's maps place much more as insets and marginalia: coats
of arms of leading local families of the county, lengthy historical and
topographical notes, much more elaborate town plans (over seventy
in all), even views of antiquities (Stonehenge on the Wiltshire map,
Verulamium on the one for Hertfordshire, inscriptions on Roman

---

[49] See Delano-Smith and Kain, *English Maps: A History*, pp. 73–4.
[50] John Norden, *Speculi Britan[n]iae Pars* (1598), sig. ¶3a. See also his discussion
of the details of his chorographical method in John Norden, *Nordens Preparatiue to
his Speculum Britanniæ* (1596).
[51] John Norden, *Speculum Britanniae* (1593), title-page.

monuments for Northumberland), a feature that stretches the human history the map records. The geography of Speed's chorography is dominated by human history: an illustration of the battle of Ludlow on the map of Herefordshire with the three suns joined in the sky, the battle of Bosworth featured on Leicestershire with an account of what happened to Richard's corpse afterwards. As Michael Neill suggests, "Speed discovers in the land itself a kind of historical 'plot' whose story can be deciphered in all those visible characters of the past—the memorials or 'monuments' . . . that antiquaries like John Weever were busy recording and preserving."[52] The maps also include plenty of material on the back, including lists of hundreds and historical data, not quite what Serjeant Raven and yeoman Dogson in *The Puritan* wanted but still important. By 1618, in Barten Holyday's *Technogamia*, written for and performed at Christchurch, Oxford, a character can complain that the priorities of cartographers were wrong and superficial:

> 'tis a maine fault of your common Geographers, that now-a-dayes doe rather garnish the margine of a Map, then materially describe it; and onely draw a companie of lines through it; as if they had rid ouer the Countrie to take notice onely of the high-wayes; which yet a Carriers Horse knowes better then they . . .[53]

Against this mapping of the human world in maps, the landscape of Lear's world, the space of the map and the space that the map represents, is pretty much unpeopled. As Francis Barker eloquently stated,

> If the land is a place of fulsomeness and abundance, it is at the same moment one of ideal emptiness, a depopulated landscape. No one lives or works in the countryside of Lear's map.[54]

It is as empty as the map that so disappointed Serjeant Puttock, a world where we cannot "see men peepe out of doore in" it. It is also a mapped world in which, again like Puttock, one cannot find one's own place, and a world which, like the *mappae mundi* with their

---

[52] Neill, "'The Exact Map or Discovery of Human Affairs': Shakespeare and the Plotting of History," p. 383.

[53] Barten Holyday, *Technogamia* (Oxford, 1619), sig. I2r.

[54] Francis Barker, *The Culture of Violence* (Manchester: Manchester University Press, 1993), pp. 3–4.

T-in-O form, represent the world as three regions, not Europe, Asia
and Africa but now Cornwall, Albany and an England that had
been intended for the Queen of France. It is a world traversed and
traveled in the shifting instabilities that mark out the play's progress
from the known and central to the dangerously marginal.

But the regions into which this country is now divided refuse in
King Lear to maintain their boundaries, to keep to their space. Lear's
remapped world is one of disturbing and disoriented fluidity of place. ·
The names people carry (Kent, Gloucester, Albany, Cornwall) mean
that the places they embody are relocated into what we might hear
as the wrong place: Cornwall and Albany are in Gloucester, but
Gloucester is probably not in Gloucester anyway, Gloucester and
Kent go to Dover. As Flahiff suggests, "[t]here is a kind of mad
pliancy about geographical reference in *King Lear*."[55]

In this wilderness of wandering beggars and kings, an unstable
geography of the placed and the displaced, there is little space for
what Brecht called "the thousands of people who were thus given
away." But if the map of 1.1 is visible there may be one such space
of note. Maps encourage us to locate ourselves. As I look at the
weather map on American TV, I usually locate South Bend, not
New York or Chicago, in England I look for Cambridge, not Bristol
or London. At a performance of *King Lear* at the Globe or at the
King's palace at Whitehall, a visible map will encourage the audience to find London, to find the place of performance. What happens when England is redivided, when the map of Lear's Britain is
divided in two, not three, when the "third more opulent than your
sisters" (1.1.86), the tract of the country nearest to both France and
Burgundy, the heart of England, the space of the *cor* in Latin that
begins *Cor*delia,[56] that expanse which must include London itself, is
split apart? Perhaps the new division runs straight through the capital, bisecting the city itself so that, as one crossed back from the
Globe to the city after a performance of *King Lear*, one might be
moving from Cornwall's territory to Albany's, passing through a border control in the middle of London Bridge. The population of
London had been "given away" by James's accession. The map had
changed. The people's history had been rewritten in the new geog-

---

[55] F. T. Flahiff, "Lear's Map" *Cahiers Elisabéthains* 30 (1986), pp. 17–33, p. 19.
[56] See Gillies, "The Scene of Cartography," p. 121.

raphy of the King of Great Britain, the king who now did rule "this sceptred isle"[57] as neither Richard II nor Elizabeth I could ever have done, making true Shakespeare's geographical blunder. But while Speed's maps were a literal celebration of the new king's world, it may be that it is *King Lear* that should most properly have been called *The Theatre of the Empire of Great Britaine*.

---

[57] *Richard II*, 2.1.40.

THE ABSENT *TRIUMPHATOR* IN THE 1610 *CHESTER'S TRIUMPH IN HONOR OF HER PRINCE*

Robert W. Barrett, Jr.

On 23 April 1610, St. George's Day, the city of Chester put on a show (subsequently titled *Chester's Triumph in Honor of Her Prince* for pamphlet publication). The occasion marked two inaugurations: the running of the first St. George's Day Race in Chester as well as Henry Frederick Stuart's upcoming creation as Prince of Wales and Earl of Chester.[1] Produced by ironmonger and sheriff-peer Robert Amery, the show was a triumphal procession, complete with death-defying acrobats, flying gods, and local boys disguised as allegorical personifications.[2] It moved down Eastgate Street, paused in front of the High Cross and the Pentice (Chester's civic center) to entertain the Mayor and the assembled aldermen, and then passed west down Watergate Street with the civic authorities following in its wake. Exiting the city via the Watergate, the procession entered the Roodee, a large tidal meadow used for a variety of ceremonial and recreational purposes. There it was met with a thunderous cannonade of greeting from a group of ships anchored in the nearby River Dee. Guarded by 240 "brauely furnished" soldiers (A4v), the audience first watched a mock-battle between a pair of ivy-clad savages and a fire-breathing dragon and then cheered on two races and a "running . . . at the Ring" (B1).[3] Characters from the procession presented the winners

---

[1] Henry's reign as Prince and Earl was cut short by his death in 1612, but the city's St. George's Day Race lives on as part of the modern-day Chester Race Company's May Festival. (The race was moved to early May in the eighteenth century, but is still run on the Roodee, site of its early modern incarnation.) See the Company's website (http://www.chester-races.co.uk) for more information.

[2] For a complete list of the show's contents, see the Appendix to this essay.

[3] Citations of the text of Amery's show are taken from the Chetham Society edition of *Chester's Triumph in Honor of Her Prince*, ed. Thomas Corser (Manchester, 1844). Corser's edition is a facsimile of the original 1610 pamphlet of the show, so it provides only signatures, not page numbers. For greater ease of reference, I have followed his lead here. I should note as well that there is no direct evidence that the mock-battle was staged on the Roodee. The dragon does not appear in the list of the show's contents found on fols. 186–86v of British Library MS Harley 2150.

with their prizes (two silver bells and a silver cup respectively), and the show ended with a return to the Pentice building for a sumptuous feast in honor of the local gentry.

Amery's show appears to have been a great success. Richard Davies, the local poet who wrote the performers' speeches, called it "a people-pleasing spectacle" (A2v). But there was something missing from the show, something crucial to its generic self-designation as a "Triumph" (B4). Simply put, there was no guest of honor. *Chester's Triumph in Honor of Her Prince* is missing its prince: Henry Frederick Stuart was nowhere near Chester on St. George's Day. Instead, he was in the south of England, giving his cousin Prince Frederick of Brunswick a tour of various military sites. John Nichols places the two princes at the Tower of London on 20 April 1610 and at Woolwich Dockyard, visiting the still unfinished *Prince Royal*, on 25 April 1610.[4] A trip to Chester was clearly not on Henry's itinerary that April.

Scholars like David M. Bergeron and David Mills have noted his absence in their accounts of *Chester's Triumph*, but no one has yet gone beyond the mere registration of this fact to discuss its ramifications for the show's sociopolitical goals.[5] In the remarks that follow, I want to directly address the absence (and absent presence) of Henry Frederick Stuart. As I will show, the pageant assumes that the Prince is present and capable of taking part in the performance, either as spectator or actor (or as both). However, this sort of virtual presence still leaves an actual vacuum at the center of the show, a performative void available for filling by other authority figures and other, more local concerns. Prince Henry's absence destabilizes the generic affiliations of the Chester triumph, transforming a procession that to some extent assumes the form of a royal entry into a

---

The pamphlet text does describe the dragon, detailing his pursuit of the savages into "their Denne" (A3v). The spatious Roodee is a more likely location for the sort of set required by this "Denne" than the crowded streets of the city proper, and I have therefore placed the battle accordingly.

[4] *Progresses of King James the First* (New York: AMS Press, 1969), Vol. 2, 307–08. For more on Henry's visit to the *Prince Royal* (and on his interest in all things maritime), see Gregory Vaughan McNamara, "'A Perfect Diamond Set in Lead': Henry, Prince of Wales and the Performance of Emergent Majesty" (Ph.D. diss., West Virginia University, 2000), 243–301.

[5] *English Civic Pageantry, 1558–1642* (London: Edward Arnold, 1971), 92; *Recycling the Cycle: The City of Chester and Its Whitsun Plays* (Toronto: University of Toronto Press, 1998), 138.

primarily Cestrian affair implicitly engaged in an oligarchic conflict contained by the city walls. As Henry recedes from view (or, rather, fails to materialize in the first place), a *psychomachia* conflict between the figures of Love and Envy comes to dominate the dramatic action of the show. What begins as a celebration of a royal heir's creation as Prince of Wales and as a ceremony situating itself within a national ritual practice ends up as a meditation on local strife, a performative act that raises the possibility of its own negation.

The final speech of *Chester's Triumph* (delivered by the boy playing Chester, the figurehead for civic self-representation) seeks to banish the discord evoked by Envy, promoting instead a sense of social integration and amity. But this same speech also cancels Love's victory over vice, implicitly recognizing ongoing civic conflict as "fact." The second part of this essay turns to a variety of civic and antiquarian records in order to clarify the role *Chester's Triumph* itself plays in local competitions over honor and finance. A pun is crucial to my analysis here: Amery takes advantage of a variant spelling of his name (Amory) to insert himself into the show as *Amor* or Love. Love's battle against Envy does more than reflect Amery's own struggle against his fellow Cestrians: it is an active part of his efforts not only to solidify, but also to expand his civic status. The text of the show counters Prince Henry's absence by performatively enhancing Amery's presence at others' expense—*Chester's Triumph*, we are told, is "a memorable and worthy project, founded, deuised, and erected *onely* by the most famous, generous, and well deseruing Citizen, Mr. ROBERT AMERIE" (A3, my emphasis). At the same time, the city records demonstrate opposition to Amery's program of self-augmentation, actions taken to rein him in (if only in favor of promoting someone else). In the end, I hope to show that the absent *triumphator* is less a rupture in an otherwise steady pattern of authority than an opportunity to recognize "the close-mouth'd rage of emulous strife" already at work in early modern Chester and in civic culture as a whole (C2).

Absence and Authority in Chester's Triumph

Scholars of royal entries and civic triumphs have observed that the presence of the triumphal honoree (the individual Gordon Kipling designates the *triumphator*) was an essential element of late medieval

and early modern pageant practice.[6] Both Kipling and Bergeron
stress the extent to which pageant-masters situate the *triumphator* within
the performance space: Kipling describes the honoree as "the protagonist of a drama which takes all London as its stage," and Bergeron
sees him or her as an "active participant in the outcome of the dramatic presentation."[7] Moreover, in both analyses, the *triumphator* is,
without a doubt, the crucial figure in pageant drama. Kipling's use
of "protagonist" hints at this centrality, but Bergeron repeatedly
emphasizes the point, arguing that, without the presence of the *triumphator*, "the meaning of the event would be incomplete."[8] This
necessary presence functions on both ideological and performative
levels: "Elizabeth, or whoever the honoured person, is not only the
thematic centre, but also the dramatic centre of the pageant entertainment."[9] The body of the *triumphator* becomes the organizing and
authenticating principle of the overall performance, the material presence compensating spectators for their otherwise fragmentary experience
of ceremonial procession.[10] He or she unifies the dramatic action,
providing a common focal point for the multiple and necessarily limited perspectives of the audience.[11]

Bergeron's reading of the *triumphator*'s relation to the pageant audience resembles Stephen Orgel's description of the spatial dynamics
at work in the Stuart masque:

---

[6] See Kipling's "Triumphal Drama: Form in English Civic Pageantry," *Renaissance Drama* n.s. 8 (1977), 37–56.

[7] "Triumphal Drama," 42; *English Civic Pageantry*, 64. Kipling includes retinues within his expanded mimetic field: "Even the henchmen marching with the *tri-umphator* in procession often donned costumes and performed crucial mimetic actions" ("Triumphal Drama," 44).

[8] *English Civic Pageantry*, 6.

[9] Ibid., 64.

[10] Ibid., 6.

[11] One might note that Bergeron's observations here about triumphal audiences are based primarily on his knowledge of London pageant routes and an underde-veloped sense of the connections between spectators' social classes and their thus varying locations relative to the performance. In *Chester's Triumph*, there is a clear socio-spatial division within the show's audience: located at the High Cross (and probably placed in an elevated position within the Pentice or on its porch), the Mayor, sheriffs, and aldermen would have been able to see and hear the entire show—the orations would most likely have been entirely directed at them. Cestrians outside of the city government would have had the more partial experience described by Bergeron.

Jones's stage subtly changed the character of both plays and masques by transforming *audiences* into *spectators*, fixing the viewer, and directing the theatrical experience toward the single point in the hall from which the perspective achieved its fullest effect, the royal throne ... through the use of perspective the monarch, always the ethical center of court productions, became in a physical and emblematic way the center as well.[12]

City streets are of course organized along different spatial principles than Inigo Jones's masquing stage, but the pageantry described by Kipling and Bergeron remains similarly focused on the figure of authority. It depends on the *triumphator*'s presence for its coherence and, in doing so, organizes the dramatic experience along hierarchical lines.[13] Absence therefore generates a crisis within the pageant performance: without a stable, central locus of attention, spectatorship becomes necessarily diffuse and distracted. The triumphal experience is once again a partial one, hardly conducive to the ideal of holistic community such performances are intended to present. The anxiety generated by James I's reluctance to participate in public rituals (whether civic triumphs or royal entries) is thus understandable: by strategically witholding his presence, James denied city governments the body they needed to authorize their own spectacles of power.[14]

However, not all moments of absence originate in explicit conflicts over access to authoritative presences. The actual, physical body of

---

[12] "The Poetics of Spectacle," *New Literary History* 2 (1971), 378.

[13] Kipling qualifies that sense of hierarchy, arguing that the *triumphator* "can be made to perform a mimetic action predetermined by the dramatic craft of the civic dramatist" ("Triumphal Drama," 45). In this way, local space and civic interests can direct the *triumphator*'s spectacle of authority to their own ends, even as they rely upon the authoritative presence to underwrite and activate such goals. Of course, monarchs could resist the interpellations of urban pageant poets and control their own performances: James's refusal to stay and hear many of the various orations and shows intended for performance at his 1604 royal entry into London is a prime example of the conflict inherent in pageantry's politics of presence. See Gail Kern Paster, "The Idea of London in Masque and Pageant," *Pageantry in the Shakespearean Theater*, ed. David M. Bergeron (Athens: University of Georgia Press, 1985), 52, for a discussion of the reciprocity inherent in the pageants' dramatic manipulation of royal presence. Also see David M. Bergeron, "Stuart Civic Pageants and Texual Performance," *Renaissance Quarterly* 51 (1998), 167, for Thomas Dekker's attempts to compensate in the printed text of *The Magnificent Entertainment* for James's reluctance to play his set part.

[14] See *English Civic Pageantry*, 74–75 and 104, and "Triumphal Drama," 54–55.

the monarch (or, in the case of *Chester's Triumph*, the Prince) can only occupy one material location at a time—it cannot be present at every ceremony requiring its authorization. Alternative strategies for the ceremonial performance of presence were therefore developed and put into practice. Roy Strong's account of the early modern observance of St. George's Day provides us with a particularly relevant instance of these strategies in operation:

> The statutes of the Order of the Garter as revised by Henry VIII made provision for the observance of the annual Feast by Knights absent from court; the Knight was bound to erect the arms of his companions in a nearby chapel or church in the same manner as it was done in the Chapel Royal at court, in imitation of the choir stalls at Windsor. He was further to wear the robes of the Order and to attend services and ceremonies corresponding to those staged at court.[15]

Principles of "imitation" and correspondence shape this remote Garter ceremony, allowing the Garter Knight to achieve a sort of virtual presence through the use of symbolic objects and gestures. The Knight uses heraldic arms to transform his local religious space into a type of Elizabeth's Chapel Royal. He takes part in a metonymic ritual, performing as if he were present at court or, to be more accurate, as if the court were present at his location. Strong sees this practice as a projection of royal authority on a national scale: "Under Elizabeth these occasions became opportunities for display on a lavish scale, opportunities for a manifestation of the ritual of royalist chivalry in the remoter parts of the realm or even abroad."[16] That is to say, St. George's Day (the date of the Garter ceremonies) serves as the temporal locus of a widespread series of celebratory rituals, stretching from Liverpool to the Netherlands, all focused on the body of the monarch and thus all implicated in a single, royally-constructed idea of the nation.[17]

Chester's Triumph relies on similar strategies of virtuality in its celebration, not only of St. George's Day, but also of the Prince's creation.[18]

---

[15] *The Cult of Elizabeth: Elizabethan Portraiture and Pageantry* (London: Thames and Hudson, 1977), 174–75.

[16] Ibid., 175.

[17] See ibid., 175, for descriptions of St. George's Day celebrations in the locations named above. Also see Gordon Kipling, *Enter the King: Theatre, Liturgy, and Ritual in the Medieval Civic Triumph* (Oxford: Clarendon Press, 1998), 47, for more on pageantry's ideological fantasy of political union.

[18] Indeed, it appears that Amery and Davies originally believed that Prince Henry

The list of performers provided by the pamphlet text describes in some detail the riders bearing the arms of both King James and Prince Henry: these shields, "very richly Haroldized" (A3v), can be seen as the functional equivalents of the arms Strong discusses in his account of the Garter observances. Their presence in the procession offers Cestrians the virtual presence of the royal figures their devices represent, a correspondence strengthened by the long-established equation of heraldic imagery with aristocratic identity in the chivalric tradition. Fame's opening address supports this connection, explaining to the audience how "these Worthies (noted by their shields) [James, Henry, and St. George]/Are (by my conduct) thus ariued here" (B2). Her remarks speak to the difficulty of establishing virtual presence: "I *Fame* . . . Haue brought them thus, as t'were against the hill/Of highest *Lets*, to celebrate this *Day*!" (B2). The speech that follows (Mercury's) increases our sense of the royal presence within Chester; this oration has proven to be so convincing in its evocation of Henry's attendance that at least one modern critic appears to have accepted its claims at face value.[19] At the start of the speech, the messenger of the gods, himself identified in song as a "Prince" (B2v), descends "in a Cloude" (most likely from the top of St Peter's or one of the buildings adjacent to the High Cross) and reports to the audience that his divine mission is "To visit Him whose rare report hath rung/Within their [the gods'] eares" (B2v–B3). Mercury continues, identifying this "Him" through gesture and direct address:

---

would be created Prince of Wales and Earl of Chester on St. George's Day in 1610. Camber states this explicitly: "Whose *Grace* is thought vpon this present day,/Which day Saint *George* hath blisfully created,/To take his Birth-right" (C1). But Henry's actual investiture ceremony took place on 4 June 1610, and Davies's preface for *Chester's Triumph* closes with the observation that Amery's "glorious Triumph, with much more, was meerely intended (as it was then thought) for the ioyfull celebration of *Cambers* boundlesse glory" (A2v).

[19] See Glynne Wickham, *Early English Stages* (London: Routledge, 1959), Vol. 2, Pt. 1, 224. Wickham places Henry at Chester on St. George's Day, stating that "A dragon spouting fire was killed for Prince Henry's amusement in Chester in April 1610." Nichols notes that Mercury's oration makes it seem "that Prince Henry was present at the time it was made; but that cannot have been the case" (*Progresses*, Vol. 2, 297), and Corser concurs in a near-paraphrase of Nichols's remarks: "It might be thought from some parts of this Show, and especially from the speech of *Mercury*, that Prince Henry was present in Chester at its representation, but we know, from other sources, that this could not have been the case" (xiv). The speech has certainly proven to be evocative in its critical afterlife.

And to this place, directed by their Powres,
I am ariu'd (in happy time I hope)
To find this happy God-beloued Man.
And loe behold on suddaine where I spie
This Fauorite so fauor'd of the Gods:
I will salute him with such courtesie
As best beseemes a wight of such account.
All haile to thee high Iustice Officer;
Mercurie, Nuntius to the Powres diuine,
Hath brought thee greetings from their Deities. (B3)

Acknowledging his Cestrian surroundings ("this place"), Mercury more specifically locates his objective ("loe behold on suddaine where I spie") and calls out to him ("All haile to thee"). Although the passage lacks an explicit stage direction, the line "I will salute him with such courtesie" suggests the precise nature of the gesture that the boy playing Mercury would then make. It also functions as the first step in its addressee's incorporation within the dramatic field of the triumph: Mercury's salute transforms the "high Iustice Officer" into Kipling's "protagonist." The entire oration prepares the audience for Camber's specific praise of Henry ("God blesse Prince HENRY Prop of Englands ioy," C1), a laudatory speech that offers spectators an identity to hang upon Mercury's "wight of such account."

The paratext of *Chester's Triumph* heightens this presence-effect. From its title page to its dedication, the pamphlet carefully prepares its readers for the identification of the "high Iustice Officer" with Prince Henry. Indeed, on page A1, just across from a dedicatory poem by Davies, the text gives us an image of the Prince's heraldic device and motto ("Ich dien"). This image offers a heightened level of virtual presence, potentially compensating for the pamphlet text's failure to provide us with the spectacle of the triumphal procession and games. The published version of *Chester's Triumph* requires the identification of the Prince as *triumphator* and takes all the steps necessary to convey that equation. These strategies of presence may stem from Amery's plan to "present" a copy of the show to Prince Henry.[20] Bergeron has argued that pageant performances did not

---

[20] This plan is first mentioned by Chester antiquarian David Rogers in the 1637 redaction of his *Brevary*. There Rogers says that Amery had Davies's speeches and verses transformed into a book, "which. booke was Imprinted and presented to that ffamos prince Henry, eldest sonne to. the blessed King Iames of famous memorie."

effectively end until they entered the realm of print culture as pamphlet texts.[21] If we accept his claim, then Amery's decision to send his triumph to London and Richmond in pamphlet form could be understood as a means of incorporating the Prince within the show. In this scenario, Henry's eventual reading of the pageant text and its evocation of his (absent) presence counts as acts of belated spectatorship and participation.

But retroactive identification of this sort takes place at a distant remove from the Chester of 23 April 1610. It does little to fill the real-time performative gap resulting from the Prince's absence, the dramatic vacuum immediately confronting the audiences gathered alongside city streets and around the High Cross. Even if the show's attempts at generating virtual presence succeed, the Henry symbolically participating in the procession still has to compete for recognition. The material fact of his absence leaves an opening in the ideological and performative field of the pageant, an empty space available for appropriation by other authorities. Without the comforting apparatus of the pamphlet text and its reassuring signals of Prince Henry's centrality to the celebration, spectators are left to their own devices when it comes to occupying the Prince's place. After all, Fame identitifies not one, but three "Worthies" in her inaugural address; moreover, when she announces Mercury's imminent arrival before the gathered crowds, she does so in vague terms: "Then for th'encrease of this triumphant Mirth,/I'le inuocate the Gods Embassadour,/To be the President of Heau'n to Earth;/And, from the Gods, salute your Gouernour" (B2). In the local context of Chester, and in the immediate material context of performance, "your Gouernour" proves to be an elusive figure. It certainly could refer to the newly created Prince in his capacity as Earl of Chester and thus to his traditional authority over Cestrians. But the phrase could also identify King James, one of Fame's three "Worthies" and

---

For all of Rogers' commentary on the St. George's Day Race, see *Chester*, ed. Lawrence M. Clopper, Records of Early English Drama (Toronto: University of Toronto Press, 1979), 434–35. (Subsequent citations from Clopper's *Chester* will be listed as *REED: Chester*.) But this appears to be wishful thinking: in the manuscript of Rogers's 1637 redaction (Liverpool University MS 23.5), the word "presented" is actually an interlinear insertion replacing a cancelled "~~deliuered~~." A "deliuered" text need never be handled or read by its dedicatee—the manuscript's unknown editor seems to be replicating Amery's strategies twenty-seven years after the fact.

[21] See "Stuart Civic Pageants," 163 and 168.

the subject of a direct address by Britaine: "Great *Britaines* Greatnesse . . .
We doe ascribe vnto thy Match-lesse worth . . . And while me (*Britaine*)
Neptune shal embrace,/Ile ruine those, that spight thee, or thy Race"
(B4v). Britaine precedes Camber in both the procession of riders and
the sequence of speeches, carefully preserving James's hierarchical
dominance over his popular son.[22] The awarding of prizes after the
race and tilt takes place along similar lines, the King's Britaine handing out "the better Bell" while the Prince's Camber has to settle for
presenting "the second Bell" (D1). Joy, the last speaker in the pageant
procession, ends her oration with an echo of Britaine's: "Wherefore
auaunt; that all the I'le may sing,/Now *Enuies* gone, in peace w'enjoy our King" (C4v). In the pre-race portion of *Chester's Triumph*,
James, not Henry, literally gets the last word.

Nevertheless, James is also nothing more a virtual figure, present
only via the operations of symbolic object and speech. The phrase
"your Gouernour" is therefore most easily appropriated by those
authorities in attendance at the show's performance, the Mayor of
Chester and his magistrates. The figure of Chester begins her speech
with a direct address to this elite audience: "Haile sage Spectators,
haile yee reu'rend Sires,/Haile yonger Brutes, whose worth self *Worth*
admires,/Whose ardent Loues both to the place, and vs,/Constraines
our Loues to entertaine yee thus" (B3v). While the gentry assembled for the race and tilt are no doubt included in Chester's address
(perhaps as the "yonger Brutes"), the civic authorities watching the
performance from the Pentice are the best candidates for the "sage
Spectators" and "reu'rend Sires" interpellated by the oration's first
line.[23] Immediately following Mercury's recognition of the "high

[22] In maintaining James's pride of place, *Chester's Triumph* reveals itself to be as
cautious as the various masques and court entertainments celebrating the Prince
and his creation during the first half of 1610. Ben Jonson's and Inigo Jones's *Barriers*
and Samuel Daniel's *Tethys' Festival* are both careful not to slight the King, and
thus both masques end up as highly qualified tributes to Prince Henry. See Norman
Council, "Ben Jonson, Inigo Jones, and the Transformation of Tudor Chivalry,"
ELH 47 (1980), 259–75; Orgel, "The Poetics of Spectacle," 367–89; Graham Parry,
"The Politics of the Jacobean Masque," *Theatre and Government under the Early Stuarts*,
eds. J. R. Mulryne and Margaret Shewring (Cambridge, UK: Cambridge University
Press, 1993), 87–117; and John Peacock, "Jonson and Jones Collaborate on *Prince
Henry's Barriers*," *Word & Image* 3 (1987), 172–94.
[23] The passage's secondary division of the elite spectators into groups of old and
young recalls the father-son dynamic of its royal references. As I will suggest below
in my discussion of Envy, generational difference, whether at court or in the mer-

Iustice Officer" whose presence works to ground the dramatic and ideological action of the triumph, Chester's speech proposes additional, local candidates for the ambiguous "Him" pointed out minutes before. If we look back at Mercury's description of the "God-beloued Man," we can see its pliability of reference:

> And know (deere Sir) thy deedes and good deserts,
> Thy well disposed nature, Minde, and thought,
> Thy zealous care to keepe their Lawes diuine,
> Thy great compassion on poore wights distrest,
> Thy prudence, iustice, temp'rance, and thy truth,
> And, to be briefe, thy vertues generall,
> Haue mou'd them all from Heau'n, with one assent,
> To send Me downe, to let thee vnderstand
> That thou art highly in their Fauors plac'd. (B3)

The "vertues generall" listed in this speech prove to be precisely that, virtues general enough to apply to both royal figures and civic officials. They could describe Prince Henry, King James, or Mayor William Leicester—each man a "high Iustice Officer" in his own right. But the spatial and mimetic effects of performance, combined with the Prince's absence, make it more likely than not that Leicester will be the recipient of Mercury's gesture of acknowledgment.

In addition, the mayor, his officers, and his colleagues in the Chester Assembly are doubly represented in the triumph's dramatic action. First, Chester's speech places them in roles reminiscent of those played by late medieval and early modern *triumphatores*; second, Chester herself embodies the corporate community ruled by these city fathers. The performative doubling of the city's representation suggests that, when Chester speaks in *Chester's Triumph*, she speaks as much to herself as she does to either King or Prince. Certainly, this is the effect conveyed in part by "Chesters last speech," the final oration of the entire triumph. Inviting "each noble worthy, and each worthy Knight,/To close their stomacke with a small repast" (the Pentice feast mentioned above), Chester concludes with a "solemne vow" marked as communal through its use of first person plural pronouns: "whilst *we* breath, *our* hearts shall honour you" (D1v, my

---

cantile institutions of the city, is a locus of competition and discord. Chester's description of the magistrates and gentlemen also calls to mind class divisions and antagonisms as it separates the "blisfull criew" of elites from "the vulgar view" of those Cestrian spectators outside the city franchise or the ranks of the gentry (B3v).

emphasis). This corporate city-self dramatically dislocates Joy's earlier celebration of the King, replacing a national consciousness with an emphasis on local hospitality and local affairs. The elite spectators on the Roodee end the show by taking part in a feast held within the building representing the institutions of Cestrian authority. Multi-national royalty is not forgotten, but the structures of locality effectively contain it and appropriate it to their own ends.

In *Chester's Triumph*, this local appropriation causes a series of identifiable shifts in the show's ideological content and dramatic practice. The first six orations of the triumph (Fame, Mercury, Chester, Britaine, Camber, and Rumor) form a static procession, concentrating on the celebration of St. George's Day in a variety of intersecting geographical and cultural spaces (England, Wales, Chester, Britain, Christendom). However, beginning with Peace's speech and its mention of "ciuill Mutinies" (C2), the drama of the show increasingly relies on dialogue and interaction between its emblematic figures.[24] The center of this performative activity is the Gorgon-like Envy: the second half of *Chester's Triumph* (running from Peace's speech all the way through the race and tilt to Chester's closing remarks) devotes itself in one way or another to Envy's destabilizing presence as well as to the various attempts to dispel that presence, to transform it into absence. A common figure in early modern civic ceremonial, Envy epitomizes the civic pageant's deployment of the English morality play tradition to resolve specifically urban anxieties.[25] Peace's anticipatory condemnation of Envy reveals the social forces, positive and negative, which the vice represents:

---

[24] See *English Civic Pageantry*, 66, for more on Jacobean pageantry's increased use of dialogue.

[25] See ibid., 7–8, for the historical and dramatic continuity linking civic pageants and morality plays, and 281–82, for a discussion of Envy's role within Elizabethan and Jacobean civic ceremonies. M. C. Bradbrook provides a complementary account of Envy in her "Politics of Pageantry: Social Implications in Jacobean London," in *Poetry and Drama, 1570–1700: Essays in Honour of Harold F. Brooks*, eds. Antony Coleman and Antony Hammond (London: Methuen, 1981), 68; she also sees the extent to which Envy is removed from its religious context of the Seven Deadly Sins and "secularized." In the remarks that follow, I will attempt to qualify Bergeron's largely moralistic account of Envy (in *English Civic Pageantry*, he includes her in a chapter devoted to "The Soul" of English civic ceremonial) by analyzing her political functions.

I'll rend the close-mouth'd rage of emulous strife,
And wound Distraction, with Connexions knife.
And when damn'd Malice comes but once in sight
I, with a vengeance, will suppresse her straight.
I'le send pale Enuie downe to hell with speed,
Where she vpon her Snakes shall onely feed.
. . . .
Which being done I'le send that base infection
(Whose onely vertue is but base) Detraction
Her to associate; where they both shall liue
As long as hell can life with horror giue: (C2v)

In Peace's description, Envy embodies social jealousy and political backbiting; she personifies the competitive drives ("emulous strife") that threaten to undermine the continued stability of urban government. In mercantile oligarchies like Chester (or London), the social and generational hierarchy of offices becomes a locus of self-aggrandizement, aggression, and desire. Those individuals located at its bottom seek to rise to the top, displacing others—both predecessors and colleagues—in their acquisition of political power and authority. Conversely, those at the top seek to maintain their control of the system, keeping their junior magistrates in place and insisting upon the measured, regular pace of governmental promotion. Both the vertically-oriented language of Peace's speech and its shift in attention from the national struggle of peoples (the Scots and the English) to the intimacies of "Domestick strife" and the administrative complexities of "this blessed State" (C2v) replicate this political structure. They present Envy as an aggressive, hostile social climber whom Peace, the representative of legitimate civic authority, must "suppresse . . . straight" and send down to her proper place in the triumph's hierarchy of virtues and vices (the dramatic parallel to Chester's own social hierarchy). Envy's lowly origins are confirmed by Peace's insistence upon the "base" status of "associate" Detraction.

Chester's Triumph therefore resembles other contemporary treatments of Envy within civic ceremonial. For example, the procession in Thomas Dekker's 1612 *Troia-Nova Triumphans* takes the new Lord Mayor of London, doubled in the pageant drama by the allegorical figure of Virtue, past the ominous castle of Envy in Cheapside en route to the Guildhall. Upon the Lord Mayor's return to Cheapside, Envy and her minions threaten the mayoral party once again. But this time, the forces of Virtue (and civic order) are ready for them: twelve gunmen accompanying the Lord Mayor discharge their weapons into the air, defeating Envy. Scholars see these twelve soldiers as the symbolic representatives of London's Twelve Great Companies, and *Troia-Nova Triumphans* has thus been read as a statement of oligarchic solidarity upon the occasion of the new Lord Mayor's election.[26] The dramatic action of *Chester's Triumph* follows a similar pattern: Love's debate with Envy ends with the vice's banishment to "the depth of deepest Stigian flood" (C4) at the virtue's command, and Joy's concluding speech widens the scope of Envy's suppression, naming all of the other speakers in the show in order to stress their shared role in the process of exclusion and condemnation.

It is almost as if Joy strips Envy of her franchise: "*Enuie* auaunt, thou art no fit Compeere/T'associate these our sweet Consociats heere" (C4v). Joy's oration makes it clear that "Compeere" and "Consociats" include her fellow personified virtues, but the terms may also be applied to the elite audience watching the show from the Pentice. Presumptuous, slandering Envy is expelled from their company as well. The show finally carries out Peace's promised suppression, restoring to the streets of Chester the "mutual concord datelesse" and "peace-procured praise" that come from the alliance of Love and Peace (C2). The relevance to urban concerns of such an alliance is confirmed early on, when Peace vows that "No forraigne Nation shall affront their force/As long as I direct them in that course./All rash dissentions and litigious braules,/I shall expell from their vnshaken walls" (C2). Even though the first couplet evokes England through the phrase "No forraigne Nation," the second couplet is explicit in its evocation of the legal battles and religious struggles which divided the supposedly uniform corporate space of the city, a unity made manifest in the passage's mention of "vnshaken walls," the material marker of late medieval and early modern *urbanitas*.[27] Thus the *psychomachia* of *Chester's Triumph*, like that of *Troia-Nova Triumphans*, resolves civic struggle in favor of virtue (defined as oligarchic order). Both

---

[26] See James Knowles, "The Spectacle of the Realm: Civic Consciousness, Rhetoric and Ritual in Early Modern London," *Theatre and Government under the Early Stuarts*, eds. J. R. Mulryne and Margaret Shewring (Cambridge, UK: Cambridge University Press, 1993), 173.

[27] Colin Platt discusses the centrality of civic defenses to urban imagination and self-representation in his *English Medieval Town* (London: Paladin-Granada Publishing, 1979), 49–50. Chester's long history as the northern bulwark of the Welsh Marches gives Peace's reference to "vnshaken walls" even greater resonance.

THE ABSENT *TRIUMPHATOR* IN THE 1610   197

shows stage dissension and strife in order to represent the vices'
active expulsion from the city community, a community whose una-
nimity is then spectacularly asserted. The triumphs posit that virtue's
victory is total.[28]

But Envy's defeat in *Chester's Triumph* ultimately proves to be a
limited and contingent one, a dramatic fantasy subsequently undone
within the field of performance itself. In retrospect, this outcome
seems inevitable: Envy may be a vice, but its character as "emulous
strife" reveals its structural necessity to the very institutions it threatens.
Emulation is an essential element in the repertoire of oligarchic
procedures and practices comprising urban government; the political aspirant follows a well-worn and clearly marked path to authority, the *cursus honorum* that ideally culminates in his assumption of
the mayoralty.[29] The jealous desires driving Envy are also those assist-
ing his emulative progress up the hierarchical ladder. Anthony
Munday's 1604 Lord Mayor's Show, *The Triumphs of Re-United Britannia*,
provides us with some London evidence for this alternate understanding of envy as an essential social force. Describing the Britannia's
Mount pageant for his readers, Munday offers an "explanation" for
its method of propulsion: "Corineus and Goemagot, appearing for
the more grace and beauty of the show, we place as guides to
Britanniae's Mount, and being fettered unto it in chains of gold,
they seem (as it were) to draw the whole frame, showing much envy
and contention who shall exceed most in duty and service" (lines
188–94).[30] Here "envy and contention" directly motivate "duty and
service"—within Munday's performance, "Britanniae's Mount," the
figure of the nation, only moves forward due to the efforts of the
monstrous figures "fettered unto it." *Triumphs of Re-United Britannia*
reconfigures Corineus and Goemagot's legendary antagonism as
socially productive competition.

Evidence for similar connections between envy and social competition can be found throughout *Chester's Triumph*, especially if we

---

[28] Arguing that Envy is "routed," Bergeron thus fully agrees with the ostensible
outcome of the show's pre-race portion (*English Civic Pageantry*, 282).

[29] For a description of Chester's particular sequence of offices, see *A History of
the County of Chester*, eds. C. P. Lewis and A. T. Thacker, Vol. 5, Pt. 1 (Woodbridge,
UK: Boydell and Brewer, 2003), 97–99.

[30] This citation is taken from the edition of *Triumphs* printed in *Renaissance Drama:
An Anthology of Plays and Entertainments*, ed. Arthur F. Kinney (Oxford: Blackwell
Publishers, 1999), 369–81.

remember the inaugural motives informing the entire show. First of all, Amery's celebration of Henry's imminent creation ends up undercut by Envy's mention of her desire "To see a Sonne the Butcher of his Sire . . . Or else to see a Father sucke the blood/Of his owne Spawne" (C3v). These grim images should not be read as knowing nods to the tension between King James and Prince Henry, but their evocation in a triumph honoring royal father and royal son nonetheless casts a momentary pall over the show. The second inauguration, Amery's establishment of an annual race and tilt, swiftly falls under Envy's jealous influence. We initially see this slippage occur in Peace's speech. She establishes an analogy between athletic and civic competition, a connection symbolized by the wreath of the champion: "I'le binde their Loues with true Loues Gordian knot,/That rude Dissentions hands vndoe it not:/And with a Wreath of euerduring Baies,/Crowne all your browes with peace-procured praise" (C2). The language of binding and unbinding at work in this passage is immediately echoed in Peace's double-edged image of "Connexions knife." Technically the personification of social concord, Peace nonetheless wields a blade that divides in order to unite: the factionalism signified by "Connexions knife" ties urban elites together even as it serves to cut out and exclude inferiors (evoked in the passage by the knife's wounding of the "rude" and thus explicitly lower-class Dissention). Chester's St. George's Day games are ludic practices marked by social class—urban and county elites provide the horses for the race and take part themselves in the tilt. The wreaths awarded to the winners are symbolically identical to those given to Peace's social victors, the urban oligarchs who join together to maintain exclusive rule over the city. In games, just as in civic politics, there are those who end up with "the better Bell" and those who must be content for now with "the second Bell."

The show also acknowledges Envy's social necessity (or at least her social inevitability) when it sends its audience mixed messages about Fame's ability to transmit honor to posterity. Introducing the presentation of prizes, Fame claims that she will preserve the winners' names "within her booke . . . till Time stayes his course . . . Maugre Detraction and fell Enuies spight" (D1). Here it is Judgment Day, and not "fell Enuies spight," that will ultimately bring a close to the victors' fame—an end which they as Christians are understood to accept. Envy's conjuration by Love appears to be eternal in duration. But four speeches later, Chester completely overturns Fame's sentence: "No Action, though admir'd for Excellence,/No Practize, though of high'st preheminence/That can escape the Poliphemian eye/Off Enuie, that for euer lookes awry" (D1v). Now it is Envy who remains eternally vigilant, and, unlike Fame, she has no limit of Doomsday placed upon her surveillance (she simply looks on jealously "for euer"). Having restored Envy to the thematic and social space of the triumph, Chester does attempt once again to exclude the vice, telling the elite audience that "Onely your Loues, which are our fairest markes,/Must muzzle Enuie" (D1v). But the displacement of exclusion onto the spectators remains a conditional one, dependent on their favor and, no doubt, their satsifaction with the show, race, and feast provided them.

Finally, even these elite viewers are susceptible to Envy's appeal, for Chester acknowledges that "the Fury barkes vnto the best" as well as the least (D1v). Envy is therefore more than a vertical phenomenon. It operates horizontally as well, extending laterally within elite levels of civic government and city culture. The vice's return to *Chester's Triumph* testifies to both the ineradicability of her dramatic presence and the necessity of her civic function. It reveals the social costs which accompany Prince Henry's absence in Chester on 23 April 1610: the performative and political spaces he fails to occupy represent both an opportunity and an instability. Multiple authorities struggle to appropriate the Prince's presence to their own ends, but the very fact of their conflict delineates the limits of the *triumphator*'s own authority. In *Chester's Triumph*, all authoritative presence—royal, civic, moral—is rendered contingent. Someone else is always waiting to take your place.

Love and Envy in the Urban Archive

Of course, there is still one candidate missing from my analysis of authority's absence in *Chester's Triumph*: Robert Amery, the show's producer. As I mentioned above, Amery takes advantage of a Latinate pun on his surname (Amery = *Amor* = Love) to cast himself in his own show. The pamphlet version of the show hints at that equation in its closing lines:

> If any Reader shall desire to know
> Who was the Author of this pleasing show:
> Let him receaue aduertizement hereby

> A Sheriffe (late of *Chester*) AMERIE.
> Did thus performe it; who for his reward,
> Desires but Loue, and competent regard.
>   ROBERT AMERIE. (D2)

According to Mills, this verse signature indicates that "Amery expected honours or preferment as a consequence" and that his primary "Reader" was meant to be Prince Henry.[31] I think it just as likely that Amery's "process of self-promotion through display" has a specifically local audience in mind.[32] *Chester's Triumph* did seek out the Prince through print publication in London, but it was performed in Chester first. The triumph is therefore not only the record of a city's (or individual citizen's) love toward Prince Henry, but of the performative processes whereby urban "Loue," the ideological fantasy of civic unity, is generated—and of that citizen's claim to individually personify that social force, to locate its authorizing power within his own act of authorship (Amery makes it clear that he, not Davies the poet, is "Author of this pleasing show").

Amery's self-authorizing performance does not go unopposed. After all, as I have argued above, Love's defeat of Envy is only temporary. But there's a clearer sense of opposition to Love's (and thus to Amery's) schemes at work in the debate sequence. Asked by Love to define "the solace *Enuie* counteth deepe," the vice responds with an extensive wish list of horrific acts (C3v).[33] However, even Envy has her limits:

> But to behold a ranke of rustick Boyes
> Shewing as childish people childish toyes
> To grace a day with; O it grates my gall
> To heare an apish Kitling catterwall.
> Is it not harsh to heare a Marmoset squeake
> Vpon a stage a most vnioynted speake?
> And then to heare some ignorant Baboone,

---

[31] *Recycling the Cycle*, 138. Appealing to Henry, soon to be Earl of Chester and thus chief officer of the Cheshire Palatinate, is analogous to the common Chester practice of sueing one's fellow freemen not in the Mayor's Portmote court but in the Earldom's Exchequer court—a practice for which Amery was called to task on at least one occasion (see below).

[32] Ibid., 138–39.

[33] Envy's list includes the anti-civic, self-consuming desire "To see a City burnt" (C3v). Can we read this as the logic of civic emulation taken to its metaphorical extreme?

Sweare that this Monky did surmount the Moone.
When as the Infants best is too too bad,
And which to heare would make a wise-man mad. (C3v–C4)

This is an amazing speech, one that threatens to undermine the entire show: what Envy denounces here is the very performance her audience is attending.[34] She attacks triumphal discourse, redefining praise of the *triumphator* as nothing more than claims that some monkey "did surmount the Moone," a slander that includes Prince Henry, King James, Mayor Leicester, and all of the other candidates for the absent *triumphator*'s authority in its scope. That said, the passage's primary target appears to be Amery himself (in his capacity as pageant-master). Put another way, Amery uses *Chester's Triumph* to stage an assault on his own authority: as Envy says earlier in the scene, "he that thinks that Loue can e're be wise,/Hath neither iudgement, wisedome, wit, nor eies" (C3). We might therefore read the debate between Love and Envy as Amery's apopotraic pre-emption of criticism. Opposition to the show (and to the civic self-promotion that it celebrates) is demonized as the ranting of a foul she-monster, and Love (Amery) emerges victorious.[35]

Chester's reluctant acknowledgement of Envy's inevitability qualifies Amery's achievement—the ironmonger's assumption of Love's identity personalizes the point I made earlier about Envy's civic necessity. The pageant's conclusion suggests Amery's awareness of the limits to his self-authorization, and so (in retrospect) does the debate: you only ward off what you fear and expect to encounter. As Amery's life-records demonstrate, he was no stranger to the social dynamics epitomized by Envy. Admitted to the civic franchise on 16 January 1598, Amery was the son and grandson of former sheriffs.[36] He

---

[34] Davies announces at the start of the pamphlet text that "The chiefest part of this people-pleasing spectacle, consisted in three Bees, *viz. Boyes, Beasts*, and *Bels . . . Boyes* of rare Spirit, and exquisite performance" (A2v).

[35] Christina M. Fitzgerald's work on the masculinity of guild culture in Chester's sixteenth-century Whitsun plays applies equally well to this seventeenth-century civic triumph. See her "Of Magi and Men: Christ's Nativity and Masculine Community in the Chester Mystery Cycle," *Varieties of Devotion in the Middle Ages and Renaissance*, ed. Susan C. Karant-Nunn (Turnhout, Belg.: Brepols, 2003), 145–62, for more information. Civic status depends in part on a publicly secure gender identity: by linking criticism of the show to the Medusa-like Envy, Amery pre-defines his opponents as effeminate (and thus lesser in nature).

[36] *The Rolls of the Freemen of the City of Chester, Part I: 1392–1700*, ed. and trans. J. H. E. Bennett (Edinburgh: Record Society of Lancashire and Cheshire, 1906), 78.

became a common councilman in 1604, a leavelooker in 1605–06, and a sheriff in 1608–09.[37] His career in government apparently reached a plateau at this point: from 1609–10 until his death on 21 September 1613, Amery is listed in the Mayor's Books as a sheriff-peer, an unofficial office between sheriff and alderman.[38]

We know that he was caught up in several instances of intra-franchise conflict: for example, on 12 April 1605, he and two other men were ordered to submit to the Assembly for punishment because they had pursued "forraine suites" against their fellow freemen in the Cheshire palatinate's Exchequer court.[39] Even more relevant to the purposes of this essay are the five shillings he was fined on 29 November 1611: "And at the same Assemblie Mr Robert Amerie for giuinge diuers vncivill speeches vnto the said Mr Button to the disturbance of this Assembly was fyned in fyve shillinges and ordered to pay to pay the same to the vse of the Maior and Citezens of the said Cittie accordinglie."[40] What Button did to merit "diuers vncivill speeches" from Amery is unclear, but we do know that he had just been "elected and chosen to be Alderman in steed and place of William Brocke Esquier learned in the lawes late Alderman deceased."[41] Did Amery feel passed over at Button's election and lash out? Was he simply launching yet another offensive in an ongoing and other-wise unrecorded feud? Whatever the answer to such questions, Robert Amery's "uncivill speeches" bear a striking resemblance to the "ciuill Mutinies" evoked by Peace in her St. George's Day speech (C2). The man who would be Love certainly knew how to play the part of Envy.

To be fair to Amery, his fellow citizens proved equally adept at portraying "Loues Misanthropos" (C4). The extant records of the 1610 St. George's Day show testify to the opposition generated by Amery's overly conspicuous attempt to fill Prince Henry's vacant spot. At first, things seem to go well. The Painters' account book

[37] Cheshire and Chester Archives MS A/B/1, fol. 282d; Cheshire and Chester Archives MS MB/28, fol. 243; and Cheshire and Chester Archives MS A/B/1, fol. 305.
[38] Cheshire and Chester Archives MS MB/29, fols. 169 and 242. Amery's will (Cheshire and Chester Archives MS WS Amery 1613) survives, revealing to us that he lived on Bridge Street in St. Bridget's parish.
[39] Cheshire and Chester Archives MS A/B/1, fol. 287d.
[40] Ibid., fol. 316d.
[41] Ibid., fol. 316.

documents a payment of twenty shillings on 18 October 1609 "to mr amery for St george," and the Beerbrewers managed to chip in a shilling.[42] All in all, Amery managed to get seventeen companies to help cover the costs of the race prizes (to the tune of approximately £36).[43] He then put together a document entitled "The maner of the showe that is if god spare life & health shalbe seene by all the behoulders vpon St Georges day next being the 23th of Aprill 1610."[44] The extant version of this text can be found in British Library MS Harley 2150, a collection of civic records compiled by the seventeenth-century Chester antiquarian Randle Holme.[45] It is essentially a program for the upcoming event, listing the various participants in their processional order. I cannot identify the precise audience for the document, but I suspect that it may have been presented to the Assembly.

My suspicions stem from Amery's signature at text's end.[46] The "maner of the showe" text ends with a direct address inviting response and commentary on the pageant: "when all is done then Iudge what you haue seene & soe speake on your mynd, as you fynde."[47] The text is then signed by "The Actor for the presente. Robart Amory."[48] Amory's decision to identify himself in his signature as "Actor" is an interesting one: at least three senses of the term are potentially active here, and all three are particularly relevant to his involvement in the planning and execution of the 1610 pageant. The first sense of *actor*—"A manager, overseer, agent, or factor"—points to his apparently self-appointed role as pageant-master.[49] The accounts of the

---

[42] *REED: Chester*, 255 and 256.

[43] Ibid., 258.

[44] Ibid., 258.

[45] The same manuscript contains the assessment of the companies' contribution to the St. George's Day Race just mentioned above.

[46] Corser claims in his notes to *Chester's Triumph* that Harley 2150 is "drawn up in the hand-writing of Mr. Amery himself" (no page number given). A look at the manuscript confirms that "the maner of the show" is written in a different hand than that of Randle Holme, a point with which Clopper agrees (*REED: Chester*, p. 260). But it does not follow that this unknown hand is Amery's own: Margaret Groombridge notes in the introduction to her *Calendar of Chester City Council Minutes, 1603–1642* (Blackpool, UK: Record Society of Lancashire and Cheshire, 1956) that scribes were routinely hired to write clean copies of petitions to the Assembly (vii).

[47] *REED: Chester*, 260.

[48] Ibid., 260.

[49] *OED*, sense 1.

Painters and Beerbrewers testify to this sense of the term, as does
the overall assessment of the company contributions provided by
Harley 2150. (We also have a 1609–1610 petition in which Amery
asks the Assembly for money to cover his personal expenses in staging the show, but I want to withhold analysis of that document for
the moment.)

The second sense of *actor* to be evoked by Amery's signature is
the one most familiar to us today: "One who personates a character, or acts a part; a stage-player, or dramatic performer."[50] This
sense, emerging in the 1580s, was potentially available to Amery. It
matters here because of a short poem placed just below Amery's signature at the document's end. It reads as follows:

> Amor is loue and Amory is his name
> that did begin this pompe and princlye game
> the Charge is great to him that all begun.
> let him be satisfyed now all is done.[51]

The pun hinted at in the pamphlet text's signatory poem is made
explicit here: "Amor is loue and Amory is his name." Written in
the same hand as the rest of the "maner of the showe" (and thus
probably of Amery's invention), the quatrain is no afterthought, but
an essential part of the document as a whole. The itemized list of
participants is the bill of fare, as it were, and Amery's poem is the
bill. Its use of the third person is an attempt to dun more effectively
the city fathers: it is some general, unlocalizable voice that seeks
reimbursement for Amery's expenses, not Amery himself. The voice
asserts that Amery's production of the "pompe and princlye game"
(the 1610 show) was motivated solely by his love for his fellow citizens and for his native city, a love identical to the one acting in
the procession proper.

The poem stands out for yet another reason: it subjects the manuscript page to the war between Love and Envy. Civic conflict manifests itself as inscription, for the last line of the quatrain has been
crossed through ("~~let him be satisfyed now all is done~~") and replaced
by a new line, "who now is Sattiffited to see all so well done."[52]

---

[50] Ibid., sense 4.
[51] *REED: Chester*, 260. The phrase "now all is done" suggests that at least the
poem, if not the entire "maner of showe," was written down after 23 April 1610.
[52] Ibid., 260.

Clopper attributes this emendation to Randle Holme. Holme's "correction" transforms the poem's meaning: instead of an imperative request for compensation on Amery's behalf as actor (in both of our first two senses of the term), we now have a subordinate clause recording Amery's aesthetic appreciation ("to see") of a task completed. Holme cancels Amery's line of verse, and, in doing so, symbolically cancels Amery's chances of getting his money back. When we consider that Holme gave Amery five shillings toward the cost of the bells and cup (the only private individual so named in the Harley 2150 assessment), we can begin to see how Amery's aggressive performance of identity backfires, evoking defensive self-assertions from his fellow citizens. What Clopper glosses as a bit of routine antiquarian practice turns out to be fairly antagonistic civic politics.

This sense of conflict brings us to the third and final sense of *actor* at work in the Amery's Harley 2150 signature: "A pleader; he who conducts an action at law . . . the plaintiff or complainant."[53] Amery's quatrain belongs to the genre of the poetic petition: "let him be satisfyed" requests payment for services rendered.[54] It also anticipates an actual document, "The humble petition of Robert Amerie."[55] Amery addresses his petition "To the right Worshipfull William Leicester Maior of the Cittie of Chester, the Alderman Sheriffes and comen Councell of the same Cittie"—in other words, to his peers (and fellow honor-competitors) in civic government.[56] In it, he claims total expenses of "the some of C li. at the leaste" and asks to be compensated for bearing this financial burden out of pocket ("to this Peticioners greate trouble & Charges").[57] Amery's assumption of this "humble" stance is ultimately a performance equivalent to those on

---

[53] *OED*, sense 2.

[54] See J. A. Burrow, "The Poet as Petitioner," *Studies in the Age of Chaucer* 3 (1981), 61–75, for a still relevant introduction to petitionary verse.

[55] *REED: Chester*, 261. Clopper dates this otherwise undated document (Cheshire and Chester Archives MS A/F/8) to 23 April 1610: its use of the phrase "did lately" with reference to Amery's staging of the triumph suggests that the show has ended by the time of the petition's composition. Groombridge notes that petitions to the Assembly "were never dated by the petitioner, who sometimes had to apply several times before he obtained an answer to his request" (*Calender of Chester City Council Minutes*, viii).

[56] *REED: Chester*, 261.

[57] Ibid., 261.

display in *Chester's Triumph*: the actor/manager producing the show becomes in turn an actor/pleader before the court of Chester's city government.

However, there is a key difference between Amery's petitionary performance and that of his allegorical double in the show. As I have argued in this essay, Love's function is to augment Amery's civic reputation. The petitioner takes an opposite tack, downplaying aggressive self-promotion in favor of a humble dedication to Chester's corporate identity. Amery claims that he proposed and carried out his plans "with the lykeinge and approbation of diuers iudicious persons within this Cittie," that he acted "for the good of the same [Chester], at home."[58] He appeals here to the spirit of communal unity and depicts his actions as directly constitutive of that unity. In doing so, he revises *Chester's Triumph*, presenting race and show as exemplars of urban—not individual—pride and self-celebration. He claims to have only ever had two aims: "the seruice of his Maiestie as occasion shall requyre" and "the present delight & Comforte of his people."[59] Moreover, his petition states that the St. George's Day Race is to serve as a perpetual monument to Cestrian community: "the greateste parte of the said Charge is bestowed vpon thinges extant, which are to remayne to future ages for the good of the said Cittie."[60] Amery's emphasis here on permanence and legacy speaks to a fantasy of endlessly unified civic purpose. His hope is that, if the Assembly members share this fantasy, they will give him his £100.

That particular gambit failed: written at the bottom of Amery's petition is the stark statement "this peticion beinge read throughte not fitt to passe to eleccion & voices at an assemblie."[61] Nonindividualized bureacratic procedures (the voice of impersonal, wholly communal civic authority) reject Amery's petition, denying him the chance to recreate the dialogic debate he staged in *Chester's Triumph*.[62]

---

[58] Ibid., 261.
[59] Ibid., 261.
[60] Ibid., 261.
[61] Ibid., 261.
[62] Groombridge's description of the petitionary process suggests that it had its performative elements: "it was often advisable to provide entertainment if support was wanted for a measure" (*Calendar of Chester City Council Minutes*, vii). For example, in 1603–04, representatives of the Painters' company spent eight pence to buy "wyne at Thomas Alertons tavern" for the Clerk of the Pentice, the civic official

Indeed, although we do have one 1610 record of a payment to Amery by the Drawers of Dee (interestingly enough, at "mr maiors request"), it nonetheless appears that Amery never recovered his expenses.[63] He did continue to look for ways to conspicuously perform his "Love" for Chester: the Assembly Book entry for 1 October 1613, ten days after his 21 September death, notes that Amery's children will be allowed to resubmit his petition requesting compensation for "newe worke in the said Cittie for the strykeinge of the quarters of howers neere the high Crosse."[64] This sort of privately-funded civic improvement—whether it takes the form of a clockworks, a horse race, or a streetside spectacle—exemplifies the Janus-like "Love" Amery celebrates in *Chester's Triumph*. Love of self meets love of city, and the performance of civic virtue generates individual honor (and envy).

Seventeenth-century Cestrians were aware of this conjunction of social forces, and I want to close with one last document testifying to that fact. It is an Assembly Book entry for 17 April 1612, the year of the third St. George's Day race:

> Allso at the same Assemblie it is thought fitt and soe ordered that those sportes and recreacions vsed of late within this Citie vpon Saint George his daie, shalbe from hencefourth vsed and Continued in such decent and Comendable manner as by the Maior for the time beinge and his brethren shalbe appoincted and allowed of as a pleasure or recreation performed and daie by Direction of the Maior and Citizens, and not by anie priuate or particuler person whatsoever.[65]

There is a hint of puritan opposition to sports and games in this entry (indicated by the phrase "decent and Comendable manner").[66] But a comment in the margin clarifies the Assembly's motives in this

---

responsible for presenting petitions to the Assembly (ibid., viii). This sort of bribe may not initially seem performative until we remember that Chester's city fathers had their own official drinking rituals: for an account of one such ritual (the "shot"), see Mary Wack, "Women, Work, and Plays in an English Medieval Town," *Maids and Mistresses, Cousins and Queens: Women's Alliances in Early Modern England*, eds. Susan Frye and Karen Robertson (New York: Oxford UP, 1999), 39.

[63] *REED: Chester*, 263.

[64] Cheshire and Chester Local Archives MS A/B/1, fol. 327.

[65] *REED: Chester*, 273.

[66] For information on the wider cultural background of Stuart-era opposition to games and "recreation," see Leah S. Marcus, *The Politics of Mirth: Jonson, Herrick, Milton, Marvell, and the Defense of Old Holiday Pastimes* (Chicago: University of Chicago Press, 1986).

matter: "The games and recreations on Stt George his day to haue contynuance by the onelie direction of the maior and cittizens."[67] Amery's aspirations for individually-directed celebration are dismissed in favor of community control over all spectacles. "Priuate or particular" persons need not apply: the Assembly order testifies to an anxious awareness of civic pageantry's ability to serve private purposes even as it ostensibly speaks to the public interest. To minimize the social damage epitomized by Envy, Chester's governors limit Love's purview. Public performance is now the sole business of the Corporation (a personified abstraction in its own right). Personal reputation is subordinated to the city's fame, and the ideal of the holistic community is used precisely to deny men like Amery the opportunity to celebrate Chester as anything other than the embodiment of official local power. In 1612, *Chester's Triumph* becomes the triumph of Chester.

Appendix: The Order of Show for the 1610 St George's Day Race and Triumph

The order of show presented here is that given in the pamphlet version of *Chester's Triumph*. The British Library MS Harley 2150 version lacks the following items: 1 (the acrobat), 16 (the rider bearing St. George's standard), and—most significantly—23 (the figure of Joy). Harley 2150 also inverts the order of items 15 and 17: the rider bearing the silver cup is listed before Rumor.

Performer/Speaker/Activity	Signature(s) of Oration
1. An acrobat who, while standing on the top of St. Peter's steeple at the High Cross, displays the colors of St. George, sounds a drum, shoots a gun, flourishes a sword, does a handstand—all accompanied by fireworks.	
2. Two "Greene-men" dressed as "Savages" and armed with both clubs and fireworks to clear the way for the show. They are accompanied by an artificial dragon (most likely the one used in	

---

[67] *REED: Chester*, 273.

Appendix (Cont.)

Performer/Speaker/Activity	Signature(s) of Oration
Chester's traditional Midsummer Show) which they will subsequently "battle" on the Roodee for the audience's entertainment (at some indeterminate point during item 24).	
3. A rider carrying the helmet and shield of St. George, accompanied by a drummer and two other attendants.	
4. Fame on horseback.	B2
5. A song summoning Mercury and performed by eight singers.	B2v
6. Mercury descends from the top of St. Peter's steeple in "a cloud," possessed of artificial wings and accompanied by a fireworks display which includes a wheel of fire. Upon completing his oration, Mercury reascends the steeple.	B2v–B3v
7. Chester on horseback.	B3v–B4
8. A rider carrying King James's arms.	
9. Britain on horseback.	B4v
10. A rider carrying a gilt bell engraved with the King's arms (first prize in the race to follow).	
11. A rider carrying Prince Henry's arms.	
12. Camber on horseback.	B4v–C1
13. A rider carrying a silver bell engraved with the Prince's arms (second prize in the race to follow).	
14. A rider carrying St. George's arms.	
15. Rumor on horseback.	C1–C1v
16. A rider carrying St. George's standard.	
17. A rider carrying a silver cup engraved with St. George's arms (the prize for the winner of the tilt to follow).	
18. St. George.	
19. Peace on horseback.	C2–C2v
20. Plenty on horseback.	C2v–C3
21. Envy on horseback (dialogue with Love).	C3–C4v
22. Love on horseback (dialogue with Envy).	C3–C4v
23. Joy on horseback.	C4v
24. The crowd (including the Mayor, sheriffs, and aldermen in scarlet) adjourns to the Roodee (guarded by 240 soldiers armed with halberds and guns). Ships in the River Dee display the arms of St. George and fire a number of volleys in honor of the day. The dedication of the bells and their presentation to the Mayor. A race held to	

Appendix (Cont.)

Performer/ Speaker/ Activity	Signature(s) of Oration
determine the winners of the bells. This is followed by a tilt (running at the ring) in which the local gentry vie for the cup.	
25. Fame "enrolls" the victors within her book.	D1
26. Britain grants both a wreath and the gilt bell ("the better Bell") to the winner of the race.	D1
27. Camber grants both a wreath and the silver bell ("the second Bell") to the runner-up.	D1
28. Rumor presents the winner of the tilt with both a wreath and the silver cup.	D1
29. Britain, Camber, and Rumor promise to spread the fame of the victors across "all times and places."	D1
30. Chester closes out the show by inviting the assembled worthies (urban and rural) to a banquet held at the Pentice (the city offices built onto the south front of St. Peter's).	D2v

HAVE HIS "CARKASSE": THE AFTERMATHS OF ENGLISH COURT MASQUES

Tom Bishop

In 1608, Ben Jonson had a volume of his first two masques for the court of King James printed, comprising *The Masque of Blackness* of 1605 and its sequel, *The Masque of Beauty* of 1608. Jonson prefaced the whole text with a note explaining this publication as a memorial of the two occasions. He was explicit about the necessity for this memorial, since, he insisted, "Little had been done to the studie of *magnificence* in these [spectacles], if presently with the rage of the people, who (as a part of greatnesse) are priuiledged by custome, to deface their *carkasses*, the *spirits* had also perished."[1] These were those same "spirits" Jonson was now proposing to call up and annotate in the more controllable medium of print.

The exact meaning of Jonson's reference to the fate of the material structures of masques remains somewhat obscure. In explaining his comment, editors and commentators have generally followed the authority, and often the wording, of E. K. Chambers' brief note on the subject. Chambers cited Jonson's remark in a footnote to *The Elizabethan Stage* to support his claim that in later masques "the Tudor custom of finishing the proceedings by rifling the pageant and the dresses of their decorations had not been wholly abandoned."[2] Chambers is, however, somewhat coy about what "not . . . wholly" might entail. Herford and Simpson, in their commentary on *Blackness*, simply quote Chambers verbatim.[3] Stephen Orgel glosses "At the end of the masque, the audience was traditionally permitted to tear down the scenery and plunder the decorations," eliding Chambers' more alarming suggestion that "the dresses" might also have been

---

[1] Quoted from the Folio text of 1616 as given in C. H. Herford and Percy Simpson, *Ben Jonson* 11 vols (Oxford: Clarendon Press, 1925–1963), 7: 169.

[2] E. K. Chambers, *The Elizabethan Stage* 4 vols. (Oxford: Clarendon Press, 1923), 1: 206.

[3] Herford and Simpson, 10: 451.

objects of spoil.[4] David Lindley, echoing both Chambers and Orgel, asserts that "the Tudor custom of permitting the audience to take down scenery and plunder decorations seems to have survived into the early Stuart period."[5] And most recently, John Astington discusses crowd management at royal entertainments, commenting more generally that "audiences at masques were also given to unruly behavior following the performance itself."[6]

The image of an emboldened audience at the Jacobean court attacking the set and perhaps the costumed masquers themselves in a concluding frenzy is a heady one, full of atavistic promise. For at least one critic, it provides important evidence to ground some anthropological and metaphysical speculations on the character of Jacobean, especially royal, subjectivity. In this account, the tumult expands to include not merely a generic audience, but also some of the courtly dancers themselves, and apparently immediately follows the entertainment, rather like a riot at a rock concert:

> The first act of voiding, or spoiling, occurred just as the revels dance with the audience ended. Suddenly, the "wild" audience (including, presumably, the as yet unrefined lady dancers) charged the stage, tore down the perspective scenery, and stripped the masquers of their rich furnishings.[7]

Jonson's note, in this critic's reading, reports a strange custom by which courtiers "actualize the insubstantiality of subjectivity lurking at the heart of all such 'private' entertainments."[8] That is, the assembled nobility and gentry themselves express a profound, perhaps partly unconscious, sense of the provisionality of all their social claims and identities by destroying what they themselves have, only moments before, asserted and enjoyed. A violent unrobing becomes a kind of apocalypse.

---

[4] Stephen Orgel ed., *Ben Jonson: The Complete Masques* (New Haven: Yale University Press, 1969), 47.

[5] David Lindley ed., *Court Masques* (Oxford: OUP, 1995), 215.

[6] John Astington, *English Court Theatre, 1558–1642* (Cambridge: Cambridge University Press, 1999), 177. Astington's remarks in general (pp. 170–78) are very useful.

[7] Patricia Fumerton, *Cultural Aesthetics* (Chicago: University of Chicago Press, 1991), 160. In fact, of course, there was usually at least some concluding passage of song and ceremonial withdrawal between the end of the dances and the conclusion of the entertainment.

[8] Ibid., 162.

Given the high drama of such a scene, it seems worth inquiring once more on what other authority it may rest. Who was in fact involved in these events? When and how did they occur? What contemporary understanding of them, if any, can be traced? Chambers' footnote is a good place to start. Chambers documents his "early Tudor custom" with a pair of passages from Hall's chronicle of the reign of Henry VIII, detailing incidents close to a century earlier. Unfortunately, neither of the passages is altogether clear in disclosing a firm custom or settled practice. Instead, the accounts seem to point to a complex process of negotiation, which was indeed sometimes violent, but not clearly so of right, among monarch, courtiers, and others in attendance over how and to whom the benefits of royal magnificence are to fall. The question of the disposal of the material effects of the masque is intimately bound up with several different kinds of economy—of prestige, of giving, of violence, of goods—at the heart of English court revel and society.

The first, and more famous, of Chambers' citations from Hall recounts an incident of 13 February, 1511, in the second year of Henry's reign. Lavish celebrations were being given at Richmond in honor of the birth of a son to Queen Katherine the previous New Year's Day.[9] After a magnificent two day tilt of unparalleled chivalric splendor, pageantry, and expense, in which Henry sported armor bearing the chivalric pseudonym *Cuer [Coeur] loyall* and, perhaps not surprisingly, himself "attained the prize," the King and Queen took a concluding supper. They then repaired to "the white hall within the said Palace" where dancing followed. During the dancing the King covertly withdrew. To a flourish of trumpets, a magnificent pageant wagon, called "the Golden Arbor in the arch yard of pleasure," was wheeled in. A gentleman "richly appareled" announced that the lords and ladies within the pageant wished "to show pleasure and pastime to the Queen and ladies" by dancing for them. Upon their being invited to do so, the pageant came closer and "a great cloth of Arras" fell from before it, revealing a pleasure grove of flowering trees "all made of satin, damask, silk, silver and gold" in which were six couples in similarly costly garments "embroidered full of H & K of gold."[10] The couples descended and danced before

---

[9] Prince Henry died on February 23rd, ten days later.
[10] The H and K, of course, referring to Henry and Katherine. See Edward Hall,

the audience. While they were doing so, however, there was trouble in paradise:

> the pageant was conveyed to the end of the place, there to tarry 'til
> the dances were finished, and so to have received the Lords and Ladies
> again, but suddenly the rude people ran to the pageant, and rent, and
> tare, and spoiled the pageant, so that the Lord Steward nor the head
> officers could not cause them to abstain, except they should have fought
> and drawn blood, and so was this pageant broken.[11]

Nor was the excitement yet over. At the conclusion of their dancing, the king indicated that the gold letters from the dancers' garments were to be given "in token of liberality" to "the ladies,
gentlewomen and the Ambassadors":

> ... which thing the common people perceiving, ran to the King, and
> stripped him into his hose and doublet, and all his companions in like-
> wise.... The ladies likewise were spoiled, wherefore the King's guard
> came suddenly, and put the people back.... So the King with the
> Queen and the ladies returned into his chamber, where they had a
> great banquet, and all these hurts were turned to laughing and game,
> and thought that all that was taken away was but for honor and
> largess.[12]

Despite the vividness of these accounts, it is not at all easy to solve
the central interpretive problem that they pose for our purpose: what
in all this melée was customary, what was unusual but licit, and
what was extraordinary and wild?

To try to sort these elements out, we should first consider that
there are two separate acts of pillage recorded, however they might
have fed one another on the occasion: first, the destruction of the
pageant wagon, and second, the attack on the masquers' costumes.
As regards the pageant wagon—which in Stuart masques would

Henry VIII 2 vols. (London: T. C. & E. C. Jack, 1904), 1: 26. The pageantry of
the two day tournament is documented on the magnificent surviving record still
held at the College of Heralds, and reproduced in *The Great Tournament Roll of
Westminster*, ed. and intro. Sydney Anglo, 2 vols. (Oxford: Clarendon Press, 1968).
Anglo discusses the whole sequence of celebrations in 1, 51–58, and also in his
Spectacle, Pageantry, and Early Tudor Policy (Oxford: Clarendon Press, 1969), 210–24.
I have modernized texts throughout this article where the original texts would
impede modern readers.
[11] Hall, *Henry VIII*, 1: 27. That the Lord Steward and his men were apparently
reluctant to shed blood on this occasion is notable.
[12] Hall, *Henry VIII*, 1: 27.

metamorphose into the "set"—it appears from Hall quite clearly that
"the Lord Steward [and] the head officers" attempted to prevent its
plunder, but it is not clear whether this was only because it was ill-
timed, the pageant being still needed for the egress. However, a
related narrative in the accounts of Richard Gibson, who was responsible for producing tournament and revels spectacles under Henry,
suggests that there was in fact no regular expectation that used properties would be made available to all comers. Though Gibson does
not mention the fate of the "Golden Arbor," he does record how
on the previous day a pageant representing a castle in a forest was
destroyed:

> This forest or pageant after the usance [was] had into Westminster
> Great Hall, and *by the King's guard and other gentlemen* rent, broken, and
> by force carried away, and the poor men that were set to keep [it],
> their heads broken two of them, and the remnant put therefrom with
> force, so that none thereof but the bare timber came near to the King's
> use nor store.[13]

Likewise Gibson notes that the four jousting pavilions from the second day's exertions "were saved to the King's use, and profit with
much pain" suggesting that a similar attack was this time foiled.[14]
Clearly in both cases Gibson is recording his expectation that these
items would remain among the resources of the Crown.

But if Gibson's remarks indicate that the plundering of pageants
was not an anticipated part of the proceedings, they also suggest the
inability or disinclination of the guard to prevent what many in attendance clearly saw as an irresistible opportunity. Nor this time is it
the "rude" or "common people" who stage the attack, but "gentlemen"—including even some of the guard! On three other occasions,
Gibson's accounts of this period (sadly incomplete) record that the
fabulous pageants which were a feature of Henry's revels ended up
"sent to the Prince's wardrobe as broken store," but whether they
were broken by being plundered or simply broken up for salvage
and reuse is not clear.[15] Once, Gibson *is* more explicit, noting that
the "tartron" fabric on a pageant "in the press of people was cut

---

[13] See *Letters and Papers, Foreign and Domestic, of the Reign of Henry VIII* (London:
Longman, 1862–1886; HMSO, 1887–1910), vol. 2 pt 2, p. 1495, my emphasis.
[14] *Letters and Papers* 2:2, p. 1495.
[15] *LP* 2:2, p. 1498; cf. pp. 1499, 1509.

away, rent and torn by strangers and others, as well the King's servants as not, and letted not for the King's presence."[16] And here
again, this does not seem like something which was approved—at
least by Gibson, who renders a careful account of the losses, and
clearly regards them as contrary to proper decorum.[17] Here again
both members of the court entourage and non-member "strangers"
are involved.

The same mixture of licensed and illicit depredation also marks
surviving records of the fate of costumes at Henry's revels. *The Great
Chronicle of London*, for instance, which also records the 1511 tournament and pageant, includes a somewhat different version of the
incident of Henry's stripping:

> ... the which Garment for the King would that it should be divided
> among the ambassadors servants, he commanded the Gentlemen Ushers
> of his Chamber that they should set the said servants at a certain place
> where he should passe by, when the disguising was ended, and that
> they should not fear to pull & tear the said Garment from his body,
> among the which strangers, were it by favor of the said Ushers or
> otherwise, a poor shearman of the city got in with them, where they
> so tarrying when the King came they spared not, but tore it off at
> the gainest, among the which this said shearman took his part. . . .[18]

In this account the event is rather more controlled than in Hall,
even if some participants—such as the shearman—were unautho-
rized. We have to do, it seems, with a deliberate gesture of diplo-
matic munificence, no doubt in the service of hospitality and
international prestige. Gibson's records for the occasion suggest the
taking was on a fairly large scale: he records a total of nearly nine-
teen pounds (troy) of gold gone, well over half the total adorning
the masquers.

The second occasion cited from Hall by Chambers backs up the
suggestion that what we have here at least begins as a controlled

---

[16] *LP* 2:2, p. 1502. Does the last phrase indicate that such actions were licit once
"the King's presence" was withdrawn?

[17] The care of Gibson's accounts is not surprising, since he was liable for precious metals not accounted for.

[18] A. H. Thomas and I. D. Thornley eds, *The Great Chronicle of London* (Gloucester:
Alan Sutton, 1983), p. 374 (fo. 348v). The reliability of the *Great Chronicle* narrator
is uncertain. For instance, he takes the letter K on Henry's garments to stand for
"King" (pp. 369, 371), though it clearly denotes "Katherine." He does not mention the fate of either pageant wagon.

largesse to specific recipients. At Tournai on 18 October 1513, after "a sumptuous banquet of [a hundred] dishes . . . the ladies danced, and then came in the king and [eleven] in a masque, all richly appareled with bonnets of gold, and when they had passed the time at their pleasure, the garments of the masque were cast off amongst the ladies, take who could take."[19] This courtly gesture is, again, very much a part of Henry's persona as fountain and knight of courtesy. But there is no record of a *customary* wild stripping of costumed masquers by the crowd at large.[20]

Hall mentions no other such disorderly incidents in his accounts of the festive life of Henry's court, but records of royal largesse at his entertainments are not hard to find for this period of his reign, and some aspect or version of these practices, revived or continued, is probably what Jonson is alluding to in 1608. It was, for instance, a quite regular part of period court entertainments to give accessories and items of costume to both noble and non-noble participants. Gibson's accounts show that on Epiphany 1513, at the conclusion of the "Rich Mount" pageant, "The Princess of Castile had, as the King's gift, her head apparel [and other items]. The other five ladies also kept their corresponding articles of attire. The lords, the six minstrels on the mount, the men at arms, the tambourines and the rebecks kept their dresses."[21] Partly these are courtly gifts to aristocratic peers and underlings, partly remuneration to employees for services. Such gifting was not universal however. Other garments from the "Rich Mount" entertainment were returned to the various court offices, sometimes disassembled. Thus "4 jackets of crimson velvet" were returned to Richard Smith, the yeoman of the robes, but their gold embellishments were ripped off and sent to Robert Amadas, the Master of the Jewels, who had issued gold for use in

---

[19] Hall, *Henry VIII*, 1: 117.

[20] It is possible that Jonson was himself aware of the incidents at Henry's court recorded by Hall, and had them in mind in writing his prefatory note. Though the evidence for Jonson's reading of Hall is slim, Herford and Simpson suggest that a barriers of May 6, 1527 may have provided a model for the one that followed *Hymenaei* in 1606. However, Jonson's note seems to refer to a contemporary rather than a former custom. See Herford and Simpson, *Jonson*, vol. 2, p. 271 fn. citing Hall, fol. 157b. For a more detailed description of the 1527 Barriers, see also in W.R. Streitberger, *Court Revels 1485–1559* (Toronto: University of Toronto Press, 1994), pp. 127–129.

[21] Quoted from the abstract of Gibson's accounts in *LP* 2:2, p. 1500.

the pageant as a whole.[22] And not all the unreturned pieces seem to have been clearly gifts: some of the gold (just over 4 oz.) was "given or for pleasure suffered to be taken" from the costumes of the King and Sir Charles Brandon.[23] This sounds suspiciously like the sort of moment Hall records more vividly, where the losses lie somewhere between largesse and theft.

Another illuminating account of the spoils of courtly revel, though still not involving explicit attack on the masquers, appears in the same *Great Chronicle* at the court of Henry VII in November 1502, where a series of jousts followed nightly by sumptuous banquets and disguisings were the means by which:

> many of the King's subjects were relieved, as well for the stuff by them sold and workmanship of the same, as by plates, spangles, roses and other conceits of silver and overgilt which fell from their garments, both of lords and ladies and gentlemen, whiles they leaped and danced, and were gathered of many poor folks standing near about and pressing in for lucre of the same.[24]

The chronicler has clearly recorded here an understanding of the specific role that largesse played in the complex material and symbolic economies of court entertainment. By linking the purveying of goods and services to the royal court through suppliers and artisans with the collection of valuable detritus fallen from the masquers during their exertions, the chronicle evokes a conception of "flowdown" from higher to lower facilitated by court extravagance. Whether by contractual payment for furnishings or by gathering a "superflux" literally shaken to them, those physically or institutionally adjacent to the court benefit from the very excesses of ruling revelry. Moreover, it seems here that they both expect and are expected to do so. The ambiguous character of such exchange helps explain the recurrent doubt in the accounts about whether this is all a matter of giving or taking. Wavering between these options marks out an area of understanding of one of the political purposes of aristocratic display:

---

[22] 375.5 oz. 2.75 dwt. of gold were issued, to be precise, i.e. 31.3 troy or 25.75 avoirdupois pounds.

[23] *LP* 2:2, 1500. Costumes returned to store were often refitted and used again on other occasions, as throughout the period. Gibson's accounts for the pageant of Troilus and Cressida of Epiphany 1515, for instance, record that a half-dozen ladies' costumes "were of the King's store, newly repaired," *LP* 2:2, 1505.

[24] *Great Chronicle*, p. 315; see also Streitberger, *Court Revels*, p. 335.

not only to showcase wealth, but also to shake it down. But it would be going a step further to read a definite 'custom' here—what seems in view rather is an area of potential license, an ongoing negotiation within a "moral economy" between wealth and need. In freely— even negligently—giving, or seeming to do so, wealth performs itself as at once insouciant and beneficent. In moving to take, need presents itself as the necessary object of charitable excess.[25]

The Revels Office records of Elizabeth's reign, imperfect though they are, bear out the perception that costumes and properties in court entertainments formed part of a network of gift or remuneration, expectations about which could be activated from both sides. But careful attention to the records reveals no evidence of wholesale pillage or regular plunder. The Revels accounts are at pains to record the care taken to maintain, preserve and recycle masquing costumes, "airing, repairing, laying abroad, turning, sewing, amending, tacking, sponging, folding, suiting, putting in order and safe bestowing" as one entry puts it.[26] Accounts of the fortunes of a given set of masque costumes (which the records refer to simply as "a masque") are often minute in their description of how the garments were repeatedly recast and remade until they were so tired they could no longer be used. A typical such entry is this one, following the fate of some cloth used in:

> 8 pair of slops parted, the one leg of . . . blue cloth of gold and the other of green cloth of silver, the green cloth . . . translated into lining of the Almains slops, and again cut in pieces to pane fishermen's slops and bodies, and again translated into a masque of mariners, and again translated into torchbearers for a masque of Turks, . . . the same being so often shown and translated was forsworn and not serviceable.[27]

Such reuse of textiles saves the expense of new purchases while still providing variety in the entertainments. In none of these careful entries is there good evidence that costumes were damaged in or after performance.

---

[25] It is notable that these vivid records are concentrated in the early years of Henry's reign. In later years, Magnificence was more restrained and his court saw nothing like the ebullient—and extravagant—occasions of the 1520s.

[26] See Albert Feuillerat ed., *Documents relating to the Office of the Revels in the time of Queen Elizabeth* (London: David Nutt, 1908), p. 147. This entry is from 1572.

[27] Feuillerat, *Revels*, p. 19. The descent from main masquers through linings to torchbearers is also typical. Cloth seems gradually to slip down a social scale as it deteriorates in quality from reuse.

As under Henry, Elizabethan costumes and other items were often
used as largesse gifts or as payment to performers. The Revels
accounts record both kinds of transaction. From a masque of Clowns
"eight aprons of white gold sarsenet edged with Venice gold fringe
[were] given away by the maskers in the Queen's presence."[28] There
are regular notations of costumes "taken for their fees" by musicians
or players.[29] Sometimes, again as with Henry, it is not entirely clear
whether costumes that walked away with their wearers were given
or taken. Some sections of the black velvet used to mimic the limbs
of "a masque of Moors" were taken away by "the Lords that
masqued," and parts of a masque of Palmers from Queen Mary's
reign could not be traced "for they were all taken away by the
Strangers and Lords that masqued in the same."[30] At least once, the
illicit withholding is explicit: in 1574, William Elom had to be paid
for "six horns garnished with silver, by him delivered into the office
for the hunters' masque on New Year's night, which horns the masquers detained and yet doth [sic] keep them against the will of all
the officers."[31] Once again, gift, payment and theft overlap.

But the document in the Elizabethan Revels accounts that most
clearly suggests costumes were carefully preserved and maintained in
good condition, despite the chronic penury of the office (to which
it also testifies), is the 1572 complaint of one Thomas Giles, a London
man with a costume hire business. Giles alleges in his complaint that
the Yeoman of the Revels:

> doth usually let to hire her said Highness' masques to the great hurt,
> spoil, and discredit of the same to all sorts of persons . . ., by reason
> of which common usage the gloss and beauty of the same garments
> is lost and cannot so well serve to be often altered and . . . showed
> before her Highness as otherwise it might and hath been used.[32]

Giles' concern is not only for the Queen: the hire of court costumes
is undercutting him "who having apparel to let . . . cannot so cheaply

---

[28] Feuillerat, p. 40. The account seems to record Her Majesty's presence as an
assurance that this gift was authorized.

[29] See Feuillerat, pp. 25, 27, 40, 41 for examples.

[30] Feuillerat, pp. 24, 23.

[31] Feuillerat, p. 202. The only explicit notation of any thefts from the masquing
arena in the accounts is a 15 s. charge in 1581 for "small lights three for them
which were stolen at Twelfthtide." Were pillage a regular conclusion to court frolic,
one would expect a much higher recorded toll.

[32] Feuillerat, p. 409.

let the same as her Highness' masques be let." And he provides a fascinating list of events to which specific sets of Revels costumes had been worn over the past year, chiefly the Inns of Court and citizen weddings (including "a tailor marriage" but also that of "the daughter of my Lord Montague") in and around London.[33] Giles notes, as part of his complaint, that the frequent wearing by those "who for the most part be of the meanest sort of men" was reducing the life of the costumes, and he suggests, as a remedy, that the masques be disassembled after each use, presumably to hinder their being rented in the interim, a practicable step since "they never come before her Highness twice in one form."[34]

The point as regards the current argument is precisely the careful notation of the use and maintenance of these valuable items of apparel as part of the resources of the Crown, even when funding for this task was barely forthcoming. Though Giles has a clear interest in insisting on the point, his petition assumes the Crown wants the costumes to be carefully safeguarded. The absence of any record of crowd damage, stripping or rifling in such circumstances speaks to the unlikelihood that regular rioting was a part of Elizabethan courtly practice.

As far as the fate of the sets, wagons or other machinery goes, the documents are frustratingly silent and we are reduced to inference. Given the resistance evident in the costume records to the reappearance of recognizable items, the elaborate painted cloths, stage "houses," and other pieces of setting furniture are perhaps unlikely to have returned year after year. Many of the settings recorded are quite generic—a city, a battlement, a mount, a country house—but we do not know whether and how they were tailored to show their particular role in that year's play "as Strato's house, Gobbyn's house, Orestio's house" of 1567–8. John Astington, reviewing Elizabethan court theater in detail, suggests that the frames on which houses and other locations were mounted "must have been reused from year to year," but this says nothing about reuse of what was *on* those frames.[35] Until detailed accounts cease in 1589, painters and set-dressers are called on to provide and decorate swaths of

---

[33] Feuillerat, p. 410. But masques also went "into Kent" and "into the country".
[34] Feuillerat, p. 409.
[35] Astington, *English Court Theatre*, p. 138.

canvas for yearly productions, though such painting duties would have included preparing the hall itself, the ceiling, the chandeliers, and any stage platform built by the Works Office.[36] What happened to such routine "extra-stage" decorations along with custom-painted stage materials once the production was done is unknown. The accounts give details recording expenses involved in *making* the sets, not in storing them after use, as they do with the costumes. May we then assume that such elements of the set and decorations of the hall were considered disposable and left to the audience or some later set of gleaners? It is at least plausible. But when and how this took place we cannot say.[37]

The unhappily little that we can glean from earlier records is by no means easy to carry forward to the Jacobean conditions and practices described by Jonson. The vivid records of mayhem around a young King Henry are one thing, and testify, if anything, to the fairly porous security that monarch permitted early in his reign. But James, whose anxiety about crowds is well documented, is unlikely to have followed Henry's example here. Though he modeled himself on, and was received as, a version of Henry in some respects, particularly in his magnificence and his headship of a royal family,

---

[36] Tracing the fate of the timber used for the sets and machinery of masques is no easier. Under Elizabeth, "houses" for court drama were built by the Office of the Revels, larger structures—such as temporary halls, risers for audiences and stage platforms—by the Works Office. Until 1565, the Surveyor of the Works retained "all demolished fabrics," perhaps including any associated with court revelry, but "in April 1565 a limited compensation was made in the shape of an allowance to the Surveyor of waste timber from the Works undertakings." (See H. M. Colvin ed., *The History of the King's Works* vol. 3 pt. 1 1485–1660, London: H. M. Stationery Office, 1975, p. 73). A later manuscript records that temporary structures for court festivities employed "used timber" and "the Windsor orders direct that some of the timber from old houses [presumably not *stage* houses, but other Crown properties] previously taken by the Surveyor to his own uses should be set aside for that purpose" (Colvin, *History*, p. 81; the MS summarized is BM Lansdowne MS 6 no 4, partly in Cecil's hand). Under James, it appears that the large construction jobs required by Jones's masque designs were contracted specially through Jones himself, separately from either the Revels' or the Works' Offices. What became of the used timber is not recorded. Precedent might suggest that Jones was entitled to it himself, in which case he would presumably not have wanted to see it stolen. This may help to explain what may have been a change of "aftermath" policy in the later Jacobean period, along with James's own innovation of having masques repeated.

[37] Even after the apparent change of policy in the late 1580s, which brought players to court with their repertoire to replace custom-built entertainments from the Revels Office, the halls would still have been elaborately trimmed for the revels, providing work for Tilney's artisans and possible leftovers for the picking.

he avoided the chivalric and martial vocabulary that Henry enjoyed. The *rex pacificus* neither danced in masques nor rode in tournaments, and when, around 1610, Prince Henry moved to refurbish the language of old chivalry, James seems to have been only partly willing to go along.[38]

Certainly, early in his reign—Jonson's note is from 1608—James was at pains to present himself as a lordly and generous monarch, given to largesses and old-fashioned royal magnificence. At his very first masque, *The Vision of Twelve Goddesses* of 1604, Queen Anne raided the late Queen's wardrobe for costumes for herself and her fellow masquers, and when the latter first shone and then walked off to the banquet in these garments, it must have seemed as though Largesse was triumphing boldly over Pick-Penny late deceased.[39] Partly, one suspects, this effect was deliberate. But if there was a regular custom of general gifting at Jacobean masquing, either inherited or revived, no clear testimony exists to shed light on its character or timing. Certainly, as Chambers notes, "some confusion" attended the ends of performances, but hardly less than that recorded at their beginnings, or than one might expect at any highly crowded venue of aggressive display. Samuel Daniel's device at *Tethys' Festival* of having a final exit procession for the masquers "in their own form" in order "to avoid the confusion which usually attendeth the dissolve of these shows" may refer to no more than the familiar scramble to get out of an overcrowded auditorium after a long night of standing immobile.[40] *Blackness* itself, subject of Jonson's obscure note, performed on the day of the creation of the young Prince Charles as Duke of York (6 Jan 1604/5), prompted Dudley Carleton to report merrily to John Chamberlain on the crush throughout:

---

[38] James forbade Henry to include an equestrian display in the planning that eventually became *Oberon* in 1610 (Herford and Simpson, *Jonson*, 10: 518). Accession Day (March 24th) tilts were yearly features of James' court, but they seem not to have been as spectacular as Elizabeth's—with the exception, notably, of the one for Henry's creation as Prince of Wales in 1610. They were discontinued altogether in 1622.

[39] For the costumes, see Dudley Carleton's letter of January 15, 1604, in *Dudley Carleton to John Chamberlain*, 1602–1624, ed. Maurice Lee (New Brunswick: Rutgers University Press, 1972), p. 55.

[40] Quoted in Chambers, *Elizabethan Stage* 3: 282. Jonson's "Love Restored" brings in Robin Goodfellow to outline some of the hazards of long waits and crowding in the masquing hall prior to the performance. By masque's end, often as late as next sunrise, it is hardly surprising if the crowd was eager for release; see "Love Restored" ll. 98 ff. in Orgel, *Complete Masques*.

The confusion in getting in was so great that some ladies lie by it and complain of the fury of the white staffs [i.e. ushers]. In the passages through the galleries they were shut up in several heaps betwixt doors and there stayed till all was ended, and in the coming out, a banquet which was prepared for the King in the great chamber was overturned, table and all, before it was scarce touched. It were infinite to tell you what losses there were of chains, jewels, purses, and suchlike loose ware, and one woman amongst the rest lost her honesty, for which she was carried to the porter's lodge, being surprised at her business on the top of the terrace.[41]

Carleton is a notorious gossip, so it is not easy to know how much of this is exaggerated, but the "confusion" he describes is logistic and accidental, or criminal, rather than customary. The overturning of the banquet is specifically an accident, and the loss of jewelry (if not of honesty) a misfortune. In a similar letter to Ralph Winwood describing a wedding masque of Juno and Hymeneus performed ten days earlier, Carleton reported that "There was no small loss . . . of chains and jewels, and many great ladies were made shorter by the skirts."[42] Is this a reference to a custom of stripping, or to bold thieving in a crowded auditorium?

Such evidence is difficult to interpret. A regular courtier like Carleton might omit to discuss customary audience depredation simply because his correspondent could take it for granted. But surviving eyewitness accounts of court masques given by foreign representatives also fail to mention any such occurrences. This is more strange given that these witnesses are prone to remark on such idiosyncrasies of English court life. Not one of the dispatches or sundry reports penned by Spanish, French, Venetian, Florentine, or Savoyard attendees speaks of any orgy of divestiture by the audience. One account which might appear to do so in fact only makes the absence of such comments the more telling. Written in Spanish by a witness to *Oberon* in 1610/11, this reports that

the king and queen with the ladies and gentlemen of the masque proceeded to the banqueting hall, going out after they had looked about and taken a turn round the table; and in a moment everything was thrown down with furious haste, according to the strange custom of the country.[43]

---

[41] Lee ed., *Dudley Carleton*, p. 68.
[42] Chambers, *Elizabethan Stage* 3: 377.
[43] *HMC: Downshire Manuscripts: Papers of William Trumbull the Elder* ed. A. B. Hinds

While it is just possible the final remark refers to the "throwing down" of the masque, it is more likely that it was the banquet in a quite different hall that was the object of "the strange custom of the country." Several other foreign reports remark on this odd English habit, which may have been merely the work of a crowd famished after a long night's exertions and overeager for their refreshments.[44]

And then there is the account of the second performance of *The Golden Age Restored* (6 Jan, 1615/16) included in despatches of the Savoy resident agent, Antonio Scarnafiggi. This describes the scenery and costumes in enough detail to identify the masque, and continues: "Afterwards a comedy was performed in the English language, and the festivity ended in very good order and the greatest content."[45] Of course the mayhem may have preceded the intervening comedy, or the latter may have subdued the former, but if so Scarnafiggi says nothing about that either.[46]

From these scattered Jacobean witnesses, it takes some imagination to construct a customary riot of masque-goers charging in to attack the set and costumed dancers, including members of the royal family, whatever may have happened under Henry VIII. Apart from Jonson's less than transparent reference, there is not one contemporary description of, or even unequivocal allusion to, a practice of set or costume stripping by the audience at the conclusion of a court masque. Though Jonson clearly was referring to something in his prefatory remarks to the 1608 volume, and something he expected

(London: H. M. Stationery Office, 1938), 3: 2. Trumbull was English resident at the court of Archduke Albert of Austria, Hapsburg regent of the Netherlands, in Brussels. It is very unlikely he himself saw the masque, but he seems to have received a report of it in Spanish. Stephen Orgel and Roy Strong attribute the report to Trumbull himself in *Inigo Jones: the Theatre of the Stuart Court* (Los Angeles: University of California Press, 1973), 1: 205.

[44] See also for instance the various references to banquet rapacity and violence recorded by Chambers, *Elizabethan Stage* 1: 207, and in John Orrell, "The London Court Stage in the Savoy Correspondence" *Theatre Research International* 4: 2 (1976), 85–6 and Astington, *Court Theatre*, p. 178.

[45] John Orrell, "London Court Stage," 83. As Orrell points out, the Savoy description clinches the previously disputed date of this masque, wrongly argued as 1614/15 by H & S 10: 545–6.

[46] Other non-official foreign attendees of masques likewise fail to mention any set-tearing. See for example the accounts of *Pleasure Reconciled to Virtue* by Orazio Busino, the Venetian chaplain (reprinted in H & S 10: 573–86), and by Francesco Quaratesi, no longer the Florentine representative (see John Orrell, "The London Stage in the Florentine Correspondence" *Theatre Research International* 3: 3 (1977), 176).

his readers not to have to strain to understand, it remains obscure to us just what and when. And since it is apparently our sole witness, it is worth looking to the specific wording of Jonson's account for what it may tell us.

Jonson's note refers to the "rage of the people who (as a part of greatnesse) are priuiledged by custome, to deface [the masques'] carkasses." Notable first is the occurrence of the same interaction of display and need that marked earlier incidents—"greatnesse" takes it as one of its "parts" to allow a "priuilege" of "rage" to its subordinates, as though recognizing how the very excess of magnificence spawns resentment that needs to be licensed, both for the affirmation and the protection of superiority. "Flowdown" is apparently still the order of the day, despite Jonson's condescending tone. But in addition, Jonson's choice of the metaphor of the "carkasse" may indicate something of the timing of this license. "Carkasse" is a specific builders' term relevant to the construction of masque sets, as Jonson, once apprenticed to a bricklayer, might be expected to know. The "carcass," according to Joseph Moxon, was "(as it were) the Skeleton of an House, before it is Lath'd and Plastered"—what we now would call, less vividly, its "frame."[47] Whether masque structures were substantial enough to have the frames under their highly decorated surfaces called "carcasses" we do not specifically know, but they were certainly, at least until Jones's innovations, called "houses." That they might be viewed so is suggested by a pun of Jonson's own in *Prince Henry's Barriers* of January, 1610, whose opening tableau presents the "House of Chivalry" as "decayed/Or rather ruined" (ll. 34–35). This ruin is elegized by the Lady of the Lake:

> O, when this edifice stood great and high,
> That in the *carcass* hath such majesty,
> Whose very *skeleton* boasts so much worth,
> What grace, what glories did it then send forth?[48]

---

[47] Joseph Moxon, *Mechanick Exercises, or The Doctrine of Handy-Works* (London: 1679). This definition is taken from the glossary in monthly issue IX, p. 165. Issue VIII also includes a section entitled "Of setting up the Carcass" describing construction. Moxon was Hydrographer to Charles II. It is highly likely that this vocabulary reflects the long-standing, traditional language of the English building trade, as Jonson would have known it. Professor Greg McNamara has pointed out to me that "carcass" is still a term used in carpentry, for instance for the shell of a set of drawers.

[48] Both quotations from Orgel and Strong, *Inigo Jones*, I: 160, ll. 34–35, 46–49,

Jonson puns on the architectural forms whose visible "skeletons" figure the decline of chivalry, employing the physical structures of the set as indices of a spiritual decay the action will overcome, when "Meliadus" (the Prince of Wales) is discovered within the "yet unde-molished" St. George's Portico. The same antithesis of carnal evanes-cence and spiritual survival—a key tension of the masque for Jonson, and a chief element of his later quarrel with Jones—appears here as in the published remark of two years before.[49] This sharpening of the term "carcass" suggests a greater precision to the 1608 note than we might have expected. If we parse "to deface their carkasses" as strictly as possible, the phrase points not to a general ravaging, but specifically to removal of the external "facing" on the wooden frames ("carcasses") of stage "houses," proscenia, and other structures.[50] The wooden frames themselves remain available for reuse, and noth-ing is implied about the costumes, which are still, after all, on the departing masquers.[51]

One other point about Jonson's wording is worth raising. Jonson refers to "the rage of the people." Though the condescension of his tone is typical, and its object not precise, are we entitled to assume from it that it was the spectators of the masque themselves who were involved in "defacing [the] carkasses"? Though we hardly know enough about the composition of these audiences to be confident here, the phrasing could suggest a populace different from the more

---

my emphasis. Jones's design for the "Fallen House of Chivalry," based on Hieronymous Cock's *Roman Ruins*, appears at I: 158.

[49] See also the same vocabulary deployed in the prefatory note to *Hymenaei* (1606). He was not the only one to make this distinction: see the letter of John Pory about this masque reprinted by Orgel and Strong, *Inigo Jones*, I: 105.

[50] Before Jones's innovations in scene design and staging, a traditional architec-tural vocabulary would have been appropriate to the separate "houses" of the action, the standard vocabulary used in the Elizabethan accounts. A Jacobean instance of the style may still be seen in Jones's designs for the 1610 *Barriers*, but this seems to have been the last time.

[51] The occasional practice of masquers sitting for portraits in costume also sug-gests the costumes were not extensively damaged. Where gentry paid for their own costumes, or costume pieces, they would perhaps have an additional interest in pre-serving them intact. Orgel and Strong report the Countess of Rutland, for instance, spending 112 li.14 s. on her costume for *Hymenaei*, in which she and other mas-quer ladies may have been painted (see Orgel and Strong, *Inigo Jones* I: 105, 114). Of this event, not financed by the Crown, John Pory reported to Sir Robert Cotton, "I think they hired and borrowed all the principal jewels and ropes of pearl both in court and city" (Orgel and Strong, I: 115). Obviously the interest in not having rented or borrowed jewels filched would be especially high.

privileged masque-goers.[52] Moreover, nothing in his remark entails that this "rage" was unleashed immediately after the masque. It is perfectly possible to imagine it postponed until hours, even days, later. It would thus be an aspect not of the performance itself, inviting comment from ambassadors and other courtier attendees, but of the process of taking down the masque and the other hall decorations. This must have been left to the Revels and Works officers, but naturally receives no attention from long-departed revelers.

The later Jacobean innovation of *repeating* masques may be a relevant consideration here. Beginning with *The Irish Masque* of 1613–14, it became the regular practice to give additional performances of court masques a few days, or weeks (on one occasion even four months!) later.[53] This raises severe problems for a theory of riotous post-performance pillaging. It seems unlikely an entire masque production, with its tremendous expense in materials and labor, could be rebuilt in, say, four days.[54] But if the undoing of the masque fabric was customarily a later event, even by a few hours, this would pose no problem: one would simply not allow it. It is also possible, given the relevant dates, that the custom to which Jonson refers in 1608 was discontinued after 1613. If so, it vanished without trace. In either case such a withdrawal of the opportunity of largesse would be a significant change in the relations of Magnificence and its subjects. Disallowing the profit made by the gleaners at Henry VII's court or the lucky shearmen at his son's would segregate two parts of what, even in its more violent manifestations under those early Tudors, seems to have been a working economic arrangement between

---

[52] On audiences at court, see Astington, *Court Theatre*, Ch. 3.

[53] Thus *The Irish Masque* (29 Dec, 1613 and 3 Jan, 1614), *Mercury Vindicated* (6 and 8 Jan, 1615), *The Golden Age Restored* (1 and 6 Jan, 1616), *The Vision of Delight* (6 and 19 Jan, 1617), *Pleasure Reconciled to Virtue* (6 Jan and, rewritten, 17 Feb, 1618), "Unknown masque" (6 Jan and 8 Feb, 1619), *News from the New World Discovered in the Moon* (17 Jan and 29 Feb, 1620), "Unknown masque" (6 Jan and 11 Feb, 1619), and *The Masque of Augurs* (6 Jan and 6 May, 1622).

[54] None of the records of the various Royal "departments" involved in paying for the masque (the Exchequer, the Treasury of the Chamber, the Office of Works, and the Office of Revels) is detailed enough to indicate whether there were extra expenses associated with a repeated masque, as the accounts were presented by the year (and sometimes several years), and do not record the dates of expenses with sufficient clarity. Exchequer accounts from the Pell book are excerpted under the respective masques in Herford and Simpson. For the Chamber accounts and those of the Works and Revels offices, see the records reprinted respectively in the *Malone Society Collections*, vol. 6 (1961), 10 (1975), and 13 (1986).

ruler and subject. The court would no longer be, in its most prodigal moment, a potential source of material benefit to the people. Such a change, be it never so slight, would mark the opening or widening of a gulf of some significance for "the rage of the people" in future Stuart history.

READING/GENRES: ON 1630S MASQUES

Lauren Shohet

The genre of court masque has occasioned some of the most finely "localized" work on Stuart politics. Such critics as Leah Marcus, Martin Butler, David Lindley, and Kevin Sharpe have decoded ways that specific court masques symbolically engage political issues *du jour*. For example, Butler and Lindley analyze how the 1615/16 *Golden Age Restored* (scripted by Ben Jonson) uses the encoded masque device to express a policy shift: in this case, to remove kingly favor from an erstwhile favorite embroiled in criminal investigation, with consequences not only for paths of courtly patronage but also for the Crown's position on the independence of the judiciary.[1] Marcus's analysis of the same masque shows how it engages another "local" context: evolving Jacobean financial policy, particularly concerning the relationship between court and the City of London.[2] Knowles, in turn, demonstrates how finely nuanced—how minutely "local"— masques' political commentary can be in an event like the "Running Masque" of 1621, whose stylistic and social Francophilia subtly expresses the masque patron's foreign-policy views (which in this case do not line up with the monarch's.)[3] In other cases, critics have shown the potential for court masque not only to articulate, but also more directly to constitute, local political action. Butler emphasizes this possibility in Caroline contexts, exploring ways that King Charles used masque as a "part of an ongoing political dialogue between the crown and its servants"; the 1640 *Salmacida Spolia* (scripted by Davenant), for example, pointedly included masquers of different religious and political persuasions, choreographed into symbolic complementarity.[4]

---

[1] Butler and Lindley, "Restoring Astraea: Jonson's Masque for the Fall of Somerset," *ELH* 61:4 (Winter 1994), 807–27.

[2] Marcus, "City Metal and Country Mettle: The Occasion of Ben Jonson's *Golden Age Restored*," in *Pageantry in the Shakespearean Theater*, ed. David Bergeron (Athens: Univ. of Georgia P, 1985), pp. 26–47.

[3] James Knowles, "The 'Running Masque' Recovered: A Masque for the Marquess of Buckingham (c. 1619–20)," *Engish Manuscript Studies* 8 (2000), 79–135.

[4] Butler, "Politics and the Masque: Salmacida Spolia," *Literature and the English Civil War*, ed. Thomas Healy and Jonathan Sawday (Cambridge: Cambridge Univ. Press, 1990), pp. 59–74, 60.

The kind of scrupulous "localism" in scholars' recreation of immediate context onto which the text of a given masque can be mapped
has proven very useful in unpacking many nuances of Caroline politics. Yet at the same time that such analysis enables the recovery
of certain historical elements, it obscures others. When critical practice flattens dramatic texts into windows onto "real" events, it can
distort history by imagining masque figuration to have been predictably consumed by homogenized receivers. Masque projects can
be complex. As the critical record I cite on *The Golden Age Restored*
demonstrates, contexts are multiple, exceeding the references unveiled
by any given "local" reading. Even more significantly, "occasional"
analysis of masque criticism has operated within the bounds of producers' intentions. The most subtle examples of such criticism acknowledge that the variety of producers involved with masque production—
patrons, composers, producers, scriptors—can pursue diverse agendas.[5]
But even if we can recover a range of masque producers' aims,
intention by no means limits meaning or reception.[6] Any investigation bound by producers' intentions—even one that acknowledges
their potential multiplicity or complexity—will necessarily deracinate
our understanding of Caroline drama. For it is in the unpredictable
hands of receivers that masque—like other genres—can have its most
significant effects.

Hence I propose that the "locales" we study must include those
of reception, which, I think, need to expand beyond the very useful but relatively rare observers' reports upon which previous remarks
about audiences have been based. Not only the exigencies of available evidence but also the nature of reception itself demands that
the spheres of audience we consider be multiple, flexible, and more

---

[5] For instance, Stephen Orgel's persuasive demonstration of varying constella-
tions of Queen Anna's, King James's, Prince Henry's, and Ben Jonson's interests
in the 1604/5 *Masque of Blackness* ("Marginal Jonson," in *The Politics of the Stuart
Court Masque*, ed. David Bevington and Peter Holbrook [Cambridge Univ. Press,
1998], pp. 144–75) or the 1608/9 *Masque of Queens* ("Jonson and the Amazons,"
Soliciting Interpretation: Literary Theory and Seventeenth-Century English Poetry, ed. Elizabeth
D. Harvey and Katharine Eisaman Maus [Chicago: Univ. of Chicago Press, 1990],
pp. 114–42.
[6] As David Lindley notes, "It is frequently a limitation of even the most sophisticated masque criticism that it assumes that those who watched were necessarily
taken over by, or in simple agreement with, the position a masque took up," *The
Trials of Frances Howard: Fact and Fiction at the Court of James I* (London: Routledge,
1993), p. 19.

copious than eyewitness accounts of a particular production. To begin
with, masque events were received in multiple formats in the seventeenth century: not only performances and sometimes repeat performances, but also published texts, public processions, ballads, and
oral news reports.[7] "Audiences" thus extend beyond spectators at a
single performance. Beyond the need to broaden the formats we
consider, we should not allow particular performance accounts to
limit our sense of how receivers understood a masque because spectacle, and perhaps especially language, are inherently multivalent.
Indeed, masque producers themselves depend upon this property:
this figure signifies both Jove and Charles; this dance encodes both
social harmony of Russells and Howards and cosmic harmony of a
well-ordered world. As the semiotic foundation of masque, this particular multivalence is exploited in purposeful ways by masque producers, but the same property also can unfold in directions producers
may not foresee or desire (as I develop in examples below). Furthermore, a masque can mean different things to different receivers, or
several things to a single receiver, or may strike a receiver differently
in different formats or different iterations. "Occasional" templates
alone cannot accommodate this nuance.

The multiplicity of context for an early modern dramatic/print
event will never be concretely recoverable. Certain references to occasion can be decoded (when a masque demonstrably engages issues
documented in other texts, as in the *Golden Age* examples above). But
we never can identify the full range of interpretive spheres for the
full range of a masque's receivers—or for the receivers of any text.
Masques allude not only to political events, but also to other masques,
to poems, to pageants, to plays, to evanescent songs and rumors.
And even if we were able to trace all such allusion, we never could
know the rich variety of how this played out for individual receivers.
As Hans Robert Jauss remarks, "In the triangle of author, work, and
public the last is no passive part, no chain of mere reactions."[8]
Instead, receivers make what they will of the texts they encounter—

---

[7] For masque publication, see my "The Masque as Book," *Reading and Literacy in
the Middle Ages and Renaissance*, ed. Ian Moulton, *Arizona Studies in the Middle Ages and
Renaissance*, vol. 8. Brussels: Brepols, 2004, pp. 143–168. On ballads, news reports,
parodies, and multiple performances, see my *Reading Masque*.

[8] Jauss, *Toward an Aesthetics of Reception*, trans. Timothy Bahti (Minneapolis: Univ.
of Minnesota Press, 1982), p. 19.

even of texts by the most controlling of producers (for instance, King
James's irritated response to Jonson's carefully scripted philosophical
rapprochement of pleasure and virtue: "What did they make me
come here for?," or D. J. Gordon's famous analysis of how observers
misunderstood elements of the Neoplatonic argument constructed in
Jonson's *Masque of Beautie*).[9]

Thus when we think about masque in its Caroline contexts, we
must take its reception, or potential receivability, as too important
to overlook, but too subtle to permit full empirical verification. As
one way to do this, I propose we take *genre* as a "locale" that can
offer as much analytic purchase as the locale of *setting*. Genre, after
all, provides receivers—perhaps early modern receivers in particular—
as many signposts for orienting understanding as the framework of
occasion. The frequently intertextual habits of court masque solidify
genre's presence in the masquing space, pointing to other masque
occasions, to habits of masque *per se*, to related forms of spectacle
such as City pageants and country-house masques. Court masques,
for instance, use the figure of Britain as a happy garden providing
refuge for the muses, and an associated pattern of virtue to all nations,
frequently enough to make variations of this theme into a leitmotif
extending across many masques. Thus when Davenant's 1637 *Luminalia*
recounts that "by the divine *mindes* of these incomparable Paire
[Charles and Henrietta Maria], the Muses . . . were received into protection, and established in this monarchy . . . the garden of the . . . Muses
of Great *Brittaine*, not inferior in beauty to that of the Hesperides . . .
Making this happy Island a pattern to all nations" (2), it recalls
moments in the Stuart masque tradition extending back to Jonson's
1608 *Masque of Beautie*:

> The glorious *Isle*, wherein [the nymphs] rest, takes place
> Of all the earth for Beautie.
> . . .
> Hither, as to their new *Elysium*,
> The spirits of the antique *Greekes* are come,
> *Poets* and *Singers*, *Linus*, *Orpheus*, all
> That haue excell'd in knowledge musicall
> Where, set in arbors made of myrtle, and gold,
> They liue, againe, these beauties to behold.

---

[9] Report of the Venetian ambassador Busino. *CSPV* XV: 111. Gordon, *The
Renaissance Imagination: Essays and Lectures* by D. J. Gordon, ed. Stephen Orgel (Berkeley:
Univ. of California Press, 1975).

And thence in flowry mazes walking forth
Sing hymnes in celebration of their worth.[10]

Like court masques, city pageants echo one another, as in the speech of Heywood's St. Katherine in the 1637 *Londini Speculum*, who remarks her representation in past pageants: "Oft have I on a passant Lyon sate,/And through your populous streets beene borne in state:/Oft have I grac'd your Triumphes on the shore,/But on the Waters was not seene before" (94). Moreover, court masques and city pageants allude not only to independent traditions, but often respond to one another, as shown in the Marcus piece cited above. Indeed, our distinctions between masque and pageant, between elite and popular spectacle, may be inaccurate. The vocabulary and practice of the period shows a significant continuum in the 1630s. Heywood's 1633 *Londini Emporia* refers to its show as an "Anti-maske," while, at court, comic antimasques previously performed by professionals can be presented by "Gentlemen of qualitie," as in the 1637 *Luminalia*. Within masques themselves, the division of labor among monarchs, aristocrats, and professionals changes. King Charles famously participates in masques as a dancer, where his father merely observed. Queen Henrietta Maria's speaking roles in court entertainments were much remarked (and famously criticized). The Ludlow masque's using the anonymous professional masquer Sabrina as the figure who resolves the masquing family's crisis shows a significantly more "public" masque semiotic than in earlier dynastic masques. Finally, the genre "masque" itself may not have been so exclusive a category as we sometimes imply. The playwright Thomas Nabbes presented "masques" at the private theatre in Salisbury Court, in 1637 and 1638. Heywood's 1636 *Loves maistresse* sports the alternative title "The Queens masque, As it was three times presented before their two Excellent Maiesties, within the space of eight dayes; in the presence of sundry forraigne ambassadors. Publikely acted by the Queens Comoedians, at the Phoenix in Drury-Lane."

Masque intertextuality long has been remarked in terms of how producers wished to "comment upon" other masque events—Milton's "critique" of the 1634 *Coelum Britannicum* in his Ludlow masque of the same year, or Jonson's "dismissal" of White's *Cupid's Banishment*

---

[10] *Ben Jonson*, ed. C. H. Herford and Percy and Evelyn Simpson. 11 vols. (Oxford: Clarendon Press, 1925–52) VII: 185. All subsequent references to Jonson masques are to this edition.

in his *Pleasure Reconcild to Vertue*—but we have not thought sufficiently about the copious interpretive horizons that allusion creates for receivers.[11] The audience positioned to respond to such intertextuality is significant. The elite audiences who attended aristocratic masques also consumed City pageantry; for instance, the Venetian ambassador reported upon the occasion of the 1632 Lord Mayor's pageant noted that "It is usual to invite the ambassadors . . . [who attend with] the great lords of the realm and . . . other lords of the royal Council."[12] Court masque audiences themselves were broader than we sometimes imagine. King Charles's endeavors to increase the size of the audience that could be accommodated at Whitehall demonstrate that court-masque audiences became larger over the course of the 1630s; in 1637, "his Majesty commanded . . . that a new temporary room of timber, both for strength and capacity of spectators, should be suddenly built."[13] Courtier Sir John Pory reveals that space was insufficient, and sometimes taken up by the relatively "public" audience of servants: "my Lord Chamberlain saith, that no chambermaid shall enter [the 1632/3 *Temple of Love*], unless she will sit cross-legged on the top of a bulk."[14] Elite masques could include city processions that encapsulated the masque device for observers in the street, such as the 1633 *Triumph of Peace* (Shirley) that the Inns of Court presented first at Whitehall and later at the Merchant Taylors' Hall. Perhaps most significantly, masques of the 1630s from all venues, including court texts, consistently were published and sold by popular London booksellers, creating the potential for wide print receivership even by audiences who did not see any of the spectacle. And print disseminated more than masque dialogue: every one of the court masques published in the 1630s includes a list of the participating masquers (a more sporadic feature in other decades), making what Leeds Barroll calls the "social text" of masque available to public readers.[15]

---

[11] For instance, Maryann Cale McGuire, *Milton's Puritan Masque* (Athens: Univ. of Georgia Press, 1983); Robert C. Evans, *Jonson and the Contexts of His Time* (Lewisburg: Bucknell Univ. Press, 1994).

[12] Gussoni in CSPV XXIII, 28.

[13] Preface to *Britannia Triumphans* in *The Dramatic Works of Sir William D'Avenant* (Edinburgh: Paterson, 1872), ii: 265. All subsequent references to Davenant's texts are to this edition unless otherwise noted.

[14] Letter to Puckering, 3 January 1632–3. *Court and Times of Charles the First* (London, 1848), ii: 214.

[15] Barroll, *Anna of Denmark, Queen of England: A Cultural Biography* (Philadelphia: Univ. of Pennsylvania Press, 2001).

One way to historicize reception, then, involves cross-reading masque performances of the 1630s within the interpretive horizon available to their receivers: a hermeneutic web that crosses boundaries of "elite" and "popular," of "masque" and "pageant." Country masques, city masques, pageants, and print forms allude to one another, both constituting and thematizing interchange; many of these texts include passages or figures that emphasize generic self-consciousness. The following table of masques and pageants between1631 and 1639, while far from exhaustive, gives a sense of the range of events in the decade.

The self-consciousness with which masques and pageants reflect upon their genre suggests a more skeptical and playful side of these

date	title	scriptor	sponsor/venue
1631	*London Ius Honorarium*	Heywood	mayor's pageant
1631	*Chloridia*	Jonson	Queen's masque
1631	*Albion's Triumph*	Townshend	King's masque
1632	*Tempe Restored*	Davenant	Queen's masque
1633	*Londini Emporia*	Heywood	mayor's pageant
1634	*Triumph of Peace*	Shirley	Inns of Court (for monarchs)
1634	*Coelum Britannicum*	Carew	King's masque
1634	*Mask at Ludlow*	Milton	country-house masque
1635	*Londini Sinus Salutis*	Heywood	mayor's pageant
1635	*Temple of Love*	Davenant	Queen's masque
1636	*Triumphs of the Prince d'Amour*	Davenant	Inns of Court
1636	*Corona Minervae*	Kinnaston	private city masque (school)
1636	*Entertainment at Richmond*	Jonson	prince's masque
1636	*Loves Mistriss*	Heywood	"queen's masque" in city
1637	*Masque at Hunsdon*	Heywood	country house masque
1637	*Microcosmus*	Nabbes	city masque (Salisbury Court)
1637	*Londini Speculum*	Heywood	mayor's show
1638	*Britannia Triumphans*	Davenant	King's masque
1638	*Luminalia*	Davenant	Queen's masque
1638	*Springs Glory*	Nabbes	city masque (Salisbury Court)
1638	*Porta pietatis*	Heywood	mayor's show
1639	*Londini status pacatus*	Heywood	mayor's show

events than appears if we treat them only as decipherable windows onto occasion. Furthermore, inter-relations among texts in different genres can reshape how their assertions play out for receivers. For example, the clearly visible, often playful, *scripting* of authority through flattering, conventional address emerges more fully when we cross-read different forms of masque and pageant than if we take court masque in isolation. We are familiar with court-masque addresses to the monarch expressing dominion and potency. In *Britannia Triumphans* (1638), for instance, Fame addresses the King as the "treasure of our sight,/That art the hopeful morn of every day,/Whose fair example makes the light,/By which heroic virtue finds her way" (ii: 284). Such places look less inherently absolutist, less specialized for monarchal purposes, when we see similar addresses annually to Lord Mayors, or to the world-upside-down "ruler" of Inns-of-Court carnivals (*Triumphs of the Prince d'Amour*). The 1637 pageant *Londini Speculum*, for example, addresses the Mayor presiding over the scene thus: "This Structure (honour'd Sir) doth title beare/Of an Imperiall Fort, apt for that spheare/In which you now move, borrowing all her grace,/As well from your owne person, as your place/For you have past through all degrees that tended/Unto that height which you have now ascended" (98). The similarity in tropes of flattery among court, country-house, and civic events—the honoree as source of virtue, illumination, transformation—need not merely suggest that civic pageants imitate royal events.[16] Rather, their ubiquity shows a culture that understands "this is how we make an authority figure."

This canniness frames representations of concerns about power, creating events that even while celebrating the uncontestable authority of the status quo allows for some (intertextual) evaluation of alternatives. When Arion in Heywood's 1632 *Londini Artium* refers to the mayor as a "Great and God like Magistrate" (p. 39), he sounds as sycophantically absolutist as, for instance, Mercury's address to Charles and Henrietta Maria in Carew's 1634 *Coelum Britannicum* (as "the Brittish Stars [to whom] this lower Globe/Shall owe its light, . . . they

---

[16] For a related discussion of relationships between Jacobean masques and Lord Mayors' pageants, see Nancy Wright, "'Rival Traditions': Civid and Courtly Ceremonies in Jacobean London," *Politics of the Stuart Court Masque*, ed. David Bevington and Peter Holbrook (Cambridge: Cambridge Univ. Press, 1998), pp. 197–217.

alone dispence/To'th'World a pure refined influence."[17] But the very similarity of panegyric tropes used for heriditary, monarchal, lifelong power on the one hand, and elected, civic, annual office on the other, invokes a diversity of authoritative modes that stands in some tension with the ostensible inevitability the rhetoric celebrates. When masques and pageants explicitly discuss different means of coming to power, they likewise bring a critical repertoire of political theory into the interpretive framework. In Heywood's 1631 *London Jus Honorarium*, for instance, Honour tells the newly elected Lord Mayor, "that Swoord/Collar, and Cap of Maintenance,/These are no things, that come by chance" [pp. 22–3]). This raises "chance" as one path to power (even as it dismisses its relevance in this case), and also brings into play the various other ways authority gets conferred.

Even panegyric that represents authority as having no competitors, that is, raises the issue of alternative models. Heywood's dedication to the new Lord Mayor lauds his self-evident preeminence: "worthily was your so free election (without either emulation, or competitorship conferred upon you) . . . that none ever in your place was more sufficient or able . . . more truly to discern . . . more advisedly to dispose . . . more maturely to dispatch . . ." (A2–A2v). This reminds spectators that emulation, competition, unfree elections also offer paths to power, even if these are not relevant to this particular moment. Or, we might ask, given the strongly emphasized conventionality of such address, might invoking lesser paths to glory here, in a generic moment that so clearly and self-consciously cannot offer anything but praise, perhaps, compromise the explicit assertion of their immediate irrelevance? Furthermore, given the overlap in structure and tropes between court masques and Lord Mayor's show, might asking such questions of the latter bring them into play regarding the former—particularly, perhaps, in the contemporary receptive framework of reading their printed texts? In *Jus Honorarium*, Honour raises the multiplicity of authoritative modes: "If Kings arrive to my profection [perfection],/Tis by Succession, or Election" (23). With his "if," Honor remarks that kings may *not* achieve honor; moreover, his speech invokes alternative monarchal modes of heridity

---

[17] Ll. 101–3. *The Poems of Thomas Carew*, ed. Rhodes Dunlap (Oxford: Clarendon, 1949), p. 155. All subsequent references to this masque are from this edition, and are given by line number in the text.

("succession") and something more democratic ("election"). The very same masque whose assertion of self-evident Caroline monarchal authority I cite above, the *Britannia Triumphans*—declaring how Charles's "fair example makes the light,/By which heroic virtue finds her way" (ii: 284)—also stages the figure of "Imposture," warning that "every thing but seemes,/And borrowes the existence it appears/To have: Imposture governs all" (ii: 5). Encoded as "light" and hence visual, Charles's power might seem particularly vulnerable to imposture within the receptive framework enabled by cross-reading multiple texts.

The Inns-of-Court Christmas masque of 1636, Davenant's *Triumphs of the Prince d'Amour*, draws out alternative political models with particular nuance and playfulness. The carnivalesque occasion of declaring a lord of misrule (the Prince of the Christmas season) is well suited to staging authority whilst flouting it; as anthropologists of carnival note, it is difficult to decide whether such inversions of order serve the radical function of making political structures available for examination or the conservative function of ritually releasing their pressure so that they may continue unchanged. This text participates in the masque/pageant tradition of half- invoking multiple political models: citing a mythic history of the Inns-of-Court carnival rulers, for instance, the Master of Ceremonies describes the Prince D'Amour's palace as "by sword, then law maintain'd,/[Where] His few, but mighty ancestors have reign'd" (i: 329). Sword, law, and ancestry offer three sources of authority, with language emerging as a fourth. The prefatory materials to this masque draw out this ambiguity in creating "majesty" in name only ("A Masque presented by His Highness [i.e., the Prince D'Amour], at his Palace" [i: 318]), and especially in the way the faux license in the imprimatur foregrounds the authority of form. Reading "This Masque may be printed. By privilege of a most ancient Record in the Roles belonging to Prince D'Amour. T. Maunsell, Master of Revels to his Highness" (i: 319), the text accedes to the necessity of majesty and of censorship—the formal fact of an imprint page—but inserts its own content into those roles. And, indeed, the masque was printed: apparently the authority of "Master of Revels to his Highness" (again, "highness" for the duration of the carnival only) suffices. Moreover, the honored guests at this masque were the dispossessed princes of Bohemia, nephews of the King, deprived of their thrones upon the Habsburg succession (which English popular opinion frequently suggested redressing): princes, that is, in name only just as much as the "Prince D'Amour."

The masque opens with the Master of Ceremonies addressing the actual Prince Elector in an ostensible aside that draws out the complications of managing succession, popular opinion, and competing modes of power:

> Although his [the Prince D'Amour's] greatness is not taught to bow,
> His subjects fear he will do homage now,
> Which he esteems no less'ning to his State
> . . .
> His jealous Barons will dislike, and cry
> I am perverted to disloyalty
> . . .
> As if my words would pull his empire down,
> Shorten his sceptre, and contract his crown.
>
> (i: 328)

Using words to dismiss the delusions of the jealous who believe that words have real power, the Master of Ceremonies (in a move that inverts Heywood's panegyric) both explicitly undercuts and implicitly celebrates his own performance. The Bohemian princes' own position as exiles, dispossessed of their thrones, and the beneficiaries of English popular opinion that holds British national pride to be damaged by their monarchs' failure militarily to reinstate these Stuart princes to the authority their father claimed (with dubious legality) connects this playful reflection to their own political situation. The potential tenuousness of even absolute-seeming power is emphasized when the Master of Ceremonies discusses succession—a process for transferring power which, notably, seems to be failing the addressees. The Master conveys that the Prince D'Amour is offering the Palatine princes the full hospitality of his palace: "Not in regard, he hath short time to live;/For so, since his successor is unknown,/You take what is his subjects', not his own" (i: 329). This invokes the political principle that under uncertain succession, power reverts to the subjects: a remarkably democratic position to announce to King Charles's nephews and to publish to the book-buying public.

As we have seen, masques and pageants coexist with emergent public print culture. Masques that thematize more and less elite forms of knowledge—particularly those that represent print forms upon the stage—offer a useful place to think about the genres' self-conscious deployment of these varying modes. Representation of relationships among genres (book and performance; encomium and mirror for magistrates) is not new in the 1630s, but rather participates in a long tradition of masques that thematically reflect upon genres occupying different segments of the continuum between elite and public culture. Some of the most striking examples of this tradition come in late Jacobean court masques. Jonson's 1619/20 *News from the New World*, for instance, features debate amongst two heralds (who proclaim news orally), a chronicler (who pens long manuscripts), a factor (who pens weekly newsletters), and a printer. In another example, the print version of Jonson's 1622 *Masque of Augurs* represents one character's speech in black-letter type—a formal property whose interestingly layered association with both the marginal status of limited literacy and the weight of official proclamation (layers that *Augurs* mines for comic effect) is available to only those receivers who encounter the masque in print.

I conclude by analyzing two masques of the 1630s that represent books upon the masque scene. In 1635 *Corona Minervae* was presented on 27 February by the College of the Museum Minervae (a medical school, more or less) to Prince Charles, Prince James, and Princess Mary.[18] This masque is "private" and "royalist" in the sense that it is unlikely to have invited in numerous outside spectators and it honored identifiable royalty, but "public" in the sense that its producers were of the middling sort, the figurative argument it presents is professionally inflected—a version of guild drama—and the text was widely sold. The masque depicts Minerva and Time rejoicing that Stuart rule is advancing truth and learning throughout the realm, celebrates the seasonal pleasures governed by Time, then proceeds to proffer "fresher objects . . ./ . . . of Armes, and Arts" to the "Princely ones'" "aspects" (C2v). The royal visitors are then "conducted by *Minerva* and *Time* towards the Chamber of *Arts*, and *Armes*," where Minerva, lauding their precocious "innate love" of learning, "begin[s] . . ./bookes to prepare/Fit for [their] studies" (C3). These "books," though "so handsomely made that no man could know but that they were very bookes indeed" (C4v), actually contain the

---

[18] Francis Cynaston [Kinneston], *Corona Minervae, or, a Masque Presented before Prince Charles, His Highness the Duke of Yorke his Brother, and the Lady Mary his Sister*. Printed for William Sheares, 1635.

various foods of the banquet. (Perhaps the Cook and Poet who argued about priority of their projects in *Neptune's Triumph* [Jonson, 1624] have set up a press in the kitchen of the Museo Minervae.) The frontispiece of each "book" is inscribed with verses explicating the pun associating the author with the food: in Minerva's words, "the sweetest quintessence/Had by allusion to each Authors name" (C3). Thus the Suetonius volume contains sweetmeats, Aulus Gellius a jelly, Origen oranges, Apuleius apples, etc.

However close this verges to camp—however dizzily it may have had Jonson spinning in his grave—this device unpacks the various functions of books in masques quite wonderfully. *Corona Minervae* represents books being presented to royalty. At the same time that this evokes a traditional gesture requesting patronage (for one's own books) or offering tutelage (by means of others' books), it also is linked to more oppositional gestures like petitioning. The gesture of pressing books on princes has an additional charge, I would argue, both because of the intense concern about books' potential to incite dissent in Caroline England and because this gesture is linked to the larger, and also charged, tradition of representing books, ballads, and news on the masque stage. In this tradition, the masque stage offers a place to think, perhaps argue, about public and elite modes of information and interpretation. (Jonsonian masques characteristically look more oppositional—as in the competition among news-sources in *News from the New World* cited above, or in the Poet's remark to the Cook in *Neptune's Triumph* that the masque celebrating Prince Charles's return had to be delayed until ballads about the journey subsided; masques of Middleton, Milton, Heywood, and Davenant tend to portray public and elite modes acting more collaboratively).

When books are exchanged in a masque, they operate on two levels. First, they are theatrical properties, their function as books (things that may be perused, annotated, digested, discussed) subsumed by a theatrical economy that limits their use to an object of exchange as directed by the script. They also signify themselves, however: they *are* books, and point up the artificiality of the theatrical economy that doesn't give them space to be read. When an audience sees an identifiable book exchanged on the stage, that is, we can ask "Wonder if the Prince has read that?"; "Wonder if he'll get around to it now?"; "Maybe I should get around to reading that"; "I wouldn't think he'd like that one." Whether or not we reach that level of explicitness in our speculations, the potential readability—and interpretability—of

books is so integral to their nature that it always spills over their
function as objects of theatrical exchange.

Despite their anomalies, the special nature of the "artificiall" books
in *Corona Minervae*, emptied of their matter in order to encase deli-
cacies, actually points up books' more general functions, in masques
and in the culture surrounding them. Minerva initially presents the
books to Prince Charles as a humanist tutor would:

> Great *Britaines* Prince, since that your innate love
> To learning doth soe soone your highnes move
> To view *Minerva's* mansion, and to be
> Admitted one of hers, Behold, and see
> How I begin . . . bookes to prepare
> Fit for your studies, now from which by sense
> You may extract the sweetest quintessance
> Had by allusion to each Authours name
> To sweeten learnings roote [,] so as the same
> To others bitter might prove sweete to you.
>
> (C3)

Unaware of the books' comestible contents, Time chides Minerva:
"How dare you use the Prince thus, schoole-mistris?/Are th'armes,
and arts you promis'd to his view/To be pick't out of bookes? This
is a new/And a course way of entertainment too,/A banquet had
been fitter" (C3v). Time here points to a tension inherent to humanist instruction of princes: yes, learning is not always purely pleasurable; yes, arms and arts *are* to be picked out of books; yes, instruction
alters the power dynamic between tutor and pupil, even royal pupil.
Although this final observation is hardly new in 1635, I suspect that
changing views of rank, virtue, and pleasure in Caroline England
make it freshly intense.

The singular device of *Corona Minervae* makes the contents of those
books consumable, rendering the prince, in Minerva's words, a "*hel-
lus librorum*" (C3v): a devourer of books. This literalization of the
appetite for learning that the masque celebrates further highlights
books' various aspects in masque. First, we should note that the
books are not entirely emptied out: their ostensible authors remain
identifiable and canonized by inclusion, for both the princes and the
masque's receivers. Second, conventional masque semiotics would ask
us to read the banquet of books allegorically—the princes do indeed
value and enjoy the nourishing "meat" proffered by the House of
Wisdom. Finally, the princes' devouring the consumable contents of

Minerva's library is a highly readable moment, by which I mean variously interpretable one. We could read this as publicly available learning as the necessary alimentation for royal survival, as a parody of royal uses of learning, as a paean to the processors-popularizers of learning who make it palatable.

In 1637, Thomas Nabbes's "morall maske" *Microcosmus* was, according to its title page, *"Presented with Generall liking, at the private house in Salisbury Court, and here Set down according to the intention of the Author."*[19] This masque of temperance and chastity shares several thematic features with Milton's Ludlow masque (performed and circulated in manuscript 1634, revised and circulated further in 1637), Carew's court masque *Coelum Britannicum* (also performed and printed in 1634), and London Lord Mayors' shows of the mid-1630s, particularly Heywood's *Londini Speculum* (performed and printed, like *Microcosmus*, in 1637). Faith, hope, and especially charity or chastity as the way to a happy life of temperate virtue are prominent in these different but significantly overlapping venues of city pageant, court masque, city masque, and country-house masque. Among other things, this shows that the court passion for Neoplatonic/high church/Catholic moral philosophy and the proto-bourgeois/Reformist interest in more Stoic versions of similar ethics are part of a conversation taking place across social boundaries—not only, as previously has been argued, vectors of social fragmentation. These texts' shared thematic concerns demonstrate that Milton's "reformed" masque is not the anomalous work of a genius who blows apart every genre he touches; that Queen Henrietta Maria's interest in the philosophy of chaste love is not an entirely rarified, continental, crypto-Catholic undertaking antithetical to Englishness.

A laudatory epistle by William Cufaude, prefixed to the print version of *Microcosmus*, highlights relationships among genres as a central feature of the masque:

---

[19] Printed by Richard Oulton for Charles Greene, and "sold at the white Lyon in Pauls Church-yard." Print copies of this masque survive in unusual numbers, suggesting that it may have been copiously printed and widely sold. This masque (not too unusually) shares a few features like five-act structure, professional masquers, and performance venue with plays and Restoration operas. Other features place it firmly in the masque genre, such as its allegorical figures and scenery, its speech/song/dance structure, and its self-designation.

> . . . thou [Nabbes] dost make by thy Poetick rage
> A Schoole of Vertue of a common Stage.
> Methinks the ghosts of Stoicks vexe to see
> Their doctrine in a Masque unmasqu'd by thee.
> Thou mak'st to be exprest by action more,
> Then was contein'd in all their Bookes before.

(A4v)

Aspects of this "common stage" sound intriguingly like burgeoning public culture. Cufaude expresses surprised admiration for Nabbes's re-mediation of classical books into more "commonly" accessible drama. The "unmasquing" of bookish "doctrine" adduces to a sense of masque as elitely recondite—but, Cufaude claims, Nabbes uses an elite genre to popularize equally elite Classical philosophy. This epistle models genre as such—and specifically the genre of masque—as dynamic. An elite genre could not popularize elite content, that is, unless it were capable of transformation rather than mere translation. In Cufaude's terms, Nabbes "unmasques" "masque" by means of masquing. Moreover, Cufaude's claim that Nabbes's masque surpasses Stoic books ("expres[sing] by action more/Then was contein'd in all their Bookes before") further suggests a dynamic relationship between masque and book: that masque does not merely stage book knowledge, but transforms it. The potential for (often exclusive) masque performance and (frequently commercially available) masque text to inflect one another makes masque into a node between aristocratic masque and the public culture that purchases records of those performances (and predictably gossips about them as part of exchanging news in the aisle of St. Paul's). That masque books were considered to be more than transparent records of their performances in this decade is indicated by the inclusion in Davenant's *Salmacida Spolia* (1639) of a song "to be printed, not sung."[20]

Not confined to the laudatory epistles, books find their way onto the proscenium stage of *Microcosmus* as well. Once the central figure Physander is converted from sensuality to temperance, the masque's "*malus genius*" decides to make a final sally against Physander's resolve. But our hero stands firm with his chastely virtuous wife Bellanima, as they rebuff the evil spirit "in their first habits" (long white robes,

---

[20] *The Dramatic Works of Sir William D'Avenant*, 5 vols. (Edinburgh: Paterson, 1872), II: 320.

with garlands of white flowers on their heads), "with Bookes in their hands" (F3). Enacting the masque, we might say, has brought those books of Stoic virtue to hand for Physander and Bellanima, and in some ways for their audience and readers as well. Physander's and Bellanima's acquisition of these books between the beginning and end of the masque suggests that we might even read Cufaude's lauda-tory comment "Thou mak'st to be exprest by action more,/Then was contein'd in all their Bookes before" to sustain a reading of "before" that understands the books themselves to have been retro-spectively transformed by Nabbes's staging of their content. The Stoic books, in this reading, contained less "before" than they do "now": masque rehearsal has rejuvenated those always-available tomes. Even if we don't take the "before" quite that far, the masque certainly has placed them as active doctrine into the hands of the masquers Physander and Bellanima; likewise, it has made the books more pub-licly "available" in the sense of renewing their interest to the masque's receivers (readers as well as audience).

Books, of course, are slippery things on which to hang an argu-ment about public and elite modes of knowledge because they func-tion in so many different ways. On the one hand, they disseminate knowledge in distinctively interpretable, debatable form—hence Habermas's emphasis upon civil discussion of shared reading as the *sine qua non* of the public sphere. How fully and immediately Caroline culture shares this sense of published books as inherently (and dan-gerously) interpretable is highlighted in discussions of reading car-ried out in the Star Chamber trial of William Prynne for his book *Histrio-mastix*, conducted in 1634 and 1637 (precisely the years of interest to us here). Once positions are disseminated in print, inter-pretation is unpredictable and uncontrollable: the Chamber rebutted Prynne's defense of his intentions with the remark that an author "doth not accompanye his booke, to make his intencion knowne to all that reades it."[21] (Note also that the Star Chamber strengthened censorship statutes, including clarifying that ephemera are subject to licensing, in this same year of 1637.) But shared books and the inter-pretive practices they draw with them are not associated only with the emergent public culture that makes civil war possible by the

---

[21] *Documents Relating to the Prosecution of William Prynne in 1634 and 1637*, ed. S. R. Gardiner (London: Camden Society, 1877), p. 16.

1640s; they also are the much more longstanding medium of humanism. We need not unequivocally resolve the question of what books
signify in order to see that masque representations of books in the
mid-1630s themselves stage the problem. The genre *is*, indeed, the
occasion.

INDEX OF PROPER NAMES

STUDIES IN MEDIEVAL AND REFORMATION TRADITIONS

(Formerly Studies in Medieval and Reformation Thought)

Founded by Heiko A. Oberman†
Edited by Andrew Colin Gow

1. DOUGLASS, E.J.D. *Justification in Late Medieval Preaching.* 2nd ed. 1989
2. WILLIS, E.D. *Calvin's Catholic Christology.* 1966 *out of print*
3. POST, R.R. *The Modern Devotion.* 1968 *out of print*
4. STEINMETZ, D.C. *Misericordia Dei.* The Theology of Johannes von Staupitz. 1968 *out of print*
5. O'MALLEY, J.W. *Giles of Viterbo on Church and Reform.* 1968 *out of print*
6. OZMENT, S.E. *Homo Spiritualis.* The Anthropology of Tauler, Gerson and Luther. 1969
7. PASCOE, L.B. *Jean Gerson: Principles of Church Reform.* 1973 *out of print*
8. HENDRIX, S.H. *Ecclesia in Via.* Medieval Psalms Exegesis and the *Dictata super Psalterium* (1513-1515) of Martin Luther. 1974
9. TREXLER, R.C. *The Spiritual Power.* Republican Florence under Interdict. 1974
10. TRINKAUS, Ch. with OBERMAN, H.A. (eds.). *The Pursuit of Holiness.* 1974 *out of print*
11. SIDER, R.J. *Andreas Bodenstein von Karlstadt.* 1974
12. HAGEN, K. *A Theology of Testament in the Young Luther.* 1974
13. MOORE, Jr., W.L. *Annotatiunculae D. Iohanne Eckio Praelectore.* 1976
14. OBERMAN, H.A. with BRADY, Jr., Th.A. (eds.). *Itinerarium Italicum.* Dedicated to Paul Oskar Kristeller. 1975
15. KEMPFF, D. *A Bibliography of Calviniana.* 1959-1974. 1975 *out of print*
16. WINDHORST, C. *Täuferisches Taufverständnis.* 1976
17. KITTELSON, J.M. *Wolfgang Capito.* 1975
18. DONNELLY, J.P. *Calvinism and Scholasticism in Vermigli's Doctrine of Man and Grace.* 1976
19. LAMPING, A.J. *Ulrichus Velenus (Oldřich Velenský) and his Treatise against the Papacy.* 1976
20. BAYLOR, M.G. *Action and Person.* Conscience in Late Scholasticism and the Young Luther. 1977
21. COURTENAY, W.J. *Adam Wodeham.* 1978
22. BRADY, Jr., Th.A. *Ruling Class, Regime and Reformation at Strasbourg, 1520-1555.* 1978
23. KLAASSEN, W. *Michael Gaismair.* 1978
24. BERNSTEIN, A.E. *Pierre d'Ailly and the Blanchard Affair.* 1978
25. BUCER, M. *Correspondance.* Tome I (Jusqu'en 1524). Publié par J. Rott. 1979
26. POSTHUMUS MEYJES, G.H.M. *Jean Gerson et l'Assemblée de Vincennes (1329).* 1978
27. VIVES, J.L. *In Pseudodialecticos.* Ed. by Ch. Fantazzi. 1979
28. BORNERT, R. *La Réforme Protestante du Culte à Strasbourg au XVIᵉ siècle (1523-1598).* 1981
29. CASTELLIO, S. *De Arte Dubitandi.* Ed. by E. Feist Hirsch. 1981
30. BUCER, M. *Opera Latina.* Vol I. Publié par C. Augustijn, P. Fraenkel, M. Lienhard. 1982
31. BÜSSER, F. *Wurzeln der Reformation in Zürich.* 1985 *out of print*
32. FARGE, J.K. *Orthodoxy and Reform in Early Reformation France.* 1985
33. 34. BUCER, M. *Etudes sur les relations de Bucer avec les Pays-Bas.* I. Etudes; II. Documents. Par J.V. Pollet. 1985
35. HELLER, H. *The Conquest of Poverty.* The Calvinist Revolt in Sixteenth Century France. 1986

36. MEERHOFF, K. *Rhétorique et poétique au XVIᵉ siècle en France.* 1986
37. GERRITS, G. H. *Inter timorem et spem.* Gerard Zerbolt of Zutphen. 1986
38. POLIZIANO, A. *Lamia.* Ed. by A. Wesseling. 1986
39. BRAW, C. *Bücher im Staube.* Die Theologie Johann Arndts in ihrem Verhältnis zur Mystik. 1986
40. BUCER, M. *Opera Latina.* Vol. II. Enarratio in Evangelion Iohannis (1528, 1530, 1536). Publié par I. Backus. 1988
41. BUCER, M. *Opera Latina.* Vol. III. Martin Bucer and Matthew Parker: Flori-legium Patristicum. Edition critique. Publié par P. Fraenkel. 1988
42. BUCER, M. *Opera Latina.* Vol. IV. Consilium Theologicum Privatim Conscriptum. Publié par P. Fraenkel. 1988
43. BUCER, M. *Correspondance.* Tome II (1524-1526). Publié par J. Rott. 1989
44. RASMUSSEN, T. *Inimici Ecclesiae.* Das ekklesiologische Feindbild in Luthers "Dictata super Psalterium" (1513-1515) im Horizont der theologischen Tradition. 1989
45. POLLET, J. *Julius Pflug et la crise religieuse dans l'Allemagne du XVIᵉ siècle.* Essai de synthèse biographique et théologique. 1990
46. BUBENHEIMER, U. *Thomas Müntzer.* Herkunft und Bildung. 1989
47. BAUMAN, C. *The Spiritual Legacy of Hans Denck.* Interpretation and Translation of Key Texts. 1991
48. OBERMAN, H.A. and JAMES, F.A., III (eds.). in cooperation with SAAK, E.L. *Via Augustini.* Augustine in the Later Middle Ages, Renaissance and Reformation: Essays in Honor of Damasus Trapp. 1991 *out of print*
49. SEIDEL MENCHI, S. *Erasmus als Ketzer.* Reformation und Inquisition im Italien des 16. Jahrhunderts. 1993
50. SCHILLING, H. *Religion, Political Culture, and the Emergence of Early Modern Society.* Essays in German and Dutch History. 1992
51. DYKEMA, P.A. and OBERMAN, H.A. (eds.). *Anticlericalism in Late Medieval and Early Modern Europe.* 2nd ed. 1994
52. 53. KRIEGER, Chr. and LIENHARD, M. (eds.). *Martin Bucer and Sixteenth Century Europe.* Actes du colloque de Strasbourg (28-31 août 1991). 1993
54. SCREECH, M.A. *Clément Marot: A Renaissance Poet discovers the World.* Lutheranism, Fabrism and Calvinism in the Royal Courts of France and of Navarre and in the Ducal Court of Ferrara. 1994
55. GOW, A.C. *The Red Jews: Antisemitism in an Apocalyptic Age, 1200-1600.* 1995
56. BUCER, M. *Correspondance.* Tome III (1527-1529). Publié par Chr. Krieger et J. Rott. 1989
57. SPIJKER, W. VAN 'T. *The Ecclesiastical Offices in the Thought of Martin Bucer.* Translated by J. Vriend (text) and L.D. Bierma (notes). 1996
58. GRAHAM, M.F. *The Uses of Reform.* 'Godly Discipline' and Popular Behavior in Scotland and Beyond, 1560-1610. 1996
59. AUGUSTIJN, C. *Erasmus. Der Humanist als Theologe und Kirchenreformer.* 1996
60. McCOOG S J, T.M. *The Society of Jesus in Ireland, Scotland, and England 1541-1588.* 'Our Way of Proceeding?' 1996
61. FISCHER, N. und KOBELT-GROCH, M. (Hrsg.). *Außenseiter zwischen Mittelalter und Neuzeit.* Festschrift für Hans-Jürgen Goertz zum 60. Geburtstag. 1997
62. NIEDEN, M. *Organum Deitatis.* Die Christologie des Thomas de Vio Cajetan. 1997
63. BAST, R.J. *Honor Your Fathers.* Catechisms and the Emergence of a Patriarchal Ideology in Germany, 1400-1600. 1997
64. ROBBINS, K.C. *City on the Ocean Sea: La Rochelle, 1530-1650.* Urban Society, Religion, and Politics on the French Atlantic Frontier. 1997
65. BLICKLE, P. *From the Communal Reformation to the Revolution of the Common Man.* 1998
66. FELMBERG, B.A.R. *Die Ablaßtheorie Kardinal Cajetans (1469-1534).* 1998

67. CUNEO, P.F. *Art and Politics in Early Modern Germany*. Jörg Breu the Elder and the Fashioning of Political Identity, ca. 1475-1536. 1998
68. BRADY, Jr., Th.A. *Communities, Politics, and Reformation in Early Modern Europe.* 1998
69. McKEE, E.A. *The Writings of Katharina Schütz Zell*. 1. The Life and Thought of a Sixteenth-Century Reformer. 2. A Critical Edition. 1998
70. BOSTICK, C.V. *The Antichrist and the Lollards.* Apocalyticism in Late Medieval and Reformation England. 1998
71. BOYLE, M. O'ROURKE. *Senses of Touch.* Human Dignity and Deformity from Michelangelo to Calvin. 1998
72. TYLER, J.J. *Lord of the Sacred City.* The *Episcopus Exclusus* in Late Medieval and Early Modern Germany. 1999
74. WITT, R.G. *'In the Footsteps of the Ancients'.* The Origins of Humanism from Lovato to Bruni. 2000
77. TAYLOR, L.J. *Heresy and Orthodoxy in Sixteenth-Century Paris.* François le Picart and the Beginnings of the Catholic Reformation. 1999
78. BUCER, M. *Briefwechsel/Correspondance.* Band IV (Januar-September 1530). Herausgegeben und bearbeitet von R. Friedrich, B. Hamm und A. Puchta. 2000
79. MANETSCH, S.M. *Theodore Beza and the Quest for Peace in France, 1572-1598.* 2000
80. GODMAN, P. *The Saint as Censor.* Robert Bellarmine between Inquisition and Index. 2000
81. SCRIBNER, R.W. *Religion and Culture in Germany (1400-1800).* Ed. L. Roper. 2001
82. KOOI, C. *Liberty and Religion.* Church and State in Leiden's Reformation, 1572-1620. 2000
83. BUCER, M. *Opera Latina.* Vol. V. Defensio adversus axioma catholicum id est criminationem R.P. Roberti Episcopi Abrincensis (1534). Ed. W.I.P. Hazlett. 2000
84. BOER, W. DE. *The Conquest of the Soul.* Confession, Discipline, and Public Order in Counter-Reformation Milan. 2001
85. EHRSTINE, G. *Theater, culture, and community in Reformation Bern, 1523-1555.* 2001
86. CATTERALL, D. *Community Without Borders.* Scot Migrants and the Changing Face of Power in the Dutch Republic, c. 1600-1700. 2002
87. BOWD, S.D. *Reform Before the Reformation.* Vincenzo Querini and the Religious Renaissance in Italy. 2002
88. PELC, M. *Illustrium Imagines.* Das Porträtbuch der Renaissance. 2002
89. SAAK, E.L. *High Way to Heaven.* The Augustinian Platform between Reform and Reformation, 1292-1524. 2002
90. WITTNEBEN, E.L. *Bonagratia von Bergamo*, Franziskanerjurist und Wortführer seines Ordens im Streit mit Papst Johannes XXII. 2003
91. ZIKA, C. *Exorcising our Demons*, Magic, Witchcraft and Visual Culture in Early Modern Europe. 2002
92. MATTOX, M.L. *"Defender of the Most Holy Matriarchs"*, Martin Luther's Interpretation of the Women of Genesis in the *Enarrationes in Genesin*, 1535-45. 2003
93. LANGHOLM, O. *The Merchant in the Confessional,* Trade and Price in the Pre-Reformation Penitential Handbooks. 2003
94. BACKUS, I. *Historical Method and Confessional Identity in the Era of the Reformation (1378-1615).* 2003
95. FOGGIE, J.P. *Renaissance Religion in Urban Scotland.* The Dominican Order, 1450-1560. 2003
96. LÖWE, J.A. *Richard Smyth and the Language of Orthodoxy.* Re-imagining Tudor Catholic Polemicism. 2003
97. HERWAARDEN, J. VAN. *Between Saint James and Erasmus.* Studies in Late-Medieval Religious Life: Devotion and Pilgrimage in The Netherlands. 2003
98. PETRY, Y. *Gender, Kabbalah and the Reformation.* The Mystical Theology of Guillaume Postel (1510–1581). 2004

99. EISERMANN, F., SCHLOTHEUBER, E. und HONEMANN, V. *Studien und Texte zur literarischen und materiellen Kultur der Frauenklöster im späten Mittelalter.* Ergebnisse eines Arbeitsgesprächs in der Herzog August Bibliothek Wolfenbüttel, 24.-26. Febr. 1999. 2004

100. WITCOMBE, C.L.C.E. *Copyright in the Renaissance.* Prints and the *Privilegio* in Sixteenth-Century Venice and Rome. 2004

101. BUCER, M. *Briefwechsel/Correspondance.* Band V (September 1530-Mai 1531). Herausgegeben und bearbeitet von R. Friedrich, B. Hamm, A. Puchta und R. Liebenberg. 2004

102. MALONE, C.M. *Façade as Spectacle: Ritual and Ideology at Wells Cathedral.* 2004

103. KAUFHOLD, M. (ed.) *Politische Reflexion in der Welt des späten Mittelalters / Political Thought in the Age of Scholasticism.* Essays in Honour of Jürgen Miethke. 2004

104. BLICK, S. and TEKIPPE, R. (eds.). *Art and Architecture of Late Medieval Pilgrimage in Northern Europe and the British Isles.* 2004

105. PASCOE, L.B., S.J. *Church and Reform.* Bishops, Theologians, and Canon Lawyers in the Thought of Pierre d'Ailly (1351-1420). 2005

106. SCOTT, T. *Town, Country, and Regions in Reformation Germany.* 2005

107. GROSJEAN, A.N.L. and MURDOCH, S. (eds.). *Scottish Communities Abroad in the Early Modern Period.* 2005

108. POSSET, F. *Renaissance Monks.* Monastic Humanism in Six Biographical Sketches. 2005

109. IHALAINEN, P. *Protestant Nations Redefined.* Changing Perceptions of National Identity in the Rhetoric of the English, Dutch and Swedish Public Churches, 1685-1772. 2005

110. FURDELL, E. (ed.) *Textual Healing: Essays on Medieval and Early Modern Medicine.* 2005

111. ESTES, J.M. *Peace, Order and the Glory of God.* Secular Authority and the Church in the Thought of Luther and Melanchthon, 1518-1559. 2005

112. MÄKINEN, V. (ed.) *Lutheran Reformation and the Law.* 2006

113. STILLMAN, R.E. (ed.) *Spectacle and Public Performance in the Late Middle Ages and the Renaissance.* 2006